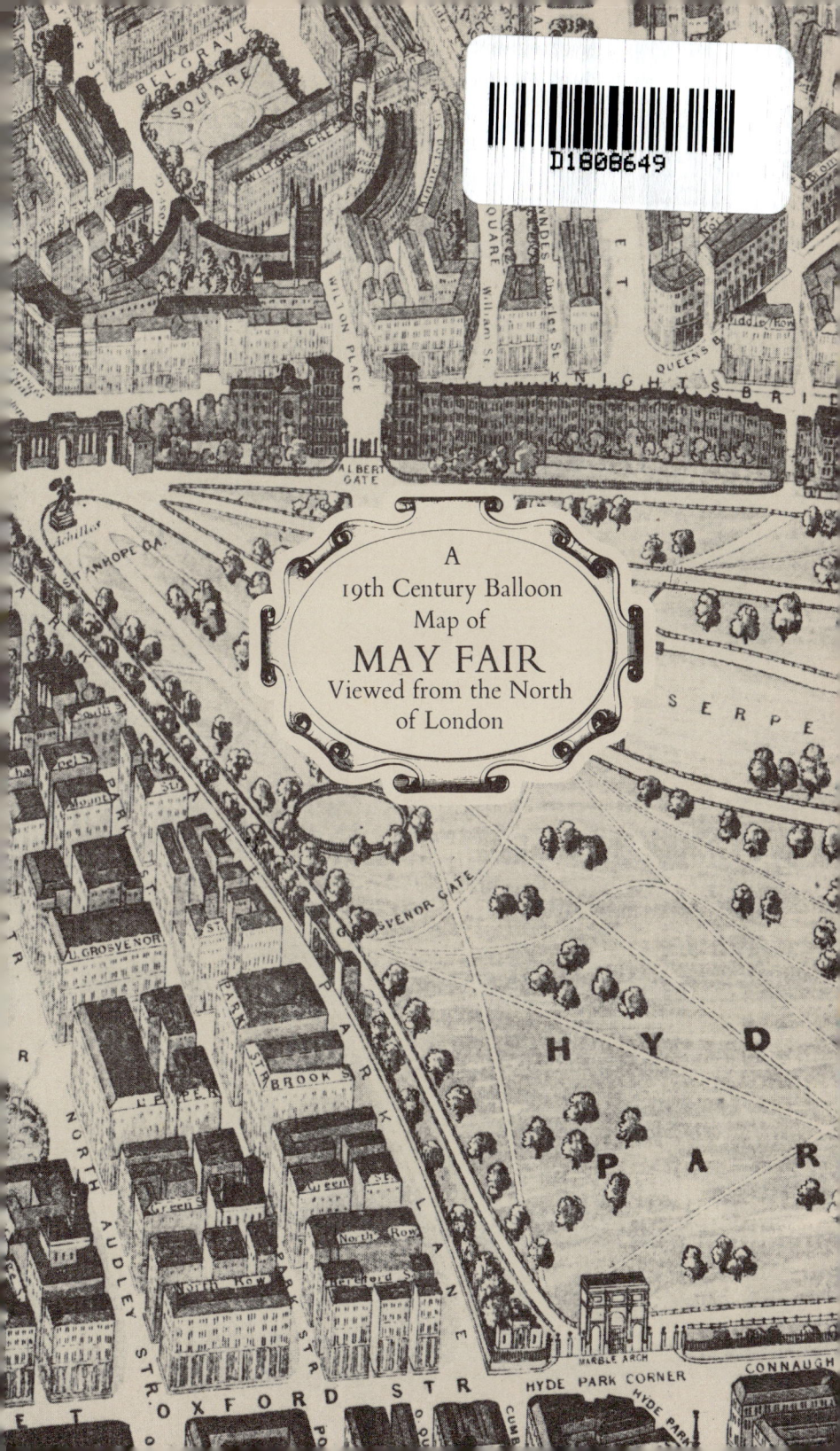

A
19th Century Balloon
Map of
MAY FAIR
Viewed from the North
of London

DIANE
A Victorian

Also by Macdonald Hastings

The 'Mr Cork' Books

CORK ON THE WATER
CORK IN BOTTLE
CORK AND THE SERPENT
CORK IN THE DOGHOUSE
CORK ON THE TELLY

Historical Novel

A GLIMPSE OF ARCADIA

A Personal History

JESUIT CHILD

War Reminiscence

PASSED AS CENSORED

Anthology

MACDONALD HASTINGS' COUNTRY BOOK

Text Books

CHURCHILL ON GAME SHOOTING
HOW TO SHOOT STRAIGHT
ENGLISH SPORTING GUNS

Biography

THE OTHER MR CHURCHILL
MARY CELESTE

For Boys

EAGLE SPECIAL INVESTIGATOR
ADVENTURE CALLING
THE SEARCH FOR THE LITTLE YELLOW MEN
MEN OF GLORY
MORE MEN OF GLORY

For Little Children

SYDNEY SPARROW

For Television

CALL THE GUN EXPERT (A SERIES)
RIVERBEAT (TWO SERIES)
VOYAGE INTO ENGLAND (A SERIES)
IN DEEPEST BRITAIN (A SERIES)
THE HATED SOCIETY: THE JESUITS

A Victorian

MACDONALD HASTINGS

LONDON
MICHAEL JOSEPH

First published in Great Britain by Michael Joseph Ltd
52 Bedford Square, London, W.C.1
1974

ISBN 0 7181 1254 7

Set and printed in Great Britain
by Northumberland Press Limited, Gateshead,
in Juliana ten on eleven and a half point,
on paper supplied by P. F. Bingham Ltd
and bound by Dorstel Press at Harlow

For Clare Hastings
In the fatherly hope that her life
will be as full as Diane's was

CONTENTS

CONTENTS

ILLUSTRATIONS

Certificate of Mrs Walter Creyke's Balloon Ascent

Diane: in early womanhood, in middle age, on the Continent, and on her hundredth birthday

Diane in a croquet tournament at Roehampton in her nineties

I

THE QUEST

N the middle fifties, when I was editing the magazine *Country Fair*, James Robertson Justice sent me a dust-laden book which he had jackdawed from the shelves of a second-hand shop in Edinburgh. Titled *Sporting Sketches*, its author had written it under the pseudonym of 'Diane Chasseresse'. It had been published in 1890.

Facing the title page J.R.J., with a flourish of his felt-tipped pen, had written: 'You may get a laugh or two out of this. It is quite preposterous.' So, in a sense, it was.

After I had read the book I lent it to A. G. Street, the author and farmer. 'Diane Chasseresse', dedicating it 'for the amusement of my children', had ended her sketches with the words: 'It may not be interesting to others.' When A.G.S. returned the book to me I noticed that he had pencilled into the margin of the last page: 'Oh, but it is.'

Years later, I learnt that David Garnett had also been captivated. But, long before I heard of that, I was hooked myself. The mysterious 'Diane Chasseresse', whomsoever she was, had aroused in me, like the Elephant's Child, an insatiable curiosity.

I was not to be disappointed.

II

HER SPORTING SKETCHES

IANE' did not pretend that her *Sporting Sketches* were other than a scrapbook, a loose collection of girlhood memories of the time when, each year, she travelled to the Highlands of Scotland with her father and mother for the fishing and the shooting. Sporting reminiscences of that sort are today as common as blackbirds; but not the reminiscences of a young girl in the period she was writing about.

She published her book in 1890 when, on her own admission, she was a matron with a growing family old enough to read. Her earliest memory of the Highlands was when she was four years old. At a hazard, that must have been about 1850, give or take a year or two.

The foundation stone of Balmoral Castle had yet to be laid. The evictions of the Highland crofters, to make way for sheep runs, were still going on. The railroad from the south terminated at Glasgow and Edinburgh. The building of the Forth railroad bridge had scarcely been contemplated. Grandsons of Highlanders in the forty-five rebellion were still alive.

In London, the first Great Exhibition was the talk of the town. The Empress Eugenie, it is said to conceal her pregnancy, was introducing the crinoline. Dickens was still writing. The Duke of Wellington was at Apsley House, and Lord Palmerston had yet to form his last administration. Prince Albert was considering patterns for the Balmoral tartan. In his studio Landseer was painting 'Monarch of the Glen'.

When we first meet her Diane, on her mother's back, was up a Highland mountain where her family, armed with hammers, were chipping specimens of mineral rock.

In her book she is at pains to conceal her own identity, and where the family went on their forays into the hills and straths. I asked Macmillan's, who published it, whether they could discover who she was. They were able to tell me that they printed an edition of 1250 copies. Although the book was widely reviewed it sold slowly, not selling out until 1907. But the vital clue was missing. The record was silent about the author who received the royalties.

So I went back to the book convinced that my dark lady, however discreet she may have intended to be, must give herself away somewhere, somehow. The sketches which begin when she was four, ended, according to my calculations, when she was in her early twenties.

Meet her, for the first time, 'when memory could not take me back any further':

'It was a fine evening and we were looking down some precipitous rocks, when all of a sudden a dense mist came on. It was not one of those cold drizzling mists that cut the mountain-tops in a straight line and wet you to the bone, but a thick white one, like rolls of cotton wool, or puffs of smoke from an engine. My little cousin, a year younger than myself, held out his hand to catch the clouds and tried to fill his pockets with them to take home to his nurse.

'A year later we went, a large party of grown-up people and children, to the top of Ben L.... There were all sorts of nice crystals and minerals to be found in Perthshire, and it was the custom for everyone to carry a hammer with a long handle to break up the stones that we expected to find and bring home. The hammers were all in proportion to the sizes of the children, and they became larger and longer until they at last reached the size of the hammer used by my father.

'There were two ponies, a black one and a white one, to divide amongst the whole party. The ponies were left on the flats, and we and our hammers went on to the top. This time a real mist came on, and we all lost our way, and what was worse still, lost the two ponies. We were miles from home, and three of us were only four, five and six years old.

'It was a question of what it was best to do; to hunt about in the dark for the two ponies, which, if they were ever found, could at most only have carried five or six out of the eight children, or to walk all the way home, without the chance of a lift. My mother settled the matter for herself and me by walking the whole way home in the dark; carrying me on her back when the heather was very long and scratched my little bare legs above my short socks; and she never rested until we got back to the Lodge. How I enjoyed my tea in my mother's bedroom! And I was allowed brown bread and butter as a great treat, instead of the sour white bread we usually had to eat.'

So she was one of a large house party which included eight children with grown-ups to match at a shooting lodge in Perthshire which had a mountain, 'Ben L....', within walking distance. It was elementary, my dear Watson, that at that time it was unlikely to be situated other than in the Western Highlands and in an area within easy staging distance of Oban. Communications on the Eastern side were still so tenuous that the only convenient way of travelling from Edinburgh to Inverness was by coastal steamer. Getting into the Western Highlands was tedious enough. At Glasgow the party would have taken the paddle steamer down the Clyde to Ardrishhaig at the mouth of the Crinan Canal. There they would have transferred to a small steamer for the nine-mile journey through fifteen locks to Crinan, and thence by another larger paddle-boat to Oban. From Oban, they would have travelled by stage coach to their destination. With eight small children, and probably a retinue of servants, it must have been quite a trek.

In the very first sketch, it emerges that Diane's father was no stern Victorian pater familias. Not for him children who are seen and not heard. When he climbed a mountain he took the infants with him. It is evident, too, that he must have been a wealthy man to entertain so hospitably. But he expected his guests, and his children, to learn to live rough:

'For many years, from the age of six or seven or so, I followed the sportsmen all over the moors in all weathers, and in clothes quite unsuited to a wet and cold climate. We had no waterproofs, and of course no umbrellas, and well I remember the feeling of the first cold drop that trickled down the back of my neck and descended to the regions below. What a shiver it gave to one's spine, and how short a time it took between the first drop of water and the last thread. How I loathed being wet through! We used to spend day after day, and sometimes week after week, wet to the skin, driving home at night cold and sodden, without a scrap of wool or flannel on our wretched bodies. Often I have walked along the road in all the puddles, which felt quite warm to my feet after the water in the hillside. On one occasion, when I was very wet, and out in a pelting storm, my mother told me to sit under the stomach of the white pony; and I was so frightened that for once I would rather have faced the rain, as I expected every moment to be kicked or trampled to death.'

Notice that mother was out in it, too. It is difficult to imagine her in a Victorian drawing room being overcome by the vapours. She must have come from a tough stock. After the soaking on the hill there was no running water, no airing cupboard, nothing better than a hip bath at the Lodge. Let's hope she enjoyed a dram of whisky. But all the discomfort didn't dim her daughter's enthusiasm.

She began sporting on her own account, fishing the burns for wee trout and shooting at small birds with a bow-and-arrow. When she was older she learnt, with the aid of a spaniel, to dig rabbits out of stone walls, subsequently releasing them in the kitchen garden where, she writes, 'they greatly assisted in the consumption of the few vegetables which were supposed to last us for the whole season'. Later, her father promoted her to greater authority.

'A celebrated artist used to stay with us every season for sketching, and I was told one day to take charge of him out shooting. It was a broiling hot day, and we began by going amongst the rocks to look for rabbits. He soon sat down to admire the view, with a pipe in his mouth and a red pocket handkerchief spread over his head, and I was left to carry the gun, loaded and at full cock, all over the roughest rocks. Then we left the rabbits and the view and went down into the valley.

'As we were passing a dark pool near the river we saw a wild duck swimming about. We stalked it with much care, and Mr. X got a shot and hit it. We were greatly excited, and went round and round the pond, I beating and he getting snap shots, till at last after the sixth shot the duck was sufficiently badly wounded to be captured and knocked on the head. We were delighted, proud and delighted, because next to a stag a wild duck was always considered the most important head of game to be bagged. But after we had secured the bird we had a little difficulty in making out what species of wild duck it belonged to. It was certainly not a mallard, nor a wigeon, nor even a teal; and we were quite puzzled; however, we went on down to the lake in high spirits, quite satisfied with our day's sport. Arrived there, we saw and hailed one of the keepers, and showing him our bag with much pride we asked him what kind of wildfowl it was.

' "And I'm thinking it's jist one of M'Gregor's tame ducks that's got away down the river." '

Here was a valuable clue. Earlier she had told how, riding the pack pony in the wake of the shooters, the saddlebags were always slipping especially when they were 'filled with kit, consisting of painting blocks and other heavy sketching materials'. Obviously they were the property of 'the celebrated artist, Mr. X'. In a latter sporting sketch, I caught her nodding. She refers to 'poor Doré'. So the artist who shot the tame duck, a friend of the family, was Gustave Doré. Magnificent painter of the Highland scene though he was, he was no sportsman. He wasn't a 'Diane'.

Her first weapon, 'a little needle rifle', was lent to her by her brother who bet her five shillings she couldn't shoot a crow on a given day. Needle guns were a transitory type of weapon between muzzleloaders and the development of centre-fire breechloaders such as we use now. They weren't all that efficient. But, on her first outing, Diane shot a grayhen, a member of the grouse family, out of the branches of a tree.

'Dear little rifle! It became mine after a time when it was beginning to wear out, and it shot very true, except when it missed fire—which was pretty often.'

Even these days, it is relatively uncommon for women to go shooting. Most women have an aversion to handling arms; indeed, they are usually clumsy with them. Diane must have had more than a streak of masculinity in her make-up. In the times in which she grew up women cultivated the pose of the shrinking violet. Dickens's clinging heroines were the models of what a young woman was supposed to be. Diane was a tomboy, and an intrepid poacher:

'My first salmon was killed, I regret to say, with a worm, long after what used to be the legal close time.

'Someone lent me a worn-out rod, much too heavy for me, and almost guiltless of rings, and I was told that I might fish the pool exactly under the ashtree where I had shot my grayhen. I was also told that there was a good chance of a salmon. After many years of small trout, hope waxeth faint, what therefore was my joy and excitement when I felt the first pull of the salmon, and the reel clicked and the line was run out. It was delightful playing the fish, but how was I to land it? I was alone, without gaff or landing net, the bank was high, and the river was deep. I might have been able to hail someone passing along the road some distance off, but as I was doing an illegal act I had to hold my tongue. For one hour and a half did I play that weary fish. The wind was high, and so cold that I had to put the skirt of my frock round my shoulders to keep a little warmth in me. The rod was so heavy, even without the fish, that I could hardly bear its weight for so long a time, and yet the fish was not sufficiently done for me to land it with rotten tackle. However, at last the struggle was over. At last I could pull it up or down the top of the water at will; and I don't know which was the most exhausted, myself or the fish, when I put the rod down, jumped down the bank, and lifted him up in my delighted arms.

'Even then my labours were not at an end, for the fish had to be carried home out of sight, hidden in the folds of my frock, and as it was very heavy with the addition of the rod, I had to sit down and rest every few yards. At last, however, I got past the high road and into the boat, where I was safe from observation, and so across the river, and home by the meadow.'

There is a sketch in the book illustrating her carrying home the fish. She can scarcely have been more than twelve or thirteen when she killed it. Its weight, she recalls, was between twelve and fourteen pounds; that's a big fish. Any salmon fisher will recognise what a remarkable feat of skill and dogged endurance the landing entailed. A man would have been proud to grass it. A stern parent, on her return to the Lodge, would have given her a talking to, and sent her to bed. That wasn't the way of Diane's father. 'Many were the jokes,' she writes, 'made by the family at the expense of me and my fish.' Indeed, her father rewarded her for the feat by giving her a salmon rod of her own, 'and flies of the best and mostly costly description'. He must have been a loving father. She made the most of it 'on one of the most difficult and sporting rivers in Scotland'.

'I have stood all day long far above my knees in the river, driving home at night in soaking petticoats, knowing that rheumatism must surely follow, rather than lose the chance of reaching the places where the best fish lay.'

She became an expert fisher. She tells how she landed a twenty-pounder:

'The excitement was so great that the coach which was passing along the high road behind us pulled up, and all the passengers got down to watch me play and land my fish, and some of them even came up and took its measure: from the tip of its nose to the end of its tail.'

A gillie who went out with her on one occasion broke his ribs when a twenty-six pounder took them downstream along the roughest part of the river bank. Diane herself fell off a rock, and missed going into the river by inches.

'How bruised I was. There were bruises all over me of every shade; violet, red, yellow, black and green. It is generally such a comfort to have something to show for a fall or an accident, but in this instance I said not one word about the matter, but walked about until my clothes were dry, and held my tongue about the bruises.'

One of her sketches is devoted to instructions on how to fish salmon. No contemporary angler could do other than agree whole-heartedly with everything she writes on fishing tactics. She speaks with the authority of a woman who had played and landed two fish, each weighing 28 lb., within the hour. It makes my own arms ache to think about it. But, if there were no legal way of catching a fish, she was still the poacher:

'I don't think I ever enjoyed a legitimate day's salmon-fishing so much as I did my only day's salmon-*chasing* with neither rod nor line. We were staying with a distant neighbour in Scotland, and as everyone else was out deer-stalking, I went up the river with a very good-looking Highlander, who was fisherman and gillie, and had the reputation himself of being something of a poacher.

'As we went along, we came upon a pool, across which we saw a salmon dart, and then hide itself under the bank. The stream was so low that the salmon could not get out at either end, so we thought we would try if we could drive it up and down the pool, and so tire it out and catch it. One of us was to go into the water, and the other to jump on the bank and frighten the fish out every time it took refuge there.

'Of course I was the one to jump into the water, so in I went, and rushed up and down the pool, poking away with a big stick, while the Highlander watched the fish from dry land, and stirred it up every time it stopped to rest. At last it got fairly exhausted, and lay quite still under the bank; so we crept very cautiously to the edge, and kneeling down, we dropped the only weapon we had with us, which was an old spoon with a triangle of three rusty hooks fastened to a bit of gimp, just over the fish.

'It was intensely exciting, and I hardly breathed as the spoon sank just beyond it so that it would not touch the fish till sufficiently low down. The supreme moment arrived. I gave a sudden and violent jerk to the end of the gimp and hooked the fish securely. Unfortunately away it went with a rush, and when we examined our spoon we found that one of the three rusty hooks were broken in halves, so we had all our work to do over again. Three times we tired out that odious fish, and each time when we got him securely hooked, he broke away with half the hook, and at last we were left with only the spoon, so we were obliged to give it up and go home with nothing.'

Diane revealed a lot of herself in that anecdote. For the first time, referring to the good-looking Highlander, she had an eye for a man. By then, she must have been a nubile young women of about seventeen or eighteen. But, characteristically, she was unwilling to play the part of the frailer sex. She was the one who plunged into the icy water, leaving the Highlander to keep his kilt dry on the bank. I felt sure that the woman I was questing would have conducted her whole life in much the same way.

'I did not take to shooting for some years after my successful debut with the grayhen; but upon one occasion a relation of ours who was staying in the neighbourhood wanted her larder filled, and went out with me and a large old-fashioned single-barrel muzzle-loading gun, to see if we could pick up a blackcock for her dinner. It was arranged that she was to load the gun, and I to shoot. We went over the moors looking about for something to stalk, when we saw some black game in a corn-field about a half a mile off. There was a wall and dyke round the field, which made it a capital place for stalking, and we made quite sure of getting a bird.

'Unfortunately someone else had equally thought there was a good chance of some sport for, as we were nearing the field, a man who had been concealed in the ditch jumped up, whisked a gun out of sight close to his side, and ran off down the glen, over the river, and up the mountain on the opposite side. I started off like the wind to give chase, delighted at the prospect of catching a poacher, but alas! I was called back and ordered not to go. It was a great disappointment, but even if we had caught the man, as we also were out with a gun and no licence, perhaps it would hardly have looked well if we had appeared in a court of justice.'

When the old rifle she had inherited from her brother had quite worn out, her father—it must have been her doting father—gave her a needle rifle,* made by Rigby, the famous London gunmakers, which she christened 'Little Death'. With the finesse of a dedicated shooter she had the sights made as fine as possible, the trigger pull very light. She painted the foresight white for shooting on dark days or in the dusk. An invention of her own was to have a thin black sight in front of the ivory one for days when the sun shone strongly. With her very first shot with 'Little Death', on her way to a hind shoot, she killed a stag. Like all needle guns, 'Little Death' constantly missed fire, especially in wet weather, as the cartridges were covered with paper and had no caps:

'Once when I had stalked some black game behind a wall, and had put the rifle through a chink to shoot, the cartridges missed fire, and the black game seeing nothing, went on quietly feeding. I had no means of getting out the cartridge, and so tried picking away at it with a strong hairpin. All at once, the hairpin touched the detonating powder, and it exploded in my face. I heard a loud report, saw a ball of fire, and thought first that my brains were

* Needle and pinfire guns were introduced in the 1840's. The needle and pin exploded the fulminate inside a paper cartridge. The breechloader superseded pinfire arms in the early 1850's.

blown out and that I was dead. Then finding that I was still alive, I thought I had been blinded in both eyes. At last I opened one eye, and found I could see, so I crawled to the little burn close by and bathed my face and eyes, and found to my great relief that there was nothing the matter except a little powder under my skin and in my eyes. But it gave me quite a shock and for a long time after I would not go into the same room as 'Little Death', and I could quite understand the horror that the maids always felt at the vicinity of an unloaded weapon.

'After a time I got over my dread; and an empty larder, and the want of a companion, and having nothing else to do, induced me to begin shooting again.'

Nothing deterred Diane for long:

'For deer-stalking I was often lent a most splendid double-barrelled rifle made by Purdey. It was terribly heavy, almost impossible to hold up to my shoulder, and it had long exploding (expanding) cartridges that went off with a terrific report. The first time I used it I was taken up to a stag and, when we were within easy shot, the rifle was given to me, loaded and cocked. I took some sort of rest and pulled the trigger. Over I went backwards down the knoll. The deer galloped happily off, not nearly so much the worse as I was.

'We had another stalk, and again the rifle kicked most horribly, though I had taken the precaution to pad my shoulder well. This time I got the deer. On reloading the rifle it was observed that two of the cartridges were missing, and it turned out that both times I had fired off the two barrels at once. I had been so used to a light single-barrelled rifle with a comparatively heavy trigger that I naturally pulled away as hard as I could. No wonder my shoulder was black and blue, and that there was such a terrific report.'

Diane, undefeatable, worked out her own methods to reduce the shock of recoil. With a woman's light frame and shoulders, she certainly needed support:

'The position I prefer and in which I always endeavour to place myself, is a sitting one, not on a rock but on the ground, so that my knees are nearly up to my chin. I then rest the rifle on my left hand with the elbow on my knees, and if the ground is level or sloping downward, I can keep pretty firm. If the deer are above me, I get the gillie to lean against my back to steady me, otherwise I generally topple over when the rifle goes off. I have sometimes shot deer resting the rifle on the stalker's back, as he knelt in front of me.

This is a capital way to shoot, unless the stalker happens to be troubled with a sense of humour, in which case he is quite sure to begin to laugh just as you have taken aim.'

She admits to one feminine weakness:

'I have never been able to cure myself of a habit of shutting my eyes tight and flinching, even when firing off a small rifle, but it does not make as much difference in the result as might be supposed; but as to firing a large rifle at a mark, nothing would induce me to do such a thing.'

But she was induced to try her hand stalking alone. It is generally recognised in the Highlands that it is the ultimate test of fieldcraft. During the Second World War, commandoes doing their battle course training in Scotland were encouraged to harden up, develop a feel for country and personal independence of action, by going into the hill after deer on their own:

'To the untrained eye everything looks so different, when you get near, to what it did from a distance, that you are often completely puzzled where to go next. You think you have made an accurate note of every stone and knoll, and when you arrive at the particular hollow in which you expect to see the deer you are after, the whole place is changed, and you get bewildered and perhaps walk on to the top of the deer, who bolts away hardly more startled than you are yourself.

'I could not believe how completely one could be deceived about distances. All I had was my little single-barrelled rifle, as I could not carry a large one. I went right over the third top of three hills that rose one above another, without finding anything. Then I went part of the way down the farther side where, to my great joy, I saw one stag lying down alone at some distance off. This was just the chance I wanted and, hastily shutting up the telescope, I went back over the top of the hill out of sight.

'After walking for some time, I thought I had got tolerably near the stag so, very cautiously and quietly, I descended by a little hollow. I considered that I was then about level with the deer, and I put my head up with the greatest care, only to find it still lying a little tiny speck in the distance. I took the landmarks more accurately this time and returned back the way I had come, over the top of the hill again.

'It seems very absurd, but in spite of all my precautions I did precisely the same thing a second and a third time. I could not have thought it possible to have been so completely deceived. At last I came to a mountain lake, and farther than that there was no more cover. I crawled on my hands and knees till I got on a level with the deer, which was 80 or 90 yards off. I was more than doubtful about getting it, as I found I had no exploding (expanding) bullets with me, and the bullets I had were so small that unless the deer was struck in a vital part, it would be sure to get away without showing a sign of being hit at all.

'I would not venture alarming it, but took a very long and steady aim, with a perfect rest on the bank of the bog, into which my blackened knees were slowly sinking. With my eyelids tightly closed (after my usual fashion), I fired my one little barrel, and had the immense satisfaction of finding that the deer could not rise. I loaded again as quick as possible, and ran forward to shoot it through the head, and thus put an end to its life.'

That night, from Diane's description of where she had dropped the beast, the professional Highland stalker, carrying a lanthorn, walked as straight as a line to its position, gralloched it, and dragged it home. Her own feat was one that a professional could respect. Over the years, the bag she made with 'Little Death' included twenty-three species (she herself, with that calamitous needle gun, could so easily have been the twenty-fourth). But there was another gentler side to her:

'It must not be supposed that I spent all my life either in fishing or shooting. We were only in Scotland in the autumn, and during the rest of the year sport was rarely even mentioned. The time devoted to sport was when I was quite alone, with nothing to do, and no companion to talk to. Sometimes I had a cousin of about my own age to go about with, and then we spent our time in a very different manner.'

It is difficult to believe that she was ever the prim little miss of the Victorian storytellers, but there is a hint of it when she describes playing 'proverbs and some other innocent games' with her cousin. She played 'follow my leader' with her:

'My cousin was neither quite so tall nor quite so strong as I, and if I jumped across the streams and she were following, she jumped into them. But that was not of the least consequence, as we used to jump straight into the sea off a high bank in all our clothes, up to our armpits, as part of the game—the grand finale before going home; and this was half the fun. And oh! how cross the maids used to be when we came home drenched with saltwater, which spoils every-thing! Not that we could be accused of wearing many clothes that would spoil, but still the things were tiresome to dry.'

No ribbons and bows for Diane. No make-up either. Living as she was in the open air of the Highlands, drying the saltwater out of her voluminous skirts and petticoats by hard exercise, her face must surely have had for that time, a most unfashionable tan. But she was beginning to enjoy the ecstatic shivers of new-found femininity:

'One evening we thought that we would like to paint a moonlight picture of the church, so we got permission for my cousin to stay the night and share my bed, and after dark we set out with our books and our paint boxes. About half-a-mile from the house was a thick wood, and through this wood was the road that led to the place from which we intended making our sketches.

'The wood was all in dark shadow, not a gleam of light came through the branches of the trees, and we did not at all fancy penetrating its blackness alone. Every step we took made us regret more and more that we had started on such a stupid expedition, and at last by mutual consent we turned tail and fled before getting into the wood.

'But it would not do to have to confess the next morning that, after all our preparations, we had been such cowards as to be afraid to go through a dark wood, so we went over the meadows down to the river, and there we sat and did our sketches, knowing quite well what the church was like either by daylight or moonlight, and as we both drew very badly the result must have been just as satisfactory as if we had sat in a place where we should have been in constant fear of tramps, gipsies, ghosts, robbers, poachers, or murderers.'

On another outing we find the two girls twittering, as young girls do, in their wet bathing gowns after a swim:

'We sat down, and fastened the skirts of our dresses round our necks so as to form a species of tent under which we dressed. Our great object was not to show the smallest speck of white, so as to avoid attracting the attention of tourists or telescopes.'

A cynic has declared that women wear modesty like a cloak. What fun girls had, before the coming of the bikini, when the flash of a well-turned ankle was enough to move any beau to stroking his whiskers. Diane had a fetish about telescopes. In her last night camping out on the hills, she and her cousin went for a bathe in a burn:

'We had not thought of bringing bathing-gowns, and there was no bank to hide us when in the water, though there was a capital nook to dress in. We knew Mac (the gillie) would have his eye on us early, to find out when he was to come over and join us, and we did not know—which would have been an immense relief—that he had left his telescope on the top of the mountain.'

What hypocrites women are. How much more the girls would have enjoyed the giggling speculation if Mac had encountered them with his telescope in its case on his shoulder. The family sometimes joined their expeditions. They had a tent which had reputedly seen service in the Crimean war. When they were alone their respective brothers plagued them, the way brothers do, by bearing down on them in a little outrigger from the sea with the intention of devouring all they could lay hands on. The girls hid the treats they had collected for their feast—such delicacies as doorsteps of bread, spread with golden syrup with slices of ham in between—in the heather, trusting that they could take the edge off the boys' appetites with fried bacon of which they had a plentiful supply. Diane records triumphantly that the ruse worked.

Her brother was certainly a pest. On another occasion, when she was deputed to look after an uncle 'who rose like an elephant in the middle of the tent, snoring and swathed in plaids and shawls' her brother excelled himself. Diane and her cousin lighted the fire, plucked and cooked the grouse for breakfast, and saw off her elephantine uncle for his day's sport:

'My brother then became very troublesome. He ate everything he could find, ran after us with a two-pronged steel fork, which he stuck into our arms whenever he caught us, and finally took the tallow candle of the lanthorn and thrust it into a cold pie, which had been provided expressly for my uncle in case he did not fancy the food we cooked.'

It is easy to imagine uncle. Most sisters will have similar recollections of their own brothers. Diane may have been a tomboy herself, but it is evident that there was a strong practical streak in her. Her parents knew that her uncle would be safe in her hands, even with her brother there to persecute her. Her father, like many men, obviously had no taste for picnics and sleeping on a bare blanket in a tent on the side of a hard Highland hill. He preferred his own dinner table and his own bed. He came once in the hope of shooting a deer when the beasts came down from the hills to the low-lying lands during the night. He didn't get his deer, and drove his daughter to distraction by demanding hot buttered toast at two o-clock in the morning.

As the Highland seasons passed it seems that the family increasingly relied on her. Her father gave her a beautiful new rifle, and it was Diane who was sent out to shoot the deer when the larder was low. It was Diane who had the art of washing and dressing the liver of a freshly killed beast for breakfast. It was Diane who brought in the blackcock, the partridges, and occasionally a pheasant, for the kitchen. It was only the grouse that the men went after with their shotguns.

Like so many hunters, she loved animals and understood them. She collected wild pets:

'I had a squirrel once, which I used to tuck into the front of the body of my riding-habit, while he was asleep, like a pocket handkerchief, and take him out riding with me. When the horse was going full gallop the squirrel would wake up and poke his head out, and was most troublesome to manage, and would never settle down comfortably to sleep again. But he used often to go out driving, and did not mind a bit.'

One of the *Sporting Sketches*, which are assembled in only casually coherent order, tells of a tame otter named 'Trots'* which when she was a married woman, she introduced to her house, big enough to have a 'foreign footman' (so perhaps it was a mansion), overlooking Hyde Park. She had a black and white tame rabbit, too, appropriately named by her 'Gnawrer', which had the exasperating habit of chewing the stuffing out of the upholstery in the furniture. The foreign footman must have loved it.

Throughout her life, she was a romanticist, too. She was one who wanted to believe in the marvellous and the strange. She would have been a sucker for the Loch Ness Monster. Indeed, she believed that she had encountered such a creature herself. Apropos of nothing, in a sketch about sea-fishing with her own children, she records:

'The other day, happening to turn over the pages of a book by the late Frank Buckland (the celebrated Victorian naturalist) called *Notes and Jottings from Animal Life*, I came upon a picture which at once took me back to an August day many years ago, when I saw a precisely similar 'ridge of fins' as it was called.

'The circumstances were as follows. I was out in the sea with an old man in an old boat on the west coast of Scotland, when there suddenly appeared what looked like a row of palings, which popped up and down, sometimes two and three at a time, and sometimes in a whole line. The old man had not an idea what they were, nor of course had I, but I loaded my rifle, and told him to row as hard as he could after them.

'We got a good deal nearer, and I had several snap shots at them, but as we advanced they receded in front of us in the direction of the shore a mile or two off. We were decidedly gaining on them, and I was in great hopes of getting a better chance when the stupid

* See Appendix (1).

old man refused to go any further. It was tolerably rough, and I believe he thought the creature, whatever it was, might turn upon us and upset the boat. It was a great pity, as we shall now never know what it was. I have been there hundreds of times since, and never seen anything the least like it, until I came upon the sketch in Mr. Buckland's work, though we have often seen both whales and porpoises much further out to sea.'

Although I felt that, by this time, I knew all about Diane as a person, I still didn't know who she was. I was really only guessing that her hunting ground was in the Western Highlands. She had written somewhere in her *Sporting Sketches*:

'To catch a 20-lb. salmon and shoot a "Royal" (a stag with twelve points to its antlers; vide "Monarch of the Glen") was once the height of my ambition, and in due time this was accomplished; but I was also anxious to add a seal to my "varieties shot with a small rifle" and that was not so easy a matter as we lived far from the sea.'

Yet, in the last sketch in the book, she writes as if the sea was on her doorstep. Perhaps over the years, the family had two different addresses.

'Late one afternoon I arranged with one of the children on the shore that she should row me over to a little island when the tide was going out, and after dropping me on it, take the boat to the nearest shore, and watch with her telescope to see if the seals who haunted it came within shot. I calculated from the way in which the wind blew, there was a possibility of some of the seals landing without scenting me, so wrapping myself in an old black mackintosh, the colour of the wet rocks, and putting seaweed on my head, I hid behind a stone and kept a sharp look-out.

'There were several seals swimming about near the rocks, and at last I saw the head of what was evidently a fine seal at the farther end of the island. I peered about very cautiously, but could not see more than the top of its head, and I think it had some sort of suspicion, as it every now and then raised its head and let it drop again.

'While I was wondering if there was any possibility of crawling nearer without rustling the seaweed, another seal came right out of the water, and looking about suspiciously, flopped up on to a stone, a good deal nearer to me, and in full view. I was so much interested in watching its movements that I did not shoot, and at last it jumped into the water and disappeared. This determined me not to throw away my only other chance; but I could not risk shooting from where I was —the bullet would only have glanced off the rock, and seals would have been frightened from coming back another day.

'It was now getting dusk, and there was no time to be lost if we meant to secure a seal that night. All at once I heard a train in the distance, and an idea flashed upon me that the seal might be distracted from watching and listening to my movements when the train passed within full view of the island; so I waited a few seconds, prepared to make a dash at the right moment. The instant the echo from the train was at its loudest, I rolled over the rock behind which I had been hiding and, bent double, hastened over the wet and slippery stones. The seaweed made a horrible noise, but my ruse answered perfectly as I got several yards nearer to the seal as the train rushed past. Still I could see the top of its head, but cocking the rifle and taking a steady aim, with a stone for a rest, I made a slight noise, just enough to make the seal bring the whole of its head into view, then fired ...'

She got her seal. The way dead seals do, it sank to the bottom. With the little girl who was in charge of the dinghy they at last sighted the animal lying on the shingle in the clear water. Diane threw an anchor over it, and rolled it closer to the rocks. At last she reached it with a boat hook and got it into the shallows. Inch by inch she and the little girl eased the carcass into the dinghy, almost overturning the boat in the process. Then, using Diane's mackintosh rigged on one of the oars as a sail, they made for home in triumph.

So ended a typical Diane adventure. She called it her 'Last Shot' suggesting that her life in the Highlands was at an end; which it wasn't. But at last, she had given me the clue I was looking for. There is only one place in the Western Highlands I know, which swarms with seals, and where the railroad runs round the arc of the bay. It must have been Oban in Argyll. Since the railroad hadn't been opened when she was first in the Highlands as a little girl, she would then have been in her twenties.

Oban was the only certain landmark I could pinpoint in the book. Earlier I had puzzled about 'Ben L....' and a ruined castle she described in which she used to play with her cousin in what I presumed were her early teens. But Scotland is littered with Bens and ruined castles, too.

I decided to fly a kite in *Country Fair* (July 1956). I wrote briefly about my discovery of *Sporting Sketches*. This was my guess, not altogether a bad one, at the time:

'Every line she writes sparkles with the brightness of truth; and I don't know why, but I have a notion that she was a raving beauty.

She had at least four, and probably more than four, children which means that one man at least must have fallen pretty hard for her ... Altogether, the aura that reaches out to me over the years is a delicious one. And I find her writing remarkably fresh and undated. After reading the book twice, I am pretty sure that she was in her forties, and still damned attractive, when she wrote it, which means that her adventures in the Highlands, which began in childhood, spread from about 1850 to the late eighties.

'The family used to take her every autumn for a Highland holiday. Most years they went to the same place, somewhere in Perthshire where there was good stalking and fishing and a ruined castle. Latterly, after her marriage, I think she may have taken her children to somewhere on the West Coast, like Oban ... She was of a well-to-do family, possibly a titled one, and she married well. She later had a house in London, with a horde of servants; and she often took rooms in the shires for the hunting season*; and I am quite sure that the artist Gustave Doré was a friend of the family ... But that's all I can find about her.

'Since the youngest of her children were clearly infants when the book was published in 1890, it's not too much to hope that some of them may still be alive to read this and to reveal to me the mystery of their mother's identity. Or perhaps there is a handsome granddaughter who will allow me to take her out to lunch; better still supper, so that I can drink champagne out of her slipper.'

Before the beginning of the partridge-shooting season in the same year I had the answer. Many readers had written to me suggesting various clues as to the identity of someone who was surely one of the pioneers of feminine emancipation in field sports. But they were all red herrings. To Mr. C. S. Minto, the City Librarian and Curator of the Scottish Central Library in Edinburgh, goes the credit of finally discovering who 'Diane Chasseresse' was. The solution was even more fascinating than I had dared to hope.

As a consequence of researches into various obscure catalogues of literature, he was satisfied that she was Mrs. Walter Creyke. Mrs. Creyke was Caroline, the daughter of Sir John Bennet Lawes Bt., of Rothamsted Park, and she was born on December 4th, 1844. She married on August 25th, 1870, Walter Pennington Creyke, the eldest son of the Ven. Archdeacon Creyke, of Bolton Percy, Yorkshire.

---

* She gave that away in her anecdote about 'Gnawrer', the black and white rabbit.

According to the records she had five children: Walter Launcelot, Everilda (m. 1910 Donald A. McAlister), Lilian (m. Eustace Henry Tylston Hodgson 1896), Diana (m. 1902 Horace Vere Clay Ker-Seymer) and Sylvia (m. Charles James Kindersley Maurice, March 23rd 1904). Mr. Minto informed me that the latter information came from *Burke's Landed Gentry* (1914) and *Burke's Peerage* (1956). (I have updated the record.)

So my guess—I still could not get used to thinking of her as Caroline—that she probably came of a titled family was not far out. Her father was a baronet. I reckoned that my hope that she might have grandchildren ought to be fulfilled. I wrote in *Country Fair*: If the family themselves do not see this perhaps a reader who knows them will draw it to their attention.'

Mr. Minto's reseaches had been so thorough that he had even unearthed her obituary from *The Times* of September 11th, 1946. Yes, 1946!

Mr. Minto's researches had been so thorough that he had even the age of 101 years and nine months. She claimed that she always kept fit by playing croquet, and she took part in tournaments until she was ninety-five. Born in Harpenden, where she is to be buried, Mrs. Creyke lived in London for the greater part of her life. Her husband was Mr. Walter Creyke, and they had six children.'

I reckoned that she must be worth a better obituary than that.

III

HER GRANDCHILDREN

T was a newsagent at Marlborough, turning the pages of *Country Fair* in September 1956, who started the train of communication with Mrs. Walter Creyke's family. Her one surviving daughter, Mrs. Maurice (Sylvia), then lived at Manton Grange in Wiltshire. The newsagent told Mrs. Maurice what I had written in my editorial. Mrs. Maurice told her son, Mr. Alec Creyke Maurice, of Enborne Chase, Newbury, in Berkshire. He told his sister, Mrs. Gerald Eastwood, wife of Brigadier Eastwood, of Hurstbourne House, Hurstbourne Tarrant, in Hampshire. She told her cousin, Barbara Ker-Seymer (grand-daughter of Diane) at her London home at The Angel, Islington.

In due course—it was after the death of Mrs. Maurice at the age of ninety-two and a half—the grandchildren welcomed me, severally and together, in their homes. The mystery of 'Diane Chasseresse's' identity was resolved. The challenge now was to unravel a hundred years of one woman's life, of one family in English social history. Mrs. Walter Creyke was no ordinary woman, as she had been no ordinary child; and hers was no ordinary family. They belonged to high society at a time when a fifth of the map of the world was painted red, when privilege drew a great divide between rulers and ruled, the very rich and the very poor, people who worked for a living if they could make one, and people to whom hereditary wealth was the right of breeding. I had already written a novel about the wretchedness of London's poor in the middle of the nineteenth century.* What beckoned me now was the elegant world, by no means to be despised, in the high sun of the British Empire.

After first encountering Mrs. Walter Creyke as 'Diane Chasseresse', her grandchildren told me that she was variously known as 'Diane', 'Ina' and, most of all, 'Skye'. She was 'Skye', a nickname I suspect bestowed on her by her father, because, like the terrier's of that name, her hair was forever tumbling windily over her face. She was 'Skye' or 'Ina', never Caroline, to her family and intimate friends throughout her long life.

* *A Glimpse of Arcadia* (1960).

Nicknames have always been a common form of family endearment. My father, for example, used to address my mother, whose name was Wilhelmina, as 'Bill'. Skye's family called her 'Gogo'.* So, henceforward, Caroline became Skye for me.

I first met Skye in the house of her grand-daughter, Jean Eastwood, in Hampshire. There were two drawings hanging on the wall, portraits of her, not unexpectedly, by Gustave Doré. Doré made them in 1879, four years before his own death, when Skye was a young matron in the pride of her womanhood. The grandchildren told me that Doré loved drawing her because he saw in Skye a resemblance to Sarah Bernhardt, for whom he had a deep admiration. Maybe....

I gazed enquiringly at his impressions of her. One was a three-quarter length study, resting a closed fan in her lap, which was clearly a preparatory sketch for the second in which he had drawn only the head and shoulders. I preferred the uninhibited line of the first when the artist was so plainly drawing from his heart rather than his hand.

Skye had the hourglass figure, the straight corseted back, that I had expected of her. On a slender neck and small shoulders her head was tilted with the proud carriage of a thoroughbred. It has been said that all women are either pekes or horses. Skye was unmistakably 'horse' with the long straight nose, high cheekbones and strong features which distinguish the type. There was an unabashed look in her eyes—I was told that they were as blue as a clear sky—which suggested that she was one on whom no man had ever been able to put a bit. Her eyebrows were plucked into an arch, and finished with a sweep of eye pencil to give a quizzical slant to her expression. She had the cupid's bow lips, shaped in the boudoir, which women affected in her time. She had tight curls with a fringe over her forehead. Her grandchildren told me that she had 'ginger' hair. But they showed me a lock of it which her mother had lovingly preserved in a miniature envelope, the size of a cigarette card, snipped from her in early childhood. It is Saxon fair. Perhaps as she grew older, as often happens, her hair became mousier with a hint of red in it. No doubt she improved on nature.

None could have described her as a classic beauty. Elegant, yes. Magnetic, yes. Intelligent, yes. Fascinating to men whose passions are aroused by the outwardly unattainable. The emanation of her, like a scent, suggested a personality who never doubted her own authority or questioned for a moment her birthright to her social position in the polite world. I fancied, too, that she never felt under

* 'Gogo' was the grandchildren's name for her before they were able to pronounce the word grandmamma.

any compulsion to conform for form's sake or, when the mood was on her refrained from behaving as wilfully as she felt inclined. On her own admission she had done just that during her childhood holidays in the Highlands.

Her own class, whatever its eccentricities, was entitled to display them. The others, to use one of her own favourite phrases, were ''Arrys', lesser people within the law. It was no fault of hers. It was the then universal attitude of the upper classes.

Later, I was to learn that Skye was a friend of the great actress Mrs. Patrick Campbell. I thought of 'Mrs. Pat' as I looked at Skye's picture. In her deep contralto voice 'Mrs. Pat' had once said to my father, to his own indignation : 'I can manage men.' I could imagine Skye saying something just like that, too. I fancied that she could be arch when she wanted to be; but for her own ends.

According to her obituary in The Times, she had six children by her husband, Walter Pennington Creyke. Burke gave her five. After talking to her grandchildren it was easy to understand why one of those infallible sources nodded. She, in fact, had four daughters and twin sons. One of the twin sons died in infancy.

It might have broken another mother's heart, even in that age when infant mortality was the common lot of large families, even privileged ones. She had lost her other twin, Walter Launcelot, when he was run over by a train in the Underground during the blitz on London. Among her voluminous papers she left no expression of grief. There is every evidence that she was a dutiful mother. There is little or no evidence that she was a fond one, or even that she was a devoted wife. All her life she was an egoist. As we would say today, she put No. 1 first. Or so it seemed to me looking at Doré's drawings and listening, during my early meetings with them, to her grandchildren. They treasured the memory of the remarkable woman, of whom they all had vivid recollections in her old age, but none of them pretended to any illusions about her. Skye, for them, was unique, formidable, artistically gifted and apparently physically indestructible. But they in their generation laughed about her as well as with her.

At last, with the grandchildren to help me, the scene of Diane Chasseresse's sporting exploits was unveiled. The autumn holidays in her early years were spent at Dalmally on Orchy Water at a convergence of glens near the north eastern extremity of Loch Awe. From 1886 to 1896 her father, Sir John Bennet Lawes, who had been created a baronet for his services to agriculture in 1882, leased

Ardchattan Priory (Ardchattan pronounced as if there were no 'C' in it) on the northern shore of Loch Etive, in the Lorn district of Argyll, about ten miles north-east of Oban, the capital of the Western Highlands. Exactly how long he was tenant at Dalmally is uncertain because all the records of the lodge named 'Craig' with its fishing and shooting, which he rented from the Breadalbane estate, were destroyed by the landlords in a fire of documents during a subsequent period of financial stringency. But it is reasonable to suppose that the lodge was occupied by the Lawes' family every autumn from the middle or late forties until they acquired the lease of Ardchattan in 1886.

Although Ardchattan Priory was altogether a more prestigious pile—it was while it was in the tenure of the family that Skye shot the seal—Dalmally was the place which held the abiding affection of the Lawes. In the last active decade of his life Ardchattan, with its fourteen thousand acres, was a worthy estate for a millionaire, and the greatest agriculturalist of his time. Sir John kept a splendid steam yacht with a tall funnel on Loch Etive, an arm of the sea stretching inland from the Sound of Mull, and the Island of Mull, for a distance of about twenty-two miles. In his steamboat Sir John would run the rapids to the open sea. The mansion, created out of the ruins of a Priory founded in the thirteenth century by an austere order of monks whose rule enjoined silence, no meat or gravy, the wearing of hair shirts and sleeping fully clothed and shod, without any mattress, was now surrounded by flower and pleasure gardens. The Mansion House, consisting of the Old Hall of the Priory and a modern wing, was described when the estate was offered for sale (though it was later withdrawn) after Sir John left in 1898. It had everything that a wealthy Victorian and his domestic staff could wish for :

'On the ground floor—low entrance-hall, morning-room, cloak-room, cellars (six divisions for wine, etc., with cold water in one), dressing room, butler's pantry, servant's hall, shoe hall, kitchen, scullery, two larders, maid's work room, maid's bedroom, two linen cupboards, two presses, plate closet, servants' W.C.

'On the first floor—front entrance hall, drawing room, dining-room, library, bedroom—known as the Prior's Bedroom—and Oratory adjoining with groined roof, three cupboards, housemaid's pantry, bathroom (both with hot and cold water), W.C., four store rooms, housemaid's firewood room, five servants' bedrooms.

'On the second floor—five bedrooms, two dressing-rooms, W.C., bath, store room (with cold water) china press.

'On the attic floor—three bedrooms, and two small store-rooms. The offices consist of laundry, larder, three bedrooms for men-servants, coach-house (eighteen by fourteen feet), stable (containing four stalls), coachman's house (containing five rooms, kitchen, scullery, closet and coal-cellar), gardener's house (containing two rooms, kitchen and scullery).

'The drainage and sanitary arrangements are in conformity with modern requirements and are in thorough working order. There is a plentiful supply of excellent water, which is laid on (hot and cold) throughout the House. The kitchen garden is enclosed by a substantial wall, and extends to about an acre. It contains a greenhouse thirty feet long, and an orchard-house one hundred feet long. There are also a fruit room, tool-house, sheds, etc. There is a private pier, with large boathouse and carpenter's shop above, within a hundred yards of the House....'*

It was nothing like that at Dalmally. Craig Lodge in the middle of the nineteenth century was a Spartan place where they slept on hard beds and fed, as Skye tells, on sour bread and what they could shoot for the pot. Although Skye complained even then of the tourists, the ''Arrys', who passed by in the limited service of stage coaches, there can only have been a handful of them. Argyll was still a poor empty place, in which the inhabitants dwelt in largely poverty-stricken bothies. Even the tourists travelled cheap. I have a copy of *Nelson's Hand-Book to Scotland for Tourists* published in 1862. 'The general charge' it says 'for a two-horse four-wheeled carriage, is 1s. 6d. per mile, with 3d. to the driver; for a one-horse four-wheeled carriage, 1s. per mile, or 15s. a day; for a gig, from 10s. 6d. to 12s. a-day; for a riding horse, from 6s. to 8s. a-day; for a pony, 5s. a-day. The general charge, in the highest hotels, for breakfast, is from 2s. to 3s.; for dinner, from 3s. to 5s.; for tea, from 2s. to 3s.; for bed, from 2s. 6d. to 4s.; for private room, from 4s. to 7s.; —in good hotels, often little inferior to the highest, for breakfast, from 1s. 6d. to 2s.; for dinner, from 2s. to 3s.; for tea, from 1s. 6d. to 2s.; for bed, from 1s. 6d. to 3s.; for private room, from 2s. 6d. to 5s.'

---

* The present owner of Ardchattan Priory, Lt.-Col. R. M. T. Campbell Preston, M.C., has told me that the only present day souvenir of Sir John Bennet Lawes's tenancy is a noxious weed Sir John introduced called Japanese Knotgrass. It appears that his notion—apparently only too fully realised— was it would provide green cover for rocky outcrops and ruinations. The estate has been trying to get rid of the rampant plant which multiplies like ground elder, and stands up to 8-feet high with clusters of small white flowers, ever since. A species of the Polygonum family, it is a living survivor of one of Sir John's few mistakes as a conservationist and agriculturalist.

Today, Craig Lodge is completely modernised. Of the old slate and granite house little remains except the gun room, lined with planking of Highland pine (which never ceases sweating) and a few small rooms left from the old structure. In Skye's day the lodge sheltered in a windbreak of great trees. The butts are still there, some of them seven feet in diameter, of Caledonian Forest Pine, beech and elm and silver spruce; felled, no doubt, for the timber when the Breadalbane estates went into decline, the decline which came to the clan of the Macgregors who once dominated Glenorchy and the surrounding glens, that clan which is commemorated in Sir Walter Scott's lament:

'The moon's on the lake, and the mist's on the brae,
   And the clan has a name that is nameless by day;
      Then gather, gather, gather, Gregalich!
Glenorchy's proud mountains, Kilchurn and her towers,
Glenstrae and Glenlyon, no longer are ours;
   We're landless, landless, landless, Gregalich!'

Ben Lui (3708), the mountain of the Macgregor's on the boundary of Perthshire and Argyll, broods as it did when little Caroline Lawes climbed it with her father and family to chip crystals off the peak. Kilchurn, a fifteenth-century stronghold on a small island at the easternmost end of the twenty-five miles of Loch Awe is the same ruined castle in which Skye and her cousin used to gambol as the hill sheep still do today. The rapids at the Western end of the Loch which Skye used to run with the gun dogs lying on an inflatable raft given to her by her father, have been tamed by the new hydro-electric dam. The salmon, which Skye fished, still run up the white waters of the Orchy, between the wild and precipitous banks from which Skye fell and bruised herself black and blue on the rocks below. The red deer, those creatures of the Highland mists, still haunt the hill; but there is no Skye now to stalk them. The head keeper keeps them under control, bringing the beasts down to the Lodge with a caterpillar tractor and trailer. The carcasses are exported to Germany. So much of the old magic has gone.

Although in her *Sporting Sketches*, Skye refers to her 'Last Shot' she returned to Dalmally, usually with some of her children, for many years after. In her childhood the family only went to the Highlands in the autumn. Latterly she travelled north for the spring-fishing as well. She fished and shot regularly until the last years of the century, latterly with a Holland and Holland breechloading rifle (No. 9456) built for her between 1870 and 1880. Her grandson, Alec, still has it in his possession.

Between them, her grandchildren unearthed for me a trunkful of papers, clipping books, albums of photographs, and quaint Victorian letters and souvenirs. Few of them concerned the sporting times in the Highlands. Most of them belonged to the seventy years when Skye was a fashionable May Fair hostess, one who only in nostalgic moments harked back to the world of her *Sporting Sketches*. In 1890, when they were published, they were reviewed with a liberality of space in the newspapers and periodicals which, contemporarily, would make an Ernest Hemingway envious. She pasted them in an album she labelled 'Gushes' with clippings of her poems (of that, later) and articles she wrote, under various pseudonyms, for the society press.

Most of the reviews are flattering effusions by people who did not know much of what they were writing about. The notion of a lady sportsman (inevitably described as 'A Feminine Nimrod') was far too novel for a considered criticism. But there were some who were shocked. The *Leeds Mercury* commented ironically :

'The book is adorned with pictures which represent this characteristic product (Diane Chasseresse) of the nineteenth century propped up on the hill-side by a stalwart Highlander, shooting the deer, pulling a dead stag by his horns through a wire fence, crouching on the rocks alone to pot a seal, or floating downstream on her back in a waterproof boat, with a rifle over her shoulder and two huge dogs sitting on her, and in other graceful and feminine attitudes. We do not think that it is at all in accordance with the eternal fitness of things for ladies to stalk over the hills and scramble over the rocks with a "dear little rifle" and a brace of dogs.'

So much for Women's Lib in the last century. On a more practical note, *The Field* rebuked her family :

'The incomprehensible part of the book is how the authoress's parents or guardians did not take better care of her. Often have we pitied the children of the working classes who are taken on Bank Holidays a journey by train, returning, it may be, wet, and certainly tired; but these hardships are as nothing compared with those suffered by "Diane Chasseresse".... Yet, apparently, the authoress's "people" went north to enjoy sport; but it must have been at a time before the Prevention of Cruelty to Children was invented.'

The Shooting Times considered it a case for marvel :

'Her adventures are of the roughest description and how she contrived her many miraculous escapes, is a perfect wonder to us, encumbered as she was with her feminine attire.'

The Society periodical *The World*, who had Skye as a contributor and almost certainly knew who she was, was ecstatic:

'We give our vote for Diane Chasseresse as the most vivacious and entertaining chronicler of sport that has arisen since Dame Juliana, of pious and immortal memory, wrote the great Boke of St. Albans.'

The Illustrated London News was puzzled, but on the whole, approving:

'We do not wish, as a matter of taste, to see the rod and the gun, fowling-piece or rifle, in the hands of every lady; killing wild creatures is hardly the best pastime for womanhood; but this Diane Chasseresse, who writes primarily for the amusement of her daughters, must have been a pleasant, amiable girl, as well as a brave one, and her experiences, which are likely to remain exceptional among her own sex, merit social toleration.'

A reviewer in Southern Australia could not believe what the 'Pommies' were coming to:

'A jury of staid British matrons sitting in judgement on this book would open their eyes in horror and amazement, and pronounce "Diane Chasseresse" guilty of all manner of sins against orthodox feminine dependence, tastes, and manner of amusement.'

The Melbourne Argus was disbelieving:

'We suspect that her weakness is to be reckoned rather more of an expert with the rod and the rifle than she is, and some of her stories are a little bit—well! coloured as is the custom with sportsmen, male and female.'

The *Birmingham Daily Post* was disgusted:

'We confess that the title of this volume repelled us. It has been among other volumes on our desk for a long time, and we have, in taking up a volume to scan, always preferred one which was not "sport". And there is much here, now that we have taken it up, that we read with a mental protest and something approaching disgust.'

The *Saturday Review* was completely disbelieving:

'We have known ladies who fished, and who even tried their hands at a little shooting, though some do not consider firearms suitable playthings for women; but so keen and determined pursuer of fur, feather and scale as Diane Chasseresse we have never met with before in life or literature ... This mortal goddess's deer seem to have been even more affable than the partridges she shot. The least thing alarms a deer, whose eyes, ears, and nostrils are ever on the alert for danger ... That is the ordinary deer, not the Diane Chasseresse variety, which latter consents to be just a little frightened, and to move with a considerate regard for the stalker's convenience....'

The *Daily News* wrote a nasty leader about her, ending: 'There is a limit to the caprices of Diane.'

Only the *Oban Times*, not surprisingly, read the authoress's secret:

'The locale of the greater number of these sketches is evidently fixed in the land of Lorn; for who can doubt but that the Orchy just above Dalmally Bridge is the scene of the waterproof boat anecdote. To this day some of the Dalmally folk speak of the novel little craft.'

So I wasn't the first to discover Diane's secret hunting ground. And, at the last, I myself thought better of her than some of her critics. She could write like this in *The World* in 1892, about Ardchattan in the autumn:

'The late heather is still in bloom, and the rowan-berries are so thick that the delicate branches of the mountain ash are bent down and almost broken by their weight. The grass is still green in the meadow, and the bracken is strong and thick on the hills, waiting for the early touch of frost or the too rare rays of a warm sun to turn it to a golden brown and to shrivel it up into little orange curls. Seldom indeed is it that we see the sun, but so changeable is the climate this season that if it rains incessantly for one whole day we may be pretty sure that it will be fine the next, though it may not be either bright or warm; while as for the wind, it never by any chance blows for twenty-four hours from the same airt. The caprices of wind and tide make the only changes in this changeless spot; but though in an inland salt-water loch there is comparatively little tide and more of the dark, gloomy-looking fresh than there is of the bright and buoyant sea-water, we have, not many miles away, a rushing torrent which affords endless excitement to the boats which have to pass up and down from the open sea into our loch. The loch is some sixteen miles in length, and debouches through a narrow channel, more than half of which is blocked by sunken rocks, into the bay below. At low tide the tangle covering the largest rock is seen, floating on the water, and one can sit in one's little boat holding on to the tough seaweeds, which look like large leather aprons, while not a ripple disturbs the calm surface of the sea; then suddenly, at the turn of the tide, there comes a rush of water flowing past in a rapid stream, and soon there will be eddies round the boat, and the sea will boil and bubble, and the seagulls will hover around

after the herring-fry, and a seal's head will appear floating down with
the tide, and shoals of fish will jump out into the air; and into the
midst of all this commotion of waters, and birds and fishes, boats
full of men and boys, with rods innumerable, will collect from all
sides and row about in the backwaters, until the tide becomes so
high that the whole channel is one big rushing stream, and boats
and fish are alike swept away ...'

So Skye on the Falls of Lorn. It seemed strange that a country
to which she was so emotionally attached she made hers so briefly.
At the end of her father's days she dismissed it like an old lover.
For the rest of her life, the glamour of London and Europe held
her as if she had never known anything beyond the thrill of a new
ball dress.

As I first muddled through the mass of papers, mementoes, letters
and press clippings, photographic albums and drawings, the residue
of Skye's world, one of her grand-daughters remarked to me: 'Of
course, grandmamma never did a hand's turn of work in her life.'
In the meaning that Skye probably never made a bed, dusted the
furniture, fixed a pin in a nappie, washed up after a meal, or got on
her knees anywhere outside a fashionable church, her grand-daughter
was almost certainly correct. Domestic work was something to which
people in her social class pulled a bell cord to have attended to.

For most society women of her time it was exertion enough to
keep up with the butterfly world of being in the right places with
the right people: the Sunday Church parade in Rotten Row: the
private view of the Royal Academy's Summer Exhibition; Ascot
Sunday with a parasol in a punt in Boulter's Lock at Maidenhead;
and, each resort in its season, Paris, Venice, Rome, Homburg, Monte
Carlo and Cowes. Entertaining and being entertained was almost a full
time occupation and, gastronomically, a testing one. A light dinner
party in the best country houses—I found plenty of lace-edged
menu cards among Skye's papers—would consist of six to eight
courses: soup, fish, *entrée* (such dishes as Ris de Veau), *relève*
(likely a choice of roast mutton, roast turkey and ham), *entremets*
(say roast chicken and asparagus), relève again of *soufflés* and various
sweets, cheeses and fruits. The silver knives and forks were laid at
each guest's place like trophies of arms. The glasses, the Victorians
had a taste for coloured goblets, were paraded like soldiers in
ascending and descending sizes on the guest's right. There was a
wine for each of them.

If there were dancing, each guest was issued with an ivory card, with a miniature pencil attached, in which to record the partners she or he had booked throughout the evening for the valse, the gavotte, the gallop and the rest. The men in their tailcoats, with a red silk handkerchief tucked negligently into their white waistcoats, wore white cotton gloves. The ladies flirted behind the shelter of their fans.

The ostrich-plumed presentations at court, the theatre, the opera, the balls, the exhibitions, provided an exhausting social roundabout in which the marriage game was played as assiduously as a poker school. Mothers with young daughters bet with them like chips for matrimonial fortunes.

In the thick of it, revelling in it, Skye paraded herself and, subsequently, her own brood. I found a leather-bound book among her papers which had begun as a Day Book, changed to an inexplicable account of household bills, and ended with a puzzling list of people she might have planned to invite to one of her musical soirées, or simply made a note on. Whatever the book was about, it is an indication of the circles she was moving in. The significance of her additional comments is anybody's guess. It includes: Thackeray and Miss Thackeray, Lady Dufferin, Dion Boucicault, Landseer (about the Prowling Lion), Hon. Mrs. Norton, George Meredith, Trentanove, sculptor?, Charles Kean, Sir John Lubbock, Sir Robert Peel, Lord Carlisle, late, Lord Egerton of Tatton (No), Lord Houghton, John Bright (with picture of dog), Duke of Manchester, Lord FitzWilliam (No), old Lady Essex, Duke of Beaufort, Lord Barrington, Lord Dudley, Adelaide Sartoris, Duke of Devonshire, George Fripp, Sir Rivers Wilson, Professor Jowett, Lord Tankerville, Lady Salisbury, Buffalo Bill (or his secretary), Mary Anderson, J. Whistler, Captain Shaw (of the Fire Brigade), Count Fleichen (Prince Victor of Hohenlo), Archbishop of York, Don Carlos, Sir Alexander Cockburn, Gustave Worms (2), Bastien Le Pape (2), Lord John Hay, Lord Elcho, Harrison Ainsworth, Mario (French, Italian and English letters), Gustave Doré*, (Count?) Arnim, Lord Tweedale, R. Daft? Cricketer, Duke of Sutherland? Lowell.'

In one of the photographic albums—Skye was obviously a keen photographer—I found autographed studio pictures of the Prince of Wales, George Booth the Salvationist, W. M. Thackeray, Sir Robert Peel, and Lord Leighton. In a brown paper parcel I came on a note by her in her jagged handwriting: 'I knew Sarah Bernhardt before she came to London when I was the guest of the Prince of Wales at

* Died 1883. So this was a list made prior to that date.

a Royal Command Performance in Paris. She asked me to be kind to her when she came to London as she knew no one.' I discovered a letter from a lady-in-waiting at Balmoral Castle saying that the Queen had been graciously pleased to accept the gift of a copy of *Sporting Sketches*. She was certainly 'in' with all the right people.

She was reported in the social columns ice-skating at Prince's in Piccadilly, as a cycling enthusiast and keen croquet player, and a follower at the fashionable meets of fox and stag hounds.

But, whatever the grandchildren said, she also worked. Indeed, she showed a breathtaking industry. Throughout her life she was a keen amateur painter of more than ordinary talent. For a time she had studied at the Slade School of Art. But, more than that, she was a journalist and poet, and a regular contributor to the leading periodicals of her day. She usually wrote her verse under the pseudonym of 'I.N.A.'. She wrote her journalism as 'Diane', 'Diane Chasseresse', 'D.C.', and, rarely, as Mrs. Walter Creyke or Caroline Lawes. Her contributions appeared regularly in *The World*, *Pall Mall Magazine*, *The Nineteenth Century*, *Fashion and Sport*, *Baily's Magazine*, *The Globe* and, occasionally, *Punch*. She also wrote plays and romances. I uncovered 'My Darling, Darling, Jack', a play in two acts; 'Not at Home', in one act; and 'Cuthbert Vale', a romance. The setting was always the social world in which she herself moved. She had no time for ' 'Arrys'.

There is no evidence that she ever had any success with her ventures into drama and fiction. But, as a journalist, she had a great success. Her series for *The World*, from 1891 to 1900 and after, called 'Pleasures of a Chaperon' was eagerly read. In her appointed field, as a commentator on the foibles of polite society, she was good, even very good and, with her background, perhaps unique. Her use of dialogue and exchanges of letters as an essay style must have seemed something quite fresh among so much turgid and ponderous writing which appeared in the Victorian prints.

And she took her journalism seriously. I was delighted to find an envelope in one of her folders on which she had written: 'The first story I ever wrote—rejected by *The World*—put away for some years—sent to *Sport and Fashion*, who said that it was the smartest piece of writing they had had and that they would take as many more in the same style as I would send. Any journalist who has ever had a rejection slip from an editor, and who hasn't?, will feel a small share in her triumph at final success.

Her clippings books record what she was paid for an article, usually between two and three guineas (remember that, at that time, the pound was a golden sovereign). In a cuttings book, which she labelled *Nuits Blanches*, she records, in June 1897, that in a few months she had made £89-4-0 from her journalistic work. In different circumstances I have no doubt that she could have made a good living out of writing.

Her verse, widely published, is heavily sentimental, but it scanned, and it suited the mood of her time. When I first got my hands on her papers, I happened on one of her lighter efforts called A *Leap-Year Reminder*. It might well have been a lyric for a moonlight duet in one of Mr. George Edwardes' then fashionable musical comedies at Daly's Theatre. Am I right that the refrain has an echo of a song which became popular many years later?

A Leap-Year Reminder

She: You know we have met once before?

He: Oh! yes—yes, of course, I remember.

She: We met in the North, at Dunmore;
You stayed there to shoot, last September.

You asked me if you might not call
In London, when up in November—
You promised to come to our ball.

He: Oh! yes—yes, I think I remember.

She: You said you would give me a box
Boxing-night, twenty-sixth of December,
For the new pantomime, Mr. Cocks—
He: No, really? I hardly remember.

She: And dine at th'Amphitryon Club,
Of which you were just made a member.
He: But I'm not, Miss Pauline—there's the rub;
Though of course—oh! of course, I remember.

She: One evening we sat hand in hand,
The fire burned down to an ember;
You called me your 'dear Pauline,' and—
He: No! Distinctly I do *not* remember!

I remember the time when you turned up your nose
At my paltry five hundred a year;
My uncle was living—you did not suppose
I might some day become a rich peer.

I remember the time when you treated with scorn
My bouquets, and bonbons, and me;
You were stately, and stuck up, and fair, and well-born—
I was nobody then, don't you see!

I remember the time when I loved you in vain,
You sneered at my suit without pity;
You turned on your heel, and you scoffed at my pain—
Poor, penniless clerk in the City!

As I shook the dust of Skye's life out of her papers, I came on a
poem dedicated to her husband by Alphonse Daudet. I found sepia
photographs with bevelled gold-edged mounts and the coats of arms
of royalty and exhibition medals on the reverse. Many of the subjects
were unidentified, bearded men with forefinger to cheek and pert
little girls in frothing skirts and high-buttoned boots. There was a
ghastly Maltese Cross in pinchbeck with a tableau of the Crucifixion
stamped into the back and, on the limbs on the face, oval photos of
Skye and her husband, and locks of their respective hair. There were
letters written, although the penny post had been introduced in 1840,
which had still travelled to their destination via the 'receivers' who
charged for transport on the weight of each package. The consequence
was that correspondence was conducted on the smallest possible
pieces of paper in doll-sized envelopes. There were still people who
adopted the exasperating illegibility of 'crossways' letters in which,
to save paper, they wrote across the grain of the lines they had
already written. It still wasn't too late in history to find handwriting
in which the 'fs' of the eighteenth century still prevailed.

I found the ornately printed programmes, of the age before
mechanical sound, in which amateur musical concerts were the order
of the evening. There was one, on Friday 13th September, 1867 at
Campsie New Town Hall in which Miss C. Lawes gave a rendering
of 'Sing, Birdie, Sing' (Gantz); another at Harpenden in 1868 in
which Skye sang, in her soprano, Offenbach's 'Je suis Alsacienne' in a
duet with 'Mr. Wade'. And there was a hand-painted programme of
amateur theatricals given by his Excellency's servants at the Chief
Secretary's Lodge in Dublin on January 21st, 1864. The programme,
tastefully decorated with a garland of shamrock and pink moss
roses, records that the Chief Secretary, the Earl of Carlisle, appeared
himself in a *petite Comedie* entitled 'Why Did You Die?'. Walter
Creyke, Skye's husband, appeared, with other members of the Chief
Secretary's staff, in the theatricals.

When Miss C. Lawes sang at the amateur concerts at Harpenden her brother Charles often appeared in the same programme with her. No doubt her father, whose ancestral seat at Rothamsted was at Harpenden, sat in the audience. They were a remarkable threesome. You couldn't really know Skye without knowing about her father and, later, her brother.

Her husband, Walter Pennington Creyke, was a more complex figure. Named in his day as one of 'the most handsome men in England', Skye appears to have worn him as she wore her jewellery. Her father and her brother, like her, loomed rather larger than ordinary life.

IV

HER FATHER

A^N anonymous contributor to the *South Australian* of November 11, 1890, ended his review of Diane Chasseresse's *Sporting Sketches* by dropping a brick:

'Further and deeper research into this work would establish the fact that there is an unimportant adjunct to the household called pater familias; that he is only unearthed when bills have to be paid, and then, if necessary, hoodwinked by his family before being relegated to his usual insignificant obscurity.'

It was a brick as monumental as the huge granite boulder, eight tons in weight, which was erected in 1893 by a grateful nation, under the patronage of the Prince of Wales (later King Edward VII), to commemorate the services to agriculture of Sir John Bennet Lawes, Diane's father. Queen Victoria had made him a baronet in 1882. As she dubbed him, before a large assembly at Windsor Castle, she said: 'Rise, Sir John, one of the greatest benefactors of man and beast.' To agriculturalists, the memory of John Bennet Lawes is still green as one of the first and greatest pioneers of agricultural science.

Mr. J. B. Priestley, in his eminent study *Victoria's Heyday*, makes no mention of John Lawes of Rothamsted Manor. As an urban man he had probably never heard of him. Yet Lawes ranks among the greatest of the great men of the nineteenth century. To him we largely owe our national pre-eminence in agricultural practice. In his world-famous laboratories and experimental station, where his lifelong work still goes on, he developed the manufacture and application of super-phosphates (artificial manures) to the soil, and benefited for ever the well-being of man and his domestic animals.

Like so many great innovators he was born to a social station in which he was under no compulsion to earn a living. For two hundred and fifty years his family, the Lawes and the Wittewronges, had been squires of Rothamsted Manor and its estates at Harpenden, near St. Albans. It was expected of him that he would settle down to the leisured life of a landed gentleman; slightly impoverished owing to his father's friendship with the Prince Regent which for his father, as for so many others, had proved extremely costly. None could write better about his early years than Lawes did himself in a document discovered posthumously among his family papers:

'I was born in the house where I now reside, and which has been in my family for 250 years, in December 1814, and am therefore in my 59th year. I have little recollection of early events, and the death of my father which occurred when I was nearly 8 years old made but a slight impression on me. This place was let during my minority and my Mother resided in a smaller house in the same parish. Shortly after my father's death I was sent to a private school at Hatfield. I remained there between one and two years learning very little and was always in mischief. I went from there to a private school at Brighton where I learned even less and was always in mischief and disgrace. I remained there about two years and at the age of 14 I went to Eton. I learnt just enough to escape punishment but no more. I took no part in the sports of the School such as football, cricket, nor did I enter the boats as one of the crew, but I was a good deal on the water in a desultory way; and most of my pursuits were more or less mischievous, such as digging mice out of the fields and moving them into my tutor's house.

'I remained at Eton between two and three years and left it without regret. My Mother rarely resided long in one place; my holidays were therefore spent at any locality where she happened to be. Twice or three times I went to France and we were in Paris during the revolution of 1830.* I thought it great fun and helped to build the barricades. After this my Mother went to reside with her parents in Oxfordshire† and I was sent to the vicar of the parish for an hour or two daily to prepare for college. The principal part of my time was spent in fishing and shooting. Of the latter sport I was passionately fond. At the age of 18 I went to Oxford where I remained two years learning little or nothing and following no particular pursuits. I did not go up for my degree.

'About this time the tenant of Rothamsted became insolvent and my Mother decided that we should live there. My education was therefore supposed to have been finished and I was set up as a country gentleman. I had no idea or wishes about farming, but the home farm was vacant and therefore I took it. Up to this period I had formed no opinions of my own on any subject. I was a Tory because most

---

* Caused by the attempt of Charles X to seize absolute power. After three days (*les trois glorieuses*) of fighting in July, Paris was left in the hands of the insurgents. Charles fled to England, and the Duke of Orleans was proclaimed 'King of the French' under the name of Louis Philippe.

† At Drayton near Banbury.

of my associates were Tories, a member of the Church of England because my Mother was a member; and although I had so far evinced a slight taste for science when in Paris by purchasing a number of bottles of acid and combustibles, I caused such destruction to my clothes and the furniture that my Mother got rid of them as quickly as possible.

'Much to my Mother's annoyance my first act after my arrival at Rothamsted was to order one of the best bedrooms to be fitted up as a Laboratory. This was done by Mr. Squire of Oxford Street. I then commenced experimenting in a very desultory manner and devoted a great deal of time in reading books of Chemistry. Thompson's *Materia Medica** and other works by the same author were much read by me. Recent discoveries had been made of two active principles of vegetable growth. In order to extract them I procured seeds of the various plants such as Belladonna, Hemlock, Madder, Saffron etc., and sowed them about the farm. I also grew some acres of Poppies and procured a considerable quantity of Opium. Having managed to make the acquaintance of Dr. A. T. Thompson I got him to allow me to work in his Laboratory at the London University. I do not however think that I learnt much or that any accurate investigations were carried on while I was there. Dr. Thompson informed me that he had invented a process for making Calomel and Corrosive Sublimate by the combustion of Mercury in Chlorine Gas, and he either persuaded me or I persuaded him to make it the subject of a patent and to manufacture it for commercial purposes. This being done I commenced turning an old barn situated about ½ a mile from this house into a chemical manufactory. I got an introduction to Tenant of Glasgow and went there to learn how to make Chlorine Gas. I spent a great deal of time trying to carry out this invention successfully on a large scale, and although I made many tons of Calomel and Corrosive Sublimate I am disposed to think the process had nothing to recommend it and was no improvement over the process commonly employed. In these failures there can be no doubt I was acquiring much knowledge which was destined to be of the greatest use to me at a later period of life. It was about the year 1837 that I commenced a few experiments upon the action of Chemical salts on the growth of Plants. Shortly after that I began to manufacture chemical products for the use of Agriculture and at the same time

* The London dispensatory: a practical synopsis of materia medica, pharmacy and therapeutics; (London 1811), by Anthony Todd Thompson (1778-1849), the first professor of materia medica and therapeutics at University College, London (then London University) and founder of the British Pharmacopoeia.

to investigate systematically the action of these substances in the growth of plants; and to these two occupations a great portion of my time has been devoted.

'As I had no male relations my Mother was the only person to influence me in my pursuits, and she was violently opposed both to science or (sic) business, although at the same time devoted to me. Home influences and education all tended to make me in pursuits an ordinary country gentleman, in Politics a conservative, in Religion an ordinary member of the Church of England accepting as truth all that they teach. Whereas for some causes to be enquired into and explained, I have been very largely engaged in manufacturing pursuits, devoted to scientific investigation, very liberal in politics, and in religion although firmly and thoroughly believing in the truth of the Christian Religion and (ready) to accept it as the guide of my life as far as I can understand it and being at the same time a regular attendant at the services of the Church of England, still I cannot admit the right of that church or of any other church to teach dogmatically what truths are necessary for my salvation; and the feelings which would cause me to resent any interference with the liberty of conscience are quite as strong in me as they were in the breast of my ancestor* when he gave up the land of his birth and property more than 300 years ago.'

John Lawes kept no diaries and made only sparse notes. For a man in his position, he delivered few speeches. Brief and direct in conversation, he played no part in the social whirl of his daughter's London life. So little is known of his early aspirations that this letter, written to the *Agricultural Gazette* (January 2, 1888) tells as much as he ever revealed from his own pen:

'In answer to your inquiries, it is always difficult to predict whether a juvenile taste will develop in after life into anything useful. To write upon the door of a dark room with a stick of phosphorous, to dissolve a penny in nitric acid, or to convey an electric shock to your old housekeeper, who "refused to touch the jar with the hand, but did not mind touching it with the end of the poker"— these are feats which, with the accompanying destruction of clothes and furniture, cause the elders of the house to look with unfavourable eyes at a boy with a taste for chemistry. In my day Eton and Oxford were not of much assistance to those whose tastes were scientific

---

* Jacques Wittewronghele (1531-93) of Ghent, who fled to London from the Spanish persecution in the Netherlands in 1564. His portrait is in the Great Drawing-room at Rothamsted Manor, which was purchased in 1623 for his grandson Sir John Wittewronge, first Baronet.

rather than classical, and, consequently, my early pursuits were of a most desultory character. Matters, however, began to look serious when, at the age of twenty, I gave an order to a London firm to fit up a complete laboratory, and I am afraid it sadly disturbed the peace of mind of my mother to see one of the best bedrooms in the house fitted up with stoves, retorts, and all the apparatus and reagents necessary for chemical research. At that time, my attention was very much directed to the composition of drugs. I almost knew the pharmocopoeia by heart, and I was not satisfied until I had made the acquaintaince of the author, Dr. A. T. Thompson.

'The active principle of a number of substances was being discovered at this time, and in order to make these substances I sowed on my farm poppies, hemlock, henbane, colchicum, belladonna, etc. Some of these are still growing about the place. Dr. Thompson had suggested a process for making calomel and corrosive sublimate by burning quicksilver in chlorine gas. I undertook to carry out the process on a large scale, and wasted a good deal of time and money on a process which was, in fact, no improvement on the process then in use. Failures, however, have their value, as I found out afterwards. All this time I had the home farm of about 250 acres in hand. I entered upon it in 1834. Farmers were suffering from the abundance of the crops, and wheat, although rigidly protected, was very low in price. For three or four years I do not remember that any connection between chemistry and agriculture passed through my mind; but the remark of a gentleman who farmed near me (Lord Dacre, of Kimpton Hoo), who pointed out that on one farm bones were invaluable for the turnip crop, and on another farm they were useless, attracted my attention a good deal, especially as I had spent a good deal of money on bones without success. Somewhere about this time a drug broker in the City of London asked me whether I could make any use of precipitated gypsum and spent animal charcoal both of which substances held at the time no market value. Some tons of these were sent down, and, as sulphuric acid was largely used by me in making chlorine gas, the combination of the two followed.

'The successful application of the superphosphate on my own fields caused me to take out a patent, and to send it out for trial elsewhere. I put up an Edge runner to grind the charcoal finer, but to manufacture the substance on a large scale profitably with a carriage of twenty-five miles by wagon was out of the question. It was, however, a serious step to set up a manufactory in London, and it did not take place for some years afterwards. All this time I was carrying on a very large number of experiments with chemical manures, but they were performed upon areas of land too small to give trustworthy acreage results. I think the *Gardener's Chronicle*, which was first published in 1840, contains the result of my earliest experiments with various chemical salts.

'The publication of Liebig's book on Agriculture Chemistry in 1840 influenced considerably the direction of our experiments, and later on brought us into a somewhat heated controversy with one of the greatest geniuses of that time. Nearly fifty years have passed since that book was written. It was a bold work; and for some years afterward everyone could give confident opinions upon all subjects relating to agriculture—but where are we now? Have we a foundation laid, and can we say that such a thing exists as a science of agriculture? Another half-century will doubtless show more rapid progress, as there are so many more brains at work on the subject in various parts of the world; but when we consider that almost every other science contributes its share to form what we call the science of agriculture, those who follow the pursuit must expect plenty of hard work and be content with a moderate amount of success.'

That John Bennet Lawes is not immediately identified with other great scientists of his period, men such as Charles Darwin and Thomas Huxley, is because his experiments were long in duration and undramatic in result. Further, to an urban layman, they were largely inexplicable. He was tackling the fundamental problem of how best to grow things, plants and domestic animals; and nature is slow to give an answer.

The Victorians, starry-eyed with the achievements of engineers like Isambard Kingdom Brunel, the manufactories of Josiah Wedgwood, the wonder of Joseph Paxton's Crystal Palace, can scarcely have been expected to be thrilled by the work of a retiring country gentleman in rural Hertfordshire who experimented with pot plants, counted under controlled conditions the density of grasses in pasture, and used charred bones doctored with sulphuric acid to make fertiliser. Like 'the girl who was so pure' most people then couldn't say the word manure.

Lawes was concerned with the conservation of phosphates wasting out to sea from the urban sewers. He scrutinised the excrement of domestic animals to learn better ways of feeding them. With the insight of genius, and a total lack of showmanship, he grappled with the basic problems of agriculture and, in his chosen field, all life. With his lifelong colleague, Joseph Henry Gilbert, later Sir Joseph, he made Rothamsted the first and greatest agricultural research station in the world, the model for all who followed.

Paxton's Crystal Palace, Brunel's steamship the *Great Eastern*, even the British Empire have passed into history. The work of Lawes and Gilbert lives. They pioneered methods of agriculture as we now know them, changing its face from an experimental industry into an expanding science. Every back gardener, fertilising his plot with a bag of artificial manure, is benefiting today from Lawes's researches.

From the beginning Lawes financed his laboratory and his soil experiments entirely out of his own pocket. Soon after he married (to Caroline, daughter of Andrew Fountaine, of Narford Hall, Norfolk) the strain on his capital compelled him to let his ancestral home. For four years, during which his daughter Caroline, the Diane and the Skye of this book, was born, he had to let his house and, with his bride, divide his residence between London and Devonshire. In 1842, the year of his marriage, he had been granted a patent for his apparently diabolical brew of 'sulphuric acid, decomposing bones, bone ash, apatite or phosporite, and other phosphoritic substances for purposes of manure'. He had to stretch his resources to the limit to finance a factory to make it at Deptford Creek in London.

He was further embarrassed by what, with characteristic courtesy, he described, in his letter to the *Agricultural Gazette* as 'a somewhat heated controversy with one of the greatest geniuses of that time'. It was all of that. The German chemist, Justus von Liebig, in whose laboratory at Giessen, Lawes' colleague Joseph Gilbert had gained his degree in Ph.D. in 1840, was determined to expose the Englishman, without a scientific degree to his name, who was challenging the theory promulgated in his own work: *Chemistry of Agriculture and Physiology*.

The illustrious Baron Liebig's theory was that all the nitrogen requirements of plants were satisfied from the ammonia in the air. Lawes and Gilbert dared to contradict him; atmospheric supplies, they insisted, were inadequate and nitrogen should be given as manure. They had proved it by field experiment supplemented in the laboratory with pot plants.

Filled with the bitterness which so often besmirches learned differences, the baron carried his war over the Channel. At the British Association Meeting at Glasgow in 1855, he denounced Lawes. It is said that he spread the slander that Lawes had dug up the bones of the dead on the field of the Battle of Waterloo to fertilise English fields. Lawes, although he must have been worried by Liebig's accusations, continued the manufacture of his superphosphates, sacking it on London River with his picture on the label.

Mr. Henry E. Armstrong, one of Lawes's henchmen, later made his own dry dismissal of Liebig's exchange of personalities: 'If we attempt to compare Lawes with Liebig, it is clear that Liebig went deeper than Lawes into the philosophy of agriculture. Not only a commanding genius, but a trained and gifted experimentalist, Liebig broadly compassed the field problems of agriculture, but he lacked Lawes's practical experience and feeling; a laboratory student, like too many academic workers today, he was content to discuss nature from a distance, but did so with infinite skill. Liebig appears never to have understood Lawes sufficiently to make allowance for his scientific limitations and so to attach the proper value to his practical work. It is sad to think that two such men should have always remained so far apart.'

Meanwhile, Lawes's fertiliser business was expanding rapidly. Unpersuaded by his friends, in days when a gentleman did not engage in trade, least of all in the manure trade, he actually advertised his product. His first advertisement appeared in the *Gardener's Chronicle* on July 1, 1843:

'J. B. LAWES PATENT MANURES, composed of Superphosphate of Lime, Phosphate of Ammonia, Silicate of Potash, etc., are now on sale at his Factory, Deptford-creek, London, price 4s. 6d. per bushel. These substances can be had separately: the Super Phosphate of Lime alone is recommended for fixing the Ammonia of Dung-heaps, Cesspools, Gas Liquor, etc. Price 4s. 6d. per bushel.'

The confusion of the illustrious Baron Liebig was complete when the practical value of Lawes's experiments was confirmed at a meeting of Hertfordshire farmers on Christmas Eve, 1853. 'It was considered,' they declared in a circular, 'that Mr. Lawes has for many years engaged in a series of scientific and disinterested investigations for the improvement of agriculture generally, which have been carried out to an extent, with an attention to accuracy and detail, and at a cost never before undertaken by any individual or even by any public institution.'

The resolution, embodying the thanks of neighbouring farmers, became national in its appeal. Over a thousand pounds was subscribed. Lawes spent the money on building a new laboratory at Rothamsted.

Inevitably, the profitability of his process, and its success, tempted other manufacturers, and it was not long before Lawes discovered that the London Manure Company and others were committing substantial infringements of his patent. Lawes went to law and won. But infringements on the part of the London Manure Company still went on. Threatened with legal action again, the rivals yielded. Lawes let them have a licence to use his patent on condition that they paid him a royalty of ten shillings per ton of phosphate used. Two other firms who had been manufacturing superphosphates without permission eventually came to terms. One of them was Fison's of Thetford. Yes, Fison's, the chemical giant of the twentieth century.

But the pickings were too good for Lawes's rivals to knuckle under for long. Chafing under his restrictions, they resolved in London in March 1852 to fight Lawes 'by every justifiable means', starting a subscription for the purpose. Lawes was undeterred. In the courts it was pointed out that Lawes had put £10,000 of his own money into his experiments and was adding to this sum at the rate of £1,500 every year, while the results were being freely published for the benefit of all concerned with agriculture; and that it would not be to the public advantage to deprive him of 'a temporary monopoly fairly granted in his favour but yet a very inadequate compensation for the large amount of time and labour and money he has expended'. He won the case hands down. Infringements of his patent ceased. He built, in 1857, a second and larger manufactory at Barking Creek; and, twenty-five years later, he was able to sell it for £300,000; in today's currency a sum equivalent to three million.

Honours poured on him. Twenty-eight years before his services to agriculture were recognised by the conferment of a baronetcy, he had been elected a Fellow of the Royal Society. Both the Royal Agricultural Society and the Chemical Society had appointed him a member of their Councils. Foreign Governments had awarded him honours; and both his own University of Oxford and then Cambridge recognised his achievements, if tardily, by conferring degrees on him, in 1893 and 1894.

As early as 1855, when he was contemplating disposing his interests in his London manufactories, he had determined to ensure the continuation of the Rothamsted experiments by placing the laboratory and the fields in the hands of trustees, together with an endowment for their maintenance. In 1872 he made it known that he had set aside £100,000 for this purpose; and in 1889 he set up the Lawes Agricultural Trust, endowing it with the money and leasing to the trust the fields on which the classical experiments were conducted, 52 acres in all, at a peppercorn rent for one hundred years.

In 1893, Rothamsted's Jubilee was celebrated to commemorate

the completion of fifty years as an experimental station. A distinguished company gathered to honour Lawes and Gilbert. An appeal for subscriptions limited to two guineas brought contributions from all over the world. The United States was represented with subscriptions from twenty-three agricultural research stations, all modelled on Rothamsted. European agricultural stations sent illuminated addresses to the mother of them all.

Apart from the monument of Westmorland granite, set up with a suitable inscription in front of the Laboratory, Sir John Lawes was presented with his portrait, painted by Hubert Herkomer, R.A. The portrait hangs today in Rothamsted Manor, the house where Lawes was born in the last months before the Battle of Waterloo, and where he died peacefully, at the age of eighty-six, on the last day of August, 1900. He had brought to Rothamsted a greater renown than any of his long line of ancestors.

He lived just late enough to see the birth of the twentieth century. A child of the nineteenth, he was one of its giants.

Herkomer's portrait of John Lawes does not appeal to me. I prefer the one which was made later by Frank Salisbury. Salisbury (1874-1962), who rose to become one of the outstanding portrait painters of his time, began as a local boy at Harpenden, working in a repairing business for bicycles. The Lawes's discovered his talent as an artist. There is little doubt that Skye and her father, with their enthusiasm for everything artistic, launched him on his way.

Salisbury's portrait reveals John Lawes as the very model of a Great Victorian. Looking at it, it would be unimaginable to write of him without a capital 'G' for great. His full white beard flows with authority. His blue eyes, hooded by lids shaped like arrowheads, flash challengingly out of the canvas as if he were putting a question to some awestruck intruder. His nose is long and sensitive. His head is leonine, and the skimped lapels of his jacket and waistcoat seem almost shrunken underneath it. With his beard decked over his collar stud he can dispense with a tie. It is said that he was under medium height but, without the inches, the majesty of his countenance was sufficient to raise him among his fellows. His contemporary, Sir Francis Galton, the founder of eugenics, would surely have given the dome of his skull full marks.

At first glance he is formidable. A longer look at his picture discloses how nearly he is breaking into a twinkling smile. His contemporaries remarked on it. He was only outwardly the remote, unapproachable and, at the height of his fame, almost legendary figure that his aura suggested. Those who approached him with a sort of reverence soon discovered a genial host eager to share his enthusiasm—he sometimes bored them with it—for the life style of every ear of corn, every blade of grass, every mud-caked pig playing a part in his experiments.

Excepting the skilled scientists in his laboratories, he recruited almost all his labour force from his local village of Harpenden. His people treated 'The Squire', as they called him, with feudal respect. He treated them with paternal courtesy. The squire was never known to raise his voice in anger, or to allow any outward pressure to disturb his equanimity. Mr. Edwin Grey, who worked for him for fifty years, rising to become Field Superintendent, records almost with bated breath an occasion when Sir John's patience was tested. He had an old and eccentric employee, whom the other men knew as 'Professor' King, who had been his scout at Oxford. One day it emerged that the 'Professor' had broken into the villagers' club house and helped himself to the beer, a gift from the brewers, which was being kept for a New Year festivity. When Sir John entered the laboratory after the deed there was a hush as it was noticed that he failed to greet one of his oldest servants. 'King', says Mr. Grey, 'never regained Sir John's esteem.' But Sir John never said anything.

The simple countrymen, men and boys who worked for him, did what he asked them in the loyal faith that anything the squire wanted must be right. It is hard to suppose that, deep in their rustic hearts, they believed other than that he was stark, staring mad.

It is told that, one morning with some of her guests from the Manor, Lady Lawes (then Mrs. Lawes) came upon a small boy laboriously separating samples of grass species. Picking out a piece of grass she asked the boy the name of it. 'That's 'Ard-'Airy, ma'am,' said the boy. 'And this?' 'That's Soft-'Airy, ma'am,' 'And how do you tell the difference?' asked Mrs. Lawes. 'One's 'airy and 'ard, and the other's 'airy and soft, and one's got a sharp point, and the other's got a round point.' The narrator adds primly that 'the species thus described were *Avena Pubescence* and *Holcus Lanatus*'.

The importance of sickling and threshing the corn on the experimental plots at harvest-time was an occupation that all the men could understand. They recognised the importance of gleaning every ear, sometimes with the help of as many as twenty-four boys, so that the yield could be measured exactly. Immediately after the threshing the figures were taken into the office where the clerks set to work tabulating the results and organising the data for Sir John's annual letter to *The Times* in which he estimated the total yield of wheat in the United Kingdom and forecast the imports required to make up the deficiency. His annual letter, starting in 1862, was issued every year until his death. But there was one year (1882) when, to the consternation of the harvesters, Sir John ordered that part of his wheat crop was not to be harvested at all. It was to be allowed to stand and shed its seed.

Their eccentric squire, as they thought him, had decided to waste a portion of the crop to ascertain how long the wheat plant would survive without man's intervention. His bewildered men looked on as the crop on which they had laboured so hard was left to take care of itself. They learnt that Sir John also wanted to find out the effect on the fertility of the soil as the natural herbage re-established itself. They watched the birds and the vermin gobbling the shed corn. They watched the weeds creeping in. Within three seasons, the wild had taken possession. In 1886, searching the allotted ground, only three or four stunted and miserable wheat plants remained. The land was covered with a host of invaders, grasses, clovers, weeds, and the seedlings of shrubs and trees. No doubt the honest workers, scratching their heads, reflected that they could have told the squire what would happen, anyway. They called the place 'The Wilderness'. It is still there at Rothamsted. The area is probably too small to be representative enough for a survey. But it demonstrates what could happen to the land if man's hand was removed; and England should 'bide till Judgement Tide, by Oak, and Ash, and Thorn!'

Although his people had long known that their squire was a great man, what with all the foreign visitors and all the comings-and-goings which attended their daily work, it was probably not until the Jubilee, celebrating fifty years of agricultural experiment, when all the big-wigs came down from London in special trains, when there were marquees on the common and everybody wore their Sunday clothes and made speeches about the Squire, that they fully realised that they themselves had shared in an achievement that had made history.

Long before, they had put their trust in the squire, and taken him to their hearts; now, they knew that he was recognised by the world. It was he who had founded a savings bank for them, before the post office savings scheme came into operation. He had administered it personally so that his men's private affairs could only be known to him. He had given all who wanted them allotments and built for the holders a club house which was reputed to be, if not the oldest, one of the oldest of its kind in England.

The club house became the centre of local life. It extended to a Store Society (a kind of Co-op), a Flour Club (because most of the women at that time cooked their own bread), a Pig Club, a Coal Club and a 'Death Fund', the object of this truly last being to assure to the relatives a certain sum of money on the death of a member or a member's wife. Whenever any new branch club or society was formed, Sir John was there to explain its workings. On one occasion he was accompanied by Charles Dickens who wrote an article describing his visit which appeared in the first number of *All the Year Round* ('The Poor Man and His Beer', April 1859).

The great event of the year in the Allotment Club was the Annual Dinner. For the Club Feast, as it was called, a marquee was erected and joints of meat were cooked in large coppers at the local brewhouse and bakehouses. The biggest piece—a huge round of beef weighing 94 to 96 lbs.—was the annual gift of Sir John, the President of the Club. When it was cooked, it required two digging forks to lift it out of the copper. Sir John himself presided over the dinner, carving the joint with a special set of carvers sent for the occasion from Rothamsted Manor.

Sir John liked living simply with his own people. But, when he made a splash, money was no object. When Skye was married to Walter Pennington Creyke, he celebrated the wedding reception at the Manor by treating all the Allotment holders with their wives to a special excursion via the Midland Railway, to the Crystal Palace. Most of them had never been in a train, never mind London. It gave them something to talk about for years. At the Jubilee of Rothamsted he also proposed sending the members of the Club to the Crystal Palace, in its new setting, to see a 'Brock's Benefit'. Twice in a lifetime was too much for the Allotment holders, many of whom were now elderly people. So the squire brought the fireworks to them. Not much to shout about these days. In Sir John's, he was doing things for his people that employers had not done before.

So much for the Australian journalist's 'pater familias who is only unearthed when bills have to be paid'. In all her own writing, Skye makes no reference to her father except once when, as Caroline Creyke, she contributed a learned paper to the *Nineteenth Century* (June 1893) on the Rothamsted Experiments. It is evident from it that she was closely informed on her father's work. No letters exist from her to him, or him to her, apart from relatively formal ones inviting her, for example, to attend his investiture, in the presence of royalty, with some honour or another. He subscribes himself formally: 'Your affectionate father, J. B. Lawes'.

Her mother 'Gogo' writes to her more intimately, mostly on trivial matters, but addressing her variously as 'Dearest Skye', 'My dear Ina' and 'Darling Caroline'. Her memory, enshrined in the anecdote of her carrying the infant Skye on her back down a Scottish mountain, is enveloped in an intangible swathe of Victorian costumiery, whalebone braced silks and satins; and what the poet Austin Dobson calls 'fal-lals and what-nots'. In faded photographs she appears as a dumpy figure, sitting formally by her husband in family groups; or, slightly out of focus, wearing a mob cap and beckoning to her little pug dog. She was undoubtedly the one who influenced Skye (and her brother) in their artistic leanings. She sketched, and she was a good water colourist. My guess is that, like many mothers, she was content to efface her own personality, to bask in her husband's fame and to enjoy the company of her two unusually gifted children. She lived to celebrate her golden wedding at Rothamsted, dying there on November 29, 1895, five years before Sir John, who, in his farming clothes, with a spud hoe for company, continued vigorously to pace his land to the end of his days, apologising to his visitors for walking too fast.

The four of them were a closely-knit family. Evidence that they were almost exclusive in their affections for one another may explain Skye's attempt to conceal her identity in the *Sporting Sketches*. Unless a lot of papers have been lost, they communicated only when they had something to tell, the sort of news which they would have passed to each other today on the telephone. I doubt whether they ever drooled amongst themselves. Self-contained, supremely confident of their social standing, and in each other, there was no call to make a demonstration of the obvious. Yet few families can have kept so close.

From those early holidays in the Highlands of Scotland to the end of Sir John's life, his children and later his grandchildren attended him as if he were the Maypole of their existence. He had them in his gloomy old manor house at Rothamsted, darkened by oak-panelling, lined with paintings of his ancestors, decorated with musty tapestries and bits of armour, and furnished with great four-poster beds. He welcomed them, year after year, in the damp shooting lodge at Dalmally and, in his last years, to the converted monastery at Ardchattan. None of his residences can have been comfortable. It was the comforting presence of their father and grandfather which made them all feel warm within.

He plainly had the rare gift of giving his children confidence without interfering with them. I am sure that it would never have occurred to him to issue a parental edict that infants of four should not climb mountains; or that they would catch their death of cold if they got wet. His own children could do what they fancied, and he watched them thrive in independence and self confidence. I'll bet that all a protesting children's nurse ever got out of him was a knowing smile. He enjoyed watching his own win their spurs.

When Skye showed that she could use a rifle, he gave her a better one. When she caught a salmon, he equipped her with the tackle to catch more. When she showed that she could row a boat he got her an inflatable one, of a kind which had never been seen in Scotland before.

When her brother began to distinguish himself as an athlete, he immediately transformed one of his precious barns at Rothamsted into a gymnasium for him. Charles was no ordinary person either.

V

HER BROTHER

ER brother Charles was the mischievous little boy who, in *Sporting Sketches*, prowled about at a picnic with a two-pronged steel fork, prodding the girls in the arms whenever he could catch them. He was a year older than Skye, and as high-spirited as she was. After the incident of the fork he grew up with a golden spoon in his mouth, that mixed blessing which Alec Waugh has aptly described as 'The Fatal Gift'.

Born to the purple, heir to a great fortune, he was endowed with a striking appearance and the physique of a Greek god. He had personal charm, all the social graces and, inherited from his mother, cultivated artistic leanings. That he possessed none of the scientific interests and aptitude for business of his father seemed irrelevant. For Charles, as Alec Waugh wrote: 'The race was won before the pistol went.'

He was born at Teignmouth in Devon on October 3rd, 1843, during the period when his father had had to sublet the family's ancestral home to conserve his finances for the development of his business. Before he was out of his infant skirts money was no longer a matter for consideration. His father grew rich, and increasingly richer; and he came to believe that he could have no greater blessing than his son. Predictably, Charles was put down for Eton, whence he went on to Trinity, Cambridge, reading for the natural sciences tripos, graduating B.A. in 1866. His scholastic achievements were unexceptional. But, on the way, he distinguished himself as the outstanding all round amateur athlete of his time.

He won his first races, the mile, quarter mile, 100 yards hurdle and the steeplechase in the school sports at Eton. In 1864, he won the 500 and 100 yards after running five heats. His father donated a 'Lawes' cup for anyone who could repeat his performance. Nobody ever has. In 1859, he took up rowing, and won the Pair oars and Tub sculling cup. The following year he added the Sculls to his credit.

At University, he continued his triumphant progress as oarsman and runner. He won the Cambridge Sculls, and Amateur Champion of the Thames. In 1862 he stroked the Cambridge Eight and won the Colquhoun Sculls. In 1863 he won the Diamond Sculls at Henley and, on the track, the Inter-University Mile. In 1865, after winning the Wingfield Sculls, he left the river to devote himself to track-running. In 1864, when the University and Inter-University sports were first established, he won the mile for Cambridge in 4 mins. 59 sec., lowering the time to 4 mins. 39 sec. in the Inter-University race the following year. He became Hon. Secretary of the University Athletic Club, presenting a Challenge Cup for the mile as a perpetual trophy.

The maids at Rothamsted must have had their time cut out polishing his own collection of trophies, silver cups and medallions. Overdoing it more than a little bit his doting father had a silver model made of him in the attitude of Apollo Belvedere, the statue in the Vatican Museum which was the Victorians' ideal of classical male beauty. He also had another one, a life-size marble statue, carved by John Henry Foley. The Great Drawing Room at the Manor was built especially for his coming of age in 1864, which was celebrated at Rothamsted with 'a ball of considerable splendour'. It would have been difficult for any man to fulfil the promise of such a gilded youth.

In fairness to him he made a brave try. Denied the discipline of having to work for a living, hampered with the inevitable disadvantages of the barrier that divides inherited wealth from truth, he did his best to achieve greatness on his own. On leaving Cambridge he conceived himself as a sculptor. As Vanity Fair put it in their feature 'Men of the Day' in 1883, when he was still hard at it with chisel and mallet in his studio near Chelsea Gardens: 'He looks neither to the right, nor the left, and foregoing not only all society, but all other things that might interfere with what he regards as his mission, he passes the whole of his days in the studio; and, if natural predilection and earnest application count for anything, should some day produce some fine work. That in sculpture as in athletics he will one day achieve fame he is persuaded; and meanwhile he holds the sculpture's art to be one which none but those with a mission should essay....'

He married in 1869 at St. Paul's Church, Knightsbridge, his first cousin Marie Amélie Rose, daughter of Charles George Fountaine, of Beaufort Gardens, South Kensington. They had an only son, John, who was born in 1872. There is no evidence that his wife, who is said to have been an exceptional beauty, ever had any special influence over him; or that he bestowed any special interest on his son. It is indicative that, in 1892, when young John Lawes was just twenty, he was shipped off, under the eye of his grandfather, to Australia, the usual haven in those days for ne'er-do-wells with a load of debts of well-connected families.* After seeing him off, his father —according to one of his nieces—hastened away to a pet shop to see about a cockatoo. He was interested in natural history.

His son, on a brief return visit to the old country brought his father a pair of Black Cockatoos from Queensland, with fearsome claws, destructive beaks and a devilish humour. He presented them, presumably in amelioration for past misdemeanours, as Jessica might have given Shylock her barbary ape. His father was delighted with the birds, and kept them to the terror of his visitors with his modelling clay and lumps of stone in his Chelsea studio.

His reputation as an eccentric extended beyond the immolation he imposed on himself in his mission as sculptor. At the age of fifty-four, at the height of cyclomania in the late nineties—the period in which Marie Lloyd sang her music hall song : 'The fellows all chi-ike, when they see me on my bike' and his sister Skye was also an enthusiastic supporter of the new fad—he took up the sport himself. He denied that it had anything to do with a wish for healthy exercise. He decried the need for exercise. He was simply fascinated to discover that he had 'a trick of pushing the treadles round quicker than most people could push them'. He took up speed cycling and, although he competed in very few races, he made several successful attacks on 'records'. He became an enthusiastic pace follower, a highly specialised form of cycle-racing in which few amateurs had the time or means to become proficient. He had both. At one time, he kept his own private pacing team at the Crystal Palace. On the track, in 1889, he set up a 25-miles amateur record of 51 mins. 15⅘ secs. During his short cycling career he had his accidents, in one of which he fractured his collar-bone. But, until the last few years of his life he regularly made the 26-mile journey from Rothamsted to his studios at Chelsea by bicycle. One of his eccentricities, on the rare occasions when he was waiting for a train, was to race on his bike up and down the platform at Harpenden Station.

In Chelsea he worked with dedicated industry to within a few days of his death. He had no taste for his sister's world, the roundabout of the London Season. He was no clubman and no man-about-town. He never followed the pursuits of a country gentleman or

* He may also have been sent to manage land which his grandfather had acquired in the new country. Perhaps it was a bit of both.

took any part, as his father did, in local affairs at his seat in Harpenden. In a polite endeavour to say the right thing in his obituary, *The Times* recorded: 'Personally, Sir Charles was a man of mark in any company, and whatever he said or did had the accent of distinction. Entirely original in his outlook and independent of current opinion, he was a stimulating talker, with his surprising practical shrewdness and power of putting aside convention.'

All he wanted was to be recognised as a great sculptor. He exhibited regularly at the Royal Academy. The large bronze group named 'The Death of Dirce' outside the Tate Galley is his work. He took a prominent part in founding the Society of Sculptors, of which he was made first President in 1909. But only an innocent could suppose that selection for the Academy Exhibition has always been ruled by purely artistic merit, or that public galleries and Royal Societies can flourish without wealthy patrons. In his lifetime he was never told the sort of thing they wrote of him after his death:

'He was not a sculptor of the first rank, although I see the words "boldness of conception" and "skill of execution" tolerantly applied to his ponderous group of "Dirce and the Bull" which lately made an earth-shaking journey to Rome.' (It won for him first prize in the Franco-British Exhibition of 1908.)

'He took seriously to the practice of art', said *The Times*, 'and became a sculptor. He frequently exhibited figures and portraits, in all of which he showed real ability, though his success was never quite equal to his ambition.... His colossal group of "Dirce and the Bull" which, carved in a sort of grey marble, was shown at the Royal Academy, and is at this moment, in spite of immense difficulties experienced in the transport, the central object in the Gallery of British Sculptors at the Rome Exhibition.* It is a work which shows a great boldness.... though whether the result is equal to the gigantic labour it must have cost is open to some doubt.

'Sir Charles Lawes's name as a sculptor will always be better known in connection with the famous lawsuit than with any work of his own....'

It was a cruel verdict, and it was a true one. Charles Lawes had dedicated his vast energies, his unremitting industry, to a vocation in which he was not gifted enough to match his achievement with his ambition. If he had been a struggling artist he would have learnt early in life that he was attempting to attain heights beyond

---

* The marble of 'The Death of Dirce', which occupied Sir Charles's latter years now stands in the Rothamsted Grounds. The bronze copy is the one at the Tate Gallery.

his own abilities. His artistic bent might well have been diverted more purposefully elsewhere. As it was his riches during his lifetime stood in the path of healthy criticism. His contemporaries, in the name of flattery, lied.

Yet, as one of his obituarists tells, he has his place in the history of sculpture. As a protagonist in the celebrated libel suit Belt v. Lawes (1882-84) he ensured for himself, if not for his works, a certain immortality. In the defence of artistic integrity he denounced one of his fashionable contemporaries, Richard Belt, as an impostor. No doubt, he was prompted into action by fellow sculptors who had greater cause to count the costs involved in a lawsuit than he had; but Lawes needed no goading. Counting it 'his privilege as well as his duty to protect the noble art of sculpture against all assaults on the part of those who may not have such a mission', he charged into the arena of the courts as pugnaciously as a bull in one of his own monumental creations.

The subsequent proceedings became at once a lawyers' Benefit Match, a contest in which Art and Fashion were ranged in opposing corners, and a contender, as it would have been today, for the *Guinness Book of Records*. It was the last English trial of importance to be held in Westminster Hall where Sir Thomas More, Ann Boleyn, Charles the First, and many other good heads for a sculptor had been condemned to lose theirs. With the exception of the Tichborne case, it was the most protracted trial—it lasted forty-three days, not counting the time taken by the various appeals—ever to be held in an English court.

In retrospect, it also has a living interest. Some of the most important exhibits in the case are still on show. On a peripatetic through the streets of London, a modern art-lover can form his own opinion of the statuary which caused such a gerfuffle during a large part of Mr. Gladstone's second ministry. You won't find Mr. Gladstone's head by Mr. Belt among all the others in the National Liberal Club. In his evidence, the plaintiff said that he had done a bust 'but (Laughter in Court) only the remnants of him remained'. In the bizarre suit the remark was typical.

The plaintiff, Richard Belt, was a self-made man and almost a self-taught artist, a rank outsider who within two or three years, had become the fashionable sculptor of his day. The Church, the Peerage and the Queen had bestowed their approval on him with commissions. It was only a short time since his statue of Byron had been ceremonially unveiled. This huge bronze, which still sits upon a slab of pink marble in the corner of Hyde Park adjoining the Duke of Wellington's Apsley House, was entered by Belt in a competition, which he won and for which the prize money was £3,500. It was his largest and most remunerative commission. Better than that, it established his status as a leading sculptor. A modern critic has described Byron's as 'one of the worst statues—if not the very worst —in London, showing him hunched up in a would-be poetic pose, half-toppling over sideways, with an apology for a dog (poor old Bo'sun) at his side'. Charles Lawes thought it rather good. His case was that Belt was himself incapable of modelling it.

Lawes at one time had employed Belt in his own studio. He had had then no high opinion of his abilities. Lawes talked with one Verhyden, another sculptor's assistant, who in turn had worked for Belt. Belt's success, they decided, was the result of an outrageous fraud. Others of their sculptor friends concurred with them. Without further ado, Lawes issued a broadside in *Vanity Fair* (August 1881) which, after suitable indemnities had been signed, the editor agreed to publish. It was headed 'Mr. Belt', and it was inflammatory stuff:

'After leaving Mr. Lawes' studio in 1875, Mr. Belt began to do business on his own account. He published as his own work a statuette of Dean Stanley, of which a good deal has been lately heard. This statuette, however, was worked up for him by Mr. Brock, as Mr. Brock himself declares. In like manner the memorial busts of Charles Kingsley and Canon Conway, which also passed as the work of Mr. Belt, were, in fact, invested by Mr. Brock—as Mr. Brock himself declares—with whatever artistic merit they possess. Mr. Brock, equally with Mr. Lawes, declares that Mr. Belt himself was incapable of doing anything in the shape of artistic work. In 1876 Mr. Belt took in partnership Mr. Verhyden. Mr. Verhyden states that the drawings that procured for Mr. Belt the Conway Monument (the bust of which was, as already stated, worked up by Mr. Brock) were his, not Mr. Belt's at all.

'Mr. Verhyden further declares that he and not Mr. Belt entirely modelled the sketch which enabled Mr. Belt to gain the victory over all the Artists of the day in the Byron competition; and that he also entirely modelled the Byron statue itself.

'In short, we are assured that all Mr. Belt's works from the year 1876 when he began on his own account up to the year 1881 were executed by Mr. Brock and Mr. Verhyden.

'Mr. Verhyden states equally with Mr. Lawes and Mr. Brock, that Mr. Belt was quite incapable of doing any artistic work whatever.

'The names we have cited are those of only some among a number of men of the highest position in the artistic world among whom our enquiries have been made, and we feel bound to say that, in the face of the detailed statements made to us, the bare outlines of which we have here set down, we find it difficult to believe that Mr. Belt has any good claim to the authorship given to the public as his or to any other title than that of a purveyor of other men's work, the editor of other men's designs, a broker of other men's sculpture. If he declared himself to be this, there would be no harm in it. But the point is that, if our information is correct, he has systematically and falsely claimed to be the author of the works for which he was only the broker, that he presents himself as a sculptor and an artist, when in reality he is but a statue jobber and a tradesman. If then the statements made to us are true—and we frankly avow that at present we fully believe them to be perfectly true—Mr. Belt has been guilty of a very scandalous imposture, and those who have admired and praised him as a genius are the victims of a monstrous deception.

'Why this deception if it be one should have been allowed to exist so long is a matter which does not concern us, though we must say that it does very greatly concern those artists who were aware of it.

'But we, having got a hint of it, and having upon this hint made very full investigations, should not be doing our duty were we to withhold from the public the result of that investigation.

'Accordingly we have set down the information we have obtained and with it the conviction which that information has produced upon us, that Mr. Belt is not the author of the works that have made him to be believed to be a sculptor of genius. Every paper in London announced on Thursday morning the fact that Mr. Belt had received from the Queen a commission to execute another statuette of Lord Beaconsfield. We shall be glad to know that Her Majesty's choice of an artist is really warranted.'

The next month Lawes sent the article to the Lord Mayor of London with the following letter:

Dear My Lord:

As the newspapers state that there is a probability of the Corporation commissioning certain works of sculpture before long, I beg to submit to your Lordship's attention the enclosed paragraph from Vanity Fair.

As this notice appeared some time ago, and as there has been no denial or refutation of the charges therein contained, though such denials have been repeatedly challenged by the Editors and others in the public press, and as also I must add that I am aware that no such denial, were it made, could possibly be substantiated, I consider it my duty to my profession to lay the matter before your Lordship.

I am, your Lordship's obedient servant,[*]

CHARLES LAWES
(Sculptor)

Mr. Belt was reluctant to take action. The public were puzzled. It was an unexpected revelation that artists used assistants; it seemed unbelievable that a sculptor's work could be any but all his own. It must be a case of professional jealousy. Opinion rallied strongly to the defence of Mr. Belt's reputation. A large sum of money was subscribed to defray the plaintiff's legal costs.

The scene in Westminister Hall, where the case finally opened, was something between submission day at the Royal Academy, the enclosure at the races and a legal light opera by Gilbert and Sullivan. Marble busts stood on every bench. Plaster casts were ranged like paper weights among the briefs, and bronzes were passed from hand to hand as if it were an art dealer's auction sale. The biggest of big-wigs (Sir Hardinge Gifford, Q.C., later Lord Halsbury, supported by three distinguished juniors, appeared for the plaintiff: Lawes was represented by Charles Russell, Q.C.—later Lord Russell of Killowen —Richard Webster, Q.C. and Lewis Coward). The seats in the court were filled with the cream of society. Twelve stolid-faced jurymen, who knew nothing about art but knew what they liked, were ranged under the judge, Baron Huddlestone, who had tried Whistler's libel action against Ruskin. That case was a pale watercolour to this one in which Lawes was ruthlessly determined to paint his rival out of sight and sound. Belt was obliged to prove his craftsmanship or withdraw from the greatness to which he had thrust himself.

The trial was so long, so repetitive, so cursed with legal tangles, that it precludes a blow by blow account. It began on June 21st, but on the 29th, it was adjourned until November. The Long Vacation of the Courts was then four months, and during that time the Judges went on assize. So when the jury returned their verdict, exactly six months had elapsed since the plaintiff appeared in the witness box. As counsel took four days delivering their final speeches, and the Judge took another four days summing-up, it was a jury, punch drunk with words, who retired to consider their verdict.

[*] This letter was wasted on the Lord Mayor who, in the subsequent trial, appeared as a witness for the plaintiff.

Gustave Doré made this charming sketch of Diane (Mrs. Walter Creyke), so different from the grotesques which constitute the larger part of his oeuvre, in 1879. He had known Diane since childhood in the Highlands of Scotland. He said that she evoked for him their mutual friend, Sarah Bernhardt.

Frank Salisbury painted this portrait of Sir John Bennet Lawes Bt. at the height of his fame and fortune. It was the patronage of the Lawes family which raised Salisbury from humble work in a bicycle repair shop in Harpenden into becoming one of the most fashionable portrait painters of his day.

Lady Lawes, never without a dog at her side, effaced herself behind her celebrated husband. He said that he was glad that she predeceased him by a few years 'because she could never have managed without me'. Still, she was a strong Victorian matriarch. Of an old Norfolk family, she was a devoted mother and grandmother.

Diane's brother, Charles, changed his name when he inherited the baronetcy, to Sir Charles Lawes Wittewronge, commemorating one of his seventeenth-century Flemish forebears. He was ancestor obsessed. In his time he had been the outstanding amateur athlete of his day, and he became a dedicated chiseller of tormented sculpture. The piece (*opposite*) 'Dirce and the Bull' still stands in the grounds of Rothamsted Manor. Another group is placed at the entrance of the Tate Gallery. But Charles is chiefly famous as the defendant in one of the most historic libel actions in the English courts when he accused a fellow sculptor, and lost his case, of being a fraud.

Diane's husband, Walter Pennington Creyke, was described as one of the most handsome men in England. Lord Leighton, then President of the Royal Academy, used him as a model for Christ in his picture 'The Wise and Foolish Virgins'. He subsequently incorporated his sitter in a mural of the same subject which can still be seen in Lyndhurst Parish Church in the New Forest. The drawing of Walter (*top left*) is by Leighton. The portraits of him (*top right and bottom left*) are by his wife. The painting (*bottom right*), also by Diane, is of the Venerable Stephen Creyke of York, Walter's father.

Gustave Doré made the finished drawing of Diane (*above*) from the preliminary sketch six pages back. It is not so effective as the first impression, although her grandchildren say that it is more like her. The Etonian (*top right*) is Diane's surviving twin son, Launcelot. She had less patience with him than she had with her daughters. Lance was killed in the underground, after a fairly dissolute life, during the London blitz. Diane called this picture (*lower right*) of her daughter, Everilda, 'The Young Lady Goes for a Walk'. Diane was an erratic artist, but she had her moments of true inspiration. The portrait of her father-in-law on the opposite page shows a considerable mastery of oil paint.

EVERILDA

LILIAN

SYLVIA

DIANA

Diane's four daughters were all as English as the rose. Everilda, the eldest, recalled here in a miniature in the Victoria and Albert Museum, left a fortune of £100,000 at the age of eighty-six. Sylvia lived into her ninety-third year. Diana, the third daughter, joined Christian Science. Only Lilian died young.

Belt had given a good account of himself in the witness box, not omitting a neat body punch or two at the defendant. He told the story of poor boy's rise to fame effectively. In a labouring boy's job under the Engineer of the House of Commons, he had taken to sketching the eminent men who thronged the lobbies. Fired with enthusiasm, he had joined an art class at a Working Men's Club and began to toy with mallet and chisel. His first head, he said—it was a good touch for the jury—he did with a nail and a hand-brush. Then, for the first time, he worked for a sculptor, named Plows, and was engaged on the head of the elephant over the Elephant House at the Zoo. Five years later became a pupil and assistant to Foley*, a Royal Academician, at a salary of £1 a week. Foley, he added wilily, was reluctant to take him because Lawes, the defendant, had been his first pupil and had turned out to be unsatisfactory. Foley was the sculptor of the figure of Prince Albert on the Albert Memorial, a work at which he (Belt) had assisted him. At this time he also made his 'probation work' for the Royal Academy—a clay copy of the Farnese Hercules—and was successful first time, while Lawes he observed, was twice 'plucked'. It was while Foley fell ill that Belt went for three or four years to Lawes's studio. Here he received his first commission, from his old employer Mr. Nicholls, the Engineer of the House of Commons. He did heads of Mr. and Mrs. Nicholls which were shown in the Royal Academy. Then came a head of Dean Stanley, which was unfortunately destroyed by the firm who were casting it. When he sued the firm for negligence, and was given £50 damages, Lawes gave evidence for him without claiming any part in the work. Soon afterwards he fell out with Lawes over an account.

Belt now took his own studio, and was an immediate success. He told how Dean Stanley had recommended him to Charles Kingsley, the clergyman and novelist who wrote *The Water Babies*. He went down to Eversley Rectory, returning with two heads, one of which, when shown in the Royal Academy, appealed so much to the Queen that she commanded a copy. He now had all the connections a fashionable sculptor could wish. As he told the story of his commissions, the appropriate work was paraded in Court—Canon Conway, Lord Stanhope, Lord Castlebury, Lord Shrewsbury, and Miss Nellie Plimsoll (who, when the sheet was removed, turned out to be 'a melancholy bronze bust of Lord Beaconsfield'). The Queen had graciously approved his Prince Imperial (Napoleon III) of whom he

* None other than the same John Henry Foley who had carved the life sized marble statue of Charles Lawes as a Grecian god.

made a posthumous bust. The Queen herself and the Royal Family at Windsor had made suggestions which he had carried out to their satisfaction. A copy of the work was eventually sent to the Queen at Windsor, and a smaller version, specially adapted to give it an appearance of greater youthfulness, to Paris. By the time he had finished his evidence there were forty or more of his sculptures in Court.

The defence had an unequivocal answer to him. In modern parlance it might be said that their case was that 'it was all done with mirrors'. The trick, 'evidently unknown to the English public, but, among sculptors, a very old one, is that a "ghost" is installed in a convenient hiding-place, and the artist proceeds to go through the accustomed forms of his profession and to show off what little he knows about modelling, accompanied by a large amount of tall and appropriate conversation. The sitting concluded, and the patron departed, the ghost comes from his hiding place, and with the aid of photographs taken during the sitting he puts the bust into artistic trim.' Verhyden testified that he entered Belt's studio in Hugh Street by climbing a ladder from an alley-way and passing through a trap-door so that he was invisible to the sitters, and also to the other men working there.

When Belt moved to a studio in Wilton Place it was said that it had similar possibilities. 'At the far end there was a curious small apartment closed off by a door which was partly a folding door and partly a sliding door. Supposing that anyone had been invited to retire beyond that sliding door he could have passed out, for there was another door closed simply by a cross-bar, which gave egress into a Mews.'

The allegations met with a warm disavowment from Belt. 'I can refer you to artists of celebrity who have seen me execute works of merit,' he protested, reeling off a list of names. 'These and many others have seen me work and stood by my side while I manipulated the clay, thousands of others have seen me, and you can all see me doing it here now, if you like.' 'If such a test should appear desirable in the course of this case', said the Judge blandly, 'I shall certainly permit it.' The loud applause in Court from the crowd in the public seating, and 'some distinguished persons who were accommodated with seats upon the bench', was immediately suppressed. But Belt had scored a bull point.

He had eighty-two witnesses, many of them distinguished men and women in society, who had sat for him and who were not going to let anybody believe that anybody could fool them. They were convinced that they saw their features being modelled before their eyes. As each one appeared in the witness box, his or her bust was placed nearby. There was Mr. Webb of Newstead Abbey, where Belt had gone to inspect the collar of Byron's dog. He stayed to do a bust of Mr. Webb. There was the Honourable Alexander Yorke, who had seen Belt at Her Majesty's request altering the expression of Napoleon the Third's eyes. There was Lord Clarence Paget who had watched Belt at work on Byron's feet and Earl Russell's head, and added modestly: 'I dabble a little in sculpture myself, having done a colossal study of Nelson on the Menai Straits, as a landmark for the Survey Department, and I once exhibited at the Royal Academy.' There was Mr. Samuel Plimsoll, of the Plimsoll Line, 'beside whom was placed, amid some merriment, a statuette in a declamatory attitude with outstretched arms'. There was a witness who had watched Belt putting the sight into Lord Beaconsfield's eye, and another who had noticed how Belt built up his face bones and skull anatomically, according to measurements taken with callipers, gradually adding muscles and tissues. 'I watched him add small pieces of clay about the size of a pea, saw it grow into a likeness. There was no way into the studio from which anyone else could have watched him and taken my bust. Sir Richard Wallace, owner of the Wallace Collection and Trustee of the National Portrait Gallery, had seen many sculptors at work and had no doubt of Belt's qualities. A Mrs. Bishoppsheim said: 'We had twelve or fifteen sittings on the ground floor—my face to the window—Mr. Belt was standing there. I was on a raised platform on a wooden box. He stood on nothing.' A daring juror rose, and asked: 'Was that the sculptor's ghost, my Lord? He stood on nothing.'

All Belt's witnesses were satisfied that, whatever his methods, he was a true artist. George Augustus Sala, the illustrious art critic of the *Daily Telegraph*, declared that he had been much struck by Belt's skill in putting on Lord Beaconsfield's hair—not the forelock, he explained, which Lord Beaconsfield cherished, but the hair on the side. As an amateur modeller himself he had paid many visits to the studio and observed that 'Belt worked accurately, turning rough clay into smooth modelling material in the manner of other sculptors'. One of Belt's studio assistants, named Schotz, had obtained all the high honours at Louvain and the Gold Medal at the Royal Academy of Antwerp.' It did emerge, however, that 'there were only two students of any consequence at Louvain—he and Verhyden. The school had gone down as the director's brain was weak.

'The gallery of fine arts in the body of the Court' wrote *The*

Times, 'was further enriched today by a large life-size plaster cast of "Hypatia", one of Mr. Belt's latest works. This greatly impeded the witnesses in giving their evidence and caused them to remove to the other side of the Court.' The list of Mr. Belt's witnesses was beginning to read like a Court Circular. The Dowager Duchess of Cleveland had had Mr. Belt down at Osterley Park which no sculptor's ghost could have haunted unseen. Dean Stanley's footman (now a verger at the Abbey) recalled that Lady Augusta had thought the Dean too tall, so he was cut through the body and the drapery remodelled. Baron Lionel de Rothschild's hairdresser told how he had been sent for by Mr. Belt so that he could find out the proper arrangement of the late baron's hair for a posthumous bust. 'The collection of busts, bronzes, statuettes, medallions etc., in the body of the Court was further enriched by a dazzling plaster cast of the Lord Mayor in his robes of office, lately done by Belt. To compensate for this, a striking bust of Edgar Vincent received so rude a shock from a barrister extracting a book from a shelf, that the bust was decapitated. This is as yet the only casualty among a vast collection of all sizes and shapes exposed to the dangers of handling by different people, and being jostled by those passing through a crowded Court.' The Lord Mayor of London gave evidence in support of the authenticity of his own statue from the Bench. 'Are not your eyebrows more arched?' asked Mr. Russell for the defence. 'You remember what the scripture said?' '"A man beholds his natural face in the glass"' replied the Lord Mayor, ' "and goes and straight away forgets what manner of man he is." It is far better looking than I think I am.' 'It is' Mr. Russell conceded, 'a fair presentable Lord Mayorish sort of person.'

Belt's evidence was corroborated, not only by all his studio assistants (except Verhyden) but also given the blessing of William Morris. William Morris was the only artist that he called. Lawes had a packful for the defence. Meanwhile, the Judge made up his mind that the only way of finding out the truth was by the practical evidence which the plaintiff had suggested. 'After Mr. Belt has finished his evidence' he pronounced quite early in the proceedings 'I propose that a stage be fitted up and some clay given to the plaintiff on which he may work before the jury. I think that it is a fair test, but I will not suggest either Mr. Russell, for the defendant or Sir Hardinge Gifford, for the plaintiff.' Belt was equal to the situation. 'I hope your Lordship will allow me to model you.' His Lordship did not dissent but, in the end, it was agreed that a room should be set apart where no one would be admitted except Belt himself, his sitter—who was to be one of his studio assistants named Pagliati—and two representatives of each side. The jury was to be allowed a peep whenever the Court was adjourned.

After the passage of many days, it was announced that the new bust of Pagliati would be produced. The exhibit was carried in like a head on a charger, preceded by Mr. Belt, followed by Mr. Pagliati. It was received with a round of applause, instantly suppressed, from the back of the Court.

Early on, Russell must have realised that the accumulation of laymen's testimony for the plaintiff, the fact that his work had received the royal 'we' of approval from Queen Victoria, and that the Lord Mayor of London himself had descended from his golden coach to give evidence for Belt, presented him with more than the usual 'difficulty'. It was obvious, too, that Belt's consummate showmanship was having an effect on the jury. He relied on two cards; Verhyden's and Brock's evidence that they had 'ghosted' for Belt, and his procession of expert witnesses, the respected leaders of the Royal Academy, for the defence.

It was obvious that 'the ghost story' had not gone down particularly well. The English jury—'middleclass, middleaged and middle-minded'—were disinclined to believe in conjuring tricks. After cross-examining Verhyden for five days, Sir Hardinge Gifford proved that a diary kept by one of the conjuror's assistants contained certain definite inaccuracies. As Sir Hardinge put it to the jury : It had been 'falsely manufactured'.

Russell, squaring into his gown, moved from a theoretical concession into all out attack. There was no dignity in this case, he said, if it was the outcome of narrow and petty jealousies within the noble profession to which Belt said that he belonged. If that was so, it was a scandal and a disgrace that it should have occupied so much of the public time. It was strong advocates' stuff. Lowering his voice in an appeal to sweet reason, he added : 'But this is not a correct view of the matter.' Rightly or wrongly, he said, there had existed in the artistic world the impression that Belt's work was not his own genuine production, but that he traded on other men's genuineness, decorating himself with plumes and feathers stolen from others. This raised an issue of importance between the parties, but a still graver question as regards the public. Pointing out that no sculptor known to fame had given evidence for Belt, he said : 'The merits of a professional man are best known to his professional brethren ... If it appears that Mr. Belt stands alone and is not supported by any body of artists, it does suggest grave consideration of how this has come out, if Mr. Belt is the man he represents himself to be.'

Sir Frederick Leighton*, President of the Royal Academy, was the first witness for the defence. 'I am the author,' he said, when the authorship of so much seemed to be in doubt 'of the "Python" in the South Kensington Museum, which has been purchased by the Nation.' On two occasions he had examined the statues in Court (private viewing days had been arranged). He stated firmly that they had not been executed by the same hand. In the Kingsley, Stanley and Plimsoll busts he recognised the work of Brock. Even in the Conway he recognised Brock's treatment of an eye. The Admiral Rous was different again. 'No artist', he asserted, 'could assimilate thoroughly the manner of another, still less the manner of two others'. (The Dutch forger, Van Meegeren, was in the next century to do just that.) The artist, said Sir Frederick, who produced the Kingsley could not have produced the Rous, and, had that been possible for any hand, it would have been impossible for the same hand or hands to have done the Duchess of Cleveland and the Lord Mayor. 'In these last two,' he said, 'there is an extreme artistic inferiority. But Rous is a work of art, while Kingsley is a very fine bust.' The President cast a critical eye upon all the busts in the Court. The earlier works, he said, were much better than the later ones (they had all been arranged in chronological order) and he did not think a young artist could have deteriorated so quickly. He praised Cardinal Newman—a statue which Verhyden had made and brought in as an exhibit—and found a strong similarity of treatment between it and some of Belt's efforts.

Asked pointedly whether he used assistants himself, he described the help he had received from Brock in completing his own 'Python'. 'I made a highly-finished sketch in clay. I put it into the hands of Mr. Brock, who caused it to be set up and descended to various operations for which so skilled a sculptor is not required, but in all cases performing myself such offices as left the artistic individuality of the work wholly mine.' There followed another burst of applause in court. It boded ill for the defence.

Hamo Thornycroft R.A., who years later was to carve the statue of Oliver Cromwell on the site where the Court then stood, completely supported the P.R.A. Laurence Alma Tadema, another R.A., said that, after studying the Byron in Hyde Park, attributed to Belt, the feeling of the composition, the rendering of the subject and the position of the limbs had struck him strongly as being the work of a Belgian sculptor. Sir William Calder Marshall R.A. scathingly

* Later Lord Leighton.

commented that Belt's sculptural method was to take a skull, and then add flesh, muscles and tissues.

Then, when at last Belt produced the bust of his assistant Pagliati, which he had made under the supervision of the Court, and placed it side by side with the original, there was a pyrotechnic display of Academic disbelief. Up till then nobody had suggested that the original bust of Pagliati was not Belt's work. Now, the President and no less than eighteen Royal Academicians (including such famous painters as Frith and Millais) came into the witness box and swore that Belt could not have done it. 'They are not done by the same hand,' said the President. 'The earlier one is the best.'

The Judge directed Mr. Belt to stand up in the well of the Court where he was sitting. With dramatic intonation and emphasis Belt declared: 'My hand alone touched that bust. My mind alone conceived the composition thereof.' There was another ominous rumble of applause.

Baron Huddleston sounded an echo to it: 'I give all due honour,' he said, 'to the gifts and character of those members of the Academy who gave unanimous testimony against the plaintiff, but it is only a matter of opinion. They are but skilful experts, and while I would if I were in doubt, hear and follow them, in a case where there is no doubt I would not yield my own opinion, founded on my own experience, to any number of Academicians, however distinguished they may be.'

It was all up for Lawes. Predictably, the jury, like the Judge, was not going to be bullied into submission by a lot of we-know-better-than-you-do experts. In the name of common sense, neither could they believe that sculpture could be produced by Maskelyne and Cooke devices. After retiring for only half-an-hour they returned to their box with a verdict for the plaintiff for £5,000 damages. The finding was greeted with an irrepressible burst of applause in the Court, echoed by a louder and deeper roar from the crowd waiting outside for the result. Mr. Belt was borne through Westminster Hall, down through the great doors, on the shoulders of his friends.

Lawes was devastated by the result. Throughout his life he had been an easy winner. Few, if any, had ever crossed him. With an obstinacy, born of shock and surprise, he appealed on the grounds that the verdict was against the weight of the evidence, that the Judge had misdirected the jury in his summing-up on the value of the evidence of the Royal Academicians, and that the damages were excessive.

The case, which had collapsed in the last trial in Westminster

Hall, came to appeal as the first case to be heard in the new Law
Courts, in the Strand. Legal brouhaha bogged down the appeal in
an embarrassing beginning. It was heard before Lord Colebridge, the
Lord Chief Justice, and Justices Denman and Manisty. The printed
copy of the Judge's notes on the first trial ran into 1,500 pages. The
Court only wished to hear counsel's arguments on the Judge's
supposed misdirection. Almost sadistically, Belt's counsel, Sir Hardinge Gifford, insisted that all the evidence be read, and the junior
judge, Mr. Justice Manisty began to do so, reading until he was tired,
when Mr. Justice Denman took up the baton. Meanwhile, having
demanded the reading of the evidence, both leading counsel left the
court. When the matter of the statues came up in the transcript of
the first trial, the Lord Chief Justice was moved to protest that a
judgement could not be formed on the evidence if a judgement was
expected on the statues, too. For nearly three days of the trial
the droning recital went on. At last Mr. Justice Manisty's voice
became so weak with fatigue that he was scarcely audible. He
ejaculated pathetically: 'What is the use of all this?' Lord Coleridge
ironically enquired: 'Might it not be as well for all three of us to
read different parts of the evidence together? It would certainly save
time and would be very much the same thing in point of utility,
and would perhaps be more lively. What do counsel say to that?'
But leading counsel were not in Court. Junior counsel felt that they
could not express an opinion and efforts to learn the whereabouts
of Sir Hardinge failed, so the reading went on. On the end of the
third day, one thousand pages still remained to be read. On the
following morning, having put his learned brethren through the
hoop, Sir Hardinge relented. But he obtained permission for the
summing up to be read by counsel on both sides. After two days of
that, Lord Coleridge had had enough: 'We are desirous of avoiding,'
he said, 'what is really likely to become a public scandal.'

The appeal didn't really begin until the fourth day, lasting twelve
days in all. To add to the confusion, the Court indicated at the end
of it that it was divided. The majority were of the opinion that
there ought to be a new trial. On the other hand they were not
agreed about their reasons for this, or on the issues upon which a
new trial should be held. There was a heartfelt hint to counsel to
settle the action before the Court delivered judgement. The parties
failed to agree to a compromise. Eventually the Court ruled that there
was to be a new trial, unless the plaintiff agreed to reduce his damages
to £500.

Belt was willing. Lawes was adamant in his refusal to bow his head to an upstart. He insisted on taking the case to a still higher Court, the new Court of Appeal. After seven more days of argument, two years after the start of the case, the verdict was unanimously in favour of the plaintiff for the full amount of £5,000. The Master of the Rolls (Sir William Britt) ruled that 'the concurrent opinion of a jury, reasonably and fairly selected, is probably safe.'

Charles Lawes, hopelessly beaten for the first and perhaps only time in his life, sought refuge in bankruptcy. Whether Belt ever got a penny of his £5,000 is a matter for doubt. Two years later, he was convicted at the Old Bailey of obtaining money by false pretences and sentenced to twelve month's hard labour. The charge related to the sale of worthless jewellery for £8,000. The new Attorney General, Sir Charles Russell, the same counsel who had defended Lawes, appeared for the prosecution. It is a footnote that, subsequently, Belt, who lived well into old age, was commissioned by the City Fathers to do the statue of Queen Anne with her attendant figures, which still stands beneath the steps of St. Paul's. Passers by of critical taste may judge whether it was the work of a ghost; or, indeed, whether it was worth doing at all.

In 1900, on the death of his father Charles inherited the baronetcy. Out of his patrimony he was at last able to pay the legal costs arising out of Belt v. Lawes. There was still plenty of money to spare to enable him to indulge a harmless, if dreary, obsession with ancestry. In 1902, he changed his name by Royal Licence, adding the name of Wittewronge, one of his forebears at Rothamsted, to his own. He assumed, in a strictly hereditary capacity, the vice-chairmanship of the Rothamsted Experimental Farm, and the chairmanship of the 'Lawes Agricultural Trust'.

As Sir Charles Lawes-Wittewronge, Bt., with an inheritance, as he supposed, of unlimited sovereigns, he indulged himself in one of the quickest ways of getting rid of them. He conceived a grandiloquent plan to transform Rothamsted into a stately home which would measure up to the presumptions of his family tree.

His obsession was to line every wall inside the house with antique linen-fold panelling. He raised the ceiling of the ballroom, which his father had built for his twenty-first birthday, into the next floor and panelled it to the ceiling. He built a library adjoining the house, with the very books barriered behind oaken planking. At best the interior of the old manor house was starved of light and windows. Charles saw to it that it was made as gloomy as a mediaeval castle.

He introduced monumental fireplaces decorated with armorial bearings. He hung the oak with portraits of his ancestors and Flemish tapestries. He furnished the rooms with great four-poster beds, and massive furniture of the sixteenth, seventeenth and eighteenth centuries. It cost him a fortune. When he died in October, 1911—he was a victim of appendicitis when, operationally, it was still a killer —he left a will of thirty-three printed foolscap pages. But there was nothing left to divide.

The whole of his collection of objets d'art and antique furniture was ultimately removed from Rothamsted by his successors to be put under the hammer at Christie's. It was too expensive to remove the oak panelling from the walls. Nobody wanted Charles's great *oeuvre* of Dirce and the Bull which, at the end of its travels, had been put in the garden; or the naiad on a fountain which Pears had used in one of their advertisements, expressing their appreciation of the sculptor's permission to reproduce it with a gift of soap.

Charles's son, John, who spent most of his life in Australia, and died there, had no interest in his father's collection. In 1936 his descendants had greater use for the money from a sale.

After that, the family of Lawes (Lawes again) passes out of the compass of this book. In 1931, on the death of the third baronet the family had decided to sell almost the whole estate, including the manor house. It was bought by public subscription and transferred to the Lawes Agricultural Trust, the governing body of Rothamsted Experimental Station. When a very old lady appeared there to attend the centenary celebrations in 1942, the officials only discovered belatedly that Mrs. Creyke was the former Caroline Lawes.

She had lived to survive three baronets. It is doubtful whether she and her brother kept up a close relationship. Their two worlds were divided. But she was there among the distinguished persons accommodated on the bench during the famous trial. Not a word should be said in her presence against the interests of another Lawes. On black-edged notepaper, mourning as the Victorians always were for somebody or another, she delivered her own verdict to her husband:

'The trial is over and Huddleston finished his discreditable summing-up by telling the jury that they were to make no comments, only to say who their verdict was for, and the amount of damages. They were away 40 minutes. I had no one to support me but Miss Davy (?) & the whole of the Court and Bench were crowded. Charlie was not there & when the verdict was given everybody naturally stared at me. Belt jumped on the bench and grasped Sir Hardinge by

the hand & there were ringing cheers all over the court and hall
which no one attempted to stop. Admiral Rous alone looked con-
temptuously down on Belt. One reporter behind me thinking he
would be civil said he was very sorry indeed that the trial had taken
place. I said I was very glad as I thought imposture ought to be shown
up. Mr. Webster got up and requested everything to be left till the
4th and Mr. Pagliati's bust sealed up. Then there were some disputes
as to who should pay for the shorthand notes, as Mr. Webster said
Huddleston would not allow them to be used. I don't know how that
ended & I enclose my correspondence with Mr. Lewis (Lawes's
solicitor). I heard two men in Westminster Hall say that 'Lawes was
to be prosecuted for perjury' so I think the sooner the new trial
comes off the better. Mrs. A. (?) says Huddleston is a horrid old
thief & tells the jury what they are to say. I called on Buckner (the
artist) on my way back & he was very glad to hear about the result
(surely she didn't mean that?) I was supported by Coward & David
(?) through the crowd into a hansom, but neither verdict nor
damages could make me feel the least as if we were not absolutely
in the right, so I required no support. David slipped off because
he said they had begun hissing him & as I left I heard the whole of
Westminster re-echoing with cheers. I must go out and make some
calls. Lady Abinger was on the bench, also Burditt (?) Coutts &
Mr. A. B. Coutts—I hope you you are having some hunting.'

Skye herself was undoubtedly on the hunt, lobbying for her
brother in the teeth, if need be, of the whole of polite society.
She had her own life in the milieu which had turned against him.
He himself had no patience with the fripperies of May Fair. It may
be that they were too much of a kind to need too much of each other's
company. But, in a crisis, the Lawes rallied together. In all their
other relationships brother and sister remained loners.

They both had a sort of ruthlessness. Unlike their father who
could say, with loving resignation, that he was glad 'Gogo' had
predeceased him because she couldn't really have managed on her
own, Charles's wife—who survived him for another seventeen years
—must have spent so much of her own life, alone. Even her only
son had been banished to Australia. It is possible that Charles did
not really need a wife. I keep on asking myself whether Skye really
needed a husband.

VI

HER HUSBAND

HEN Walter Pennington Creyke married Caroline Lawes on August 25th, 1870, she was twenty-five and he was forty-two. He had lived two-thirds of his life already. On the evidence of the Creyke Family Bible, he was not expected at his birth on October 17th, 1828, to live at all. He was baptised on the day he was born. He was vaccinated against smallpox at two months. In his case it was considered precautionary to record that he had whooping cough in 1835 and measles in 1842. He was to become a lifelong invalid.

No love letters from him to her, or her to him, survive; none of those emotional protestations on violet-scented deckle-edged paper such as the Victorians were wont to exchange with the object of their affections, and squirrel away in ribboned bundles in bottom drawers. If they were there, they have gone with the lace-edged Valentines and the arrow-pierced hearts. No photograph appears to exist even of the wedding group at Harpenden where the nuptials were performed in such ceremony by the Lord Bishop of Rochester, and celebrated in such style by the bride's father.

It is said that Walter was introduced to Skye at a house party at his family home at Bolton Percy in Yorkshire. The couple may have been drawn together by a mutual interest in art. Fluttering behind her fan, Skye was not unaware of Walter's good looks. In a pre-Raphaelite world he had the reputation of being one of the most handsome men in England. Of a very old county family he was rich and immensely well-connected. She, too, was of an old family with the prospect of a fine dowry. From a Jane Austen viewpoint it was a splendid match. Romantically it was certainly a strange one.

Walter had been intended for the Church. As a younger son of one of the best families he was expected either to take a commission in the Services, which his health precluded, or enter into Holy Orders. For a young man with a private income and social connections it offered at that time a very good life. His father, another younger son, had risen to become the Ven. Stephen Creyke, archdeacon and Canon of York and rector of Bolton Percy. I have his diary of 1822-23 in which he records his leisurely peregrinations, on horseback or in his carriage, through the dales, sporting with his friends, following hounds, and enjoying a succession of 'capital meals'. His clerical duties seem to have been little more than incidental in his social scene.

He himself prepared Walter for a career in episcopal gaiters. From the age of ten he had him under his own headmastership at St. Peter's School, York. In 1840, he sent him to Rugby; to Marival House, now known as School Field, in the last year of the reign of the redoubtable Dr. Thomas Arnold. In the period of *Tom Brown's Schooldays*, it would appear to have been the last place to send a boy of weak constitution. But it was a time when the discipline of the rod was thought to have a therapeutical value. Dr. Arnold could be trusted, from his own severe and lofty estimate of duty, to instil discipline and piety into the young gentlemen in his care. For Walter, like so many other more robust boys in his generation, it must have been sheer hell.

At his father's wish he was later ordained deacon, and went to Corfu as chaplain to Sir Henry George Ward, Lord High Commissioner of the Ionian Islands, (1849-55). The Ionian Islands, off Greece, were then a British Protectorate. If ever influence got a man a job it was that one. Walter's delicacy, so it is recorded, hardly allowed him to take 'the slightest public duty'. For the benefit of his health, Sir Henry allowed him, during most of his service, to convalesce in Italy. In Corfu, when he was there, he formed 'an intimate friend-ship' with the Earl of Carlisle who, on becoming Lord Lieutenant of Ireland (1855-64), urged him to accept the chaplaincy. But Walter, having decided not to take Holy Orders*, became his lordship's assistant private secretary in Dublin. At the end of Lord Carlisle's term of office, Walter's professional career, such as it was, came to an end. He never did anything which could pass as work again. He was thirty-six.

He was cursed not only by his wretched health but, by the standards of his periods, embarrassingly good looks. The photographs of him, which are just too numerous, show a man with soulful blue eyes, Grecian nose, and carefully coiffeured chestnut beard and hair. He wears a Byronic neckerchief, loosely tied, to set off his classic features. His appearance might be described today as insipid, even decadent. To the pre-Raphaelites, he was the Beau Ideal. When Frederick Leighton (later Lord Leighton) wanted a model for Christ

* It was said to be a matter of conscience. He was not prepared to affirm the Thirty-Nine Articles.

in his painting of 'The Wise and Foolish Virgins' which he exhibited at the Royal Academy in 1851, he chose Walter Creyke. Walter Creyke was the model for the Saviour in the fresco of the same subject which Leighton painted over the altar of Lyndhurst Parish Church in the New Forest in 1862. It is still there.

His first patron, Lord Carlisle, was devoted to Walter, and Walter to him, from the time they first met in Corfu in the early fifties. Carlisle, the seventh earl, was George William Frederick, K.G., P.C., Chief Secretary for Ireland 1835-41, Chief Commr. of Woods and Forests 1846-50, Chancellor of the Duchy of Lancaster 1850-52, and Lord Lieutenant of Ireland 1855-64. His seats were Castle Howard in Yorkshire and Naworth, Carlisle. He died, in his sixties, in 1889. He was unmarried.

Two significant letters survive between them. One, written by Carlisle at Naworth Castle, to Walter at an hotel in Nice, in 1856:

'My dear Creyke,

I was just going to write to say I could not stand not hearing from you any longer when I have just received Dr. Brett's letter. On the whole it gives me much pleasure. He seems to think decidedly that there is not much amiss with your heart; from what I know of it I should have thought it very unaccountable if there had been. But you will be aware that he harps on the old string of "very careful", so pray do not be bumptious and insolent with whatever urge you may at times feel.... I find I cannot put up with long pauses without hearing about you, so if you should not feel disposed ever to write a line yourself, perhaps either your kind Mother or one of your sisters would give me that pleasure.

Affectionately yours

Carlisle'

The second, from Walter to Carlisle, is written on unheaded notepaper without a date. I guess that it belongs to the early sixties. It was returned to Walter by the executors after Carlisle's death in 1889. His wife filed it:

'My dearest and best friend,

I know you will let me call you so, for it is now more than eleven years since you said to me on the Esplanade of Corfu: "Will you promise always to be my friend?"

I have never forgotten that, but looking back now through all these years I feel how very little I have ever been able to do in return for all you have done for me, for all your friendship and all your kindnesses.

I am only writing now these very few lines to say, what I trust you knew before, that if I can be of any use or comfort to you in any way, I hope you will tell me. It may be that you would prefer being alone at first, but, if at any moment you would care to have me, so as to be in the way if wanted either to write for you, read aloud if you feel tired*, or do anything that could be of use, remember always it would be the greatest pleasure and happiness you could give me.

Yours most affect.,

Walter Creyke.'

From the words they wrote to each other it seems that the two must have had a homosexual relationship. Among the Victorians you can never be quite sure. It is probably true that the incidence of sexual perversity is constant in any period of human society. But in Victorian times, the probability was not accepted, and the reality was not supposed to exist outside the regulations of the Royal Navy. I am told by elderly members of London Clubs that the subject was not regarded as proper for discussion in male company even after the Oscar Wilde case brought it to public notice. Women were supposed not even to know that such deviations existed.

It is possible that the relationship between Carlisle and Walter was one of those emotional things such as the relationship between the artist Holman Hunt and his fellow pre-Raphaelite John Everett Millais. They, too, had associations with each other which were embarrassingly intimate. Here's what Diana Holman Hunt wrote of her grandfather when he heard Millais announced as the winner of the gold medal at the Academy for drawing for the antique:

'An angelic-looking blue-eyed boy was passed hand to hand over the heads of the laughing, applauding audience. Although fourteen he looked much younger, a little Lord Fauntleroy. His doting parents cultivated this image. Long fair curls tumbled round his pink face and over his lace collar. He wore a tunic, velvet shorts, white socks and buckled pumps of patent leather ... For Hunt, it was love at first sight. He had wanted for so long to see his idol. As he cheered with the others tears streamed down his face. They were to love one another all their lives. Neither of them felt in the least self-conscious about the emotion they showed.'

Latterly, in one of his lovelorn letters to Hunt, Millais could write of 'his slender thighs' as if that was the sort of secret that men normally shared together. It may be that, in the affair between

---

* Carlisle was going blind.

Holman Hunt and Millais, between Carlisle and Walter, there was a lot of empty sexuality. None of it was decorative, but none of it exclusive of a normal marriage with a woman.

It became a lifelong affair, continuing until the end of Carlisle's and Walter's lives. Carlisle's last existing letter is written for him by a secretary:

'Villa Sotte Riotis,
Sorino, Near Corfu.

My dear Walter,

Here I am, on my fifty-ninth birthday, a blind old man, in the beautiful island, which we had better have kept, where I first saw you in the year 1853, as Burton would say in his translation of the Arabian Nights, like a full moon....'

It is a long letter and an unhappy one. 'The deaths of so many friends is saddening....' 'This is a sort of begging letter, with padding in it, written solely with a hope of getting a letter from you.' Surprisingly, he adds: 'If I fail to hear from you, I shall write to Mrs. Creyke. She always writes me the most charming and amusing letters, and how she finds time to do so or, indeed, how she finds time to do everything better and more beautifully than anyone else is to me a mystery. Will you tell her that I lay my blind eyes at her feet. She will probably say that they are no good to her or to anyone else, but I still have my ears left, and shall hope some day to hear her again sing.'

He signs himself 'The Count', which was clearly a nickname. When he died, a few years later, his brother, who inherited the title, wrote to Walter briefly that Carlisle had left him an annuity of one hundred pounds in his will. Skye, it is puzzling to guess why, preserved the letters. Perhaps she herself never wondered. Or did she?

Walter, spoilt by admiration of his looks, was a Narcissus. In studio and group photographs, in which most of the contemporary 'subjects' hang grimly on to tables to steady themselves for the prolonged exposure to the 'little dicky bird', Walter invariably throws himself into a pose of languorous and studied ease. Undoubtedly, those long Italian vacations brought him into company where flattery was over fulsome and the *dolce vita* dangerous. Cultivating his taste for art and music, he made his friends among the opera singers and the dancers; the greatest of them, Signor Mario (Conte di Candia), the most famous tenor of his age.

Walter's photographic album, carefully annotated, has half-a-dozen portraits of Mario, inscribed *el amico*. He shares the album with a star-spangled collection of Italian and French dancers and opera singers, all higgledy-piggledy with the English nobility and gentry, and prelates of the Church. I wondered at one man who appears twice in the album in skin tights.

I had to be told that Monsieur Leotard, who improbably appears among the company of Walter's artistic friends, was the one who invented the style of dress, which ballet dancers wear for practice, called to this day a 'leotard'. Raymond Mander, that authority on everything theatrical, tells me that Monsieur Leotard's act was the inspiration of George Leybourne's music hall song:

> 'He flies through the air with the greatest of ease,
> That daring young man on the flying trapeze.'

In spangled 'leotards' he was the inventor of the trick, dying at the age of twenty-eight in the year that Walter married Skye. There is only one picture of Skye in the album. It is a small oval print pasted in where somebody else's photo has been taken out. Walter appears in it often in various fancy dresses, singing parts like Maurico in *Trovatore* in amateur theatricals. Surprisingly, too, there is a full page photograph of Lord Carlisle's coachman in Dublin, a watery-eyed young man in a brown derby who seems even more out of keeping with the people in the rest of the photographs than Monsieur Leotard.

Walter's 'pose' was not all of him. When he was well enough, he was a good game shot, a fine horseman and a keen cricketer. He liked shooting with Skye in Scotland. After his death, a fox-hunting journalist wrote of him: 'He always rode a good horse and saw the finish of more of our best runs than many of us, before his long illness kept him out of the saddle.' Skye used to tell that one of his fears when he married her was that she might not be able to keep up with him in the hunting field. He need not have worried.

His cricket belongs to a time when the game first became a social cult. In 1858, he was elected a member of the exclusive cricket club, I Zingari. With its overtones of class, playing the game with waggish patronage, with more than a hint of the show-off, it suited Walter. He liked his cricket, and he also liked dressing up and, in common with most of his generation, wearing funny hats.

I Zingari was formed in July 1845, at the Blenheim Hotel in Bond Street, by the 6th Earl of Bessborough (then F. G. B. Ponsonby), Sir Spencer Ponsonby-Fane (then S. Ponsonby), J. L. Baldwin and

R. P. Long. The name for the wandering cricket club derived from the Italian—some pundits say Egyptian—and means 'the gypsies'. The pompous name laid a trap for people who were outside the magic circle. The in-people pronounced it I Zing-gah-ree and wrote it without a dot after the I. The club colours were black, red and gold, indicating 'out of darkness, through fire into light'. Membership was by invitation to people who had 'learnt their manners'. Rule 6 made the heavy joke 'that the entrance shall be nothing, and that the annual subscription shall not exceed the entrance'. The I Z's were described as 'A cheerful carefree lot ... whose followers pitch their tents where'er they please, and always find a home'. The latter, I imagine, is a quote from their 'anthem' sung lustily at annual dinners. The founder members must have been a boorish lot; but it is proper to add that it was the I Z's who raised the status of cricket to a national game. For better or worse, it moulded the image of the M.C.C., to which Walter was elected in 1874.

He is described as 'a distinctly useful club bowler, certainly no rabbit', and I believed that I had discovered a nugget when a rumour reached me from one of the statisticians in the Long Room at Lords that he had once caught and bowled the great W. G. Grace for a duck. It wasn't true. But he did play against W.G. in what must have been Grace's first match at Lord's when the future G.O.M. of cricket was not quite seventeen. It was not Walter who caught and bowled Grace, it was Grace who caught and bowled Creyke, W. for 0.

In the summary for the I Z's season in 1865 Walter had 11 innings, made 70 runs (highest 35), and his 'outings' (wickets) with the ball amounted to 10. He is classed in the club records as a 5th-category cricketer which was reasonably high because H.R.H. the Prince of Wales in the next season, was classified as 10th class, last on the list with the Earl of Coventry and the Hon. E. Stanhope. It was a name-dropping side. In the I Z team against Charterhouse were Lord Guernsey, Lord Hyde, Lord Lennon, Earl of Gosford, Sir Ivor Guest, Lord G. Pratt; and, in the match against Westminster School, the Earl of Dalkeith and the Earl of Gosforth are both marked 'absent'.

W. Creyke is often marked 'absent' too. He organised I Z tours in Ireland when he was assistant private secretary at Vice-Regal Lodge; but, again and again, he was not fit enough to turn out in the field. In a club which relished nicknames none is ascribed to him. He knew all the right people, and all the right people knew him. He was a member of the top West End clubs, Brook's, St. James's, Devonshire and the rest. He was financially independent; but, undoubtedly, he

fitted more easily into the châteaux and palazzi of the Continent—
he was a good linguist—and the salons of May Fair, than the
boisterous company of hard-living, hard-drinking English milords, the
Corinthian world to which he belonged by birth, but not inclination.
His great uncle Ralph of Rawcliffe in the West Riding, Master of the
York and Ainsty Hounds and owner of over five thousand broad acres,
was a Creyke of the old school. Walter, beautiful as he was, was a
runt.

Gentle and unassuming, undemonstrative and forgiving, his
melancholy temperament found relaxation in music, and his books,
paper backed editions of French and Italian authors bound in leather
for his own library, in the French works by Balzac (illustrated by
Doré), Flaubert and Zola. He needed a mother figure. He married
Caroline Lawes.

On New Year's Eve, 1869, sitting in romantic reverie in the
Yorkshire Club at York, withdrawn from the back-slapping toasts
which must have been going on all about him, he wrote a letter :

'Dear Miss Lawes,
    There is only one more hour left of the year, and I have been
writing letters all the evening, to various friends—and thinking over
the events of the year which is dying out. As I can remember nothing
which gave me so much pleasure as your singing and the pleasant
days I spent at Rothamsted, I venture to write and wish you every
possible happiness for the New Year and many years to come; and
let me add that I hope I may hear again before very long : "Oh why
did you break on my dream?" and the Faust song, both of which have
haunted me ever since. Since I saw you I have been at a great many
country houses and shot many coverts. I spent a very pleasant
fortnight at Castle Howard at the partridge shooting in Sept., and
after Sir J. Wombwell, Lady M. Vigners (?) ending my shooting
at Lord de Grey's at the end of November. Since then I have been
hunting six days a week till stopt by the frost on Xmas Day. We
begin again tomorrow. All this is very pleasant and healthy, but
I have never heard a note of music ! May I hope to hear from you
when I come to town?
                        Yrs. always very sincerely, Walter Creyke.'

    So began the formal Victorian approach to a proposal. Meanwhile,
his-soon-to-be-betrothed' was keeping in good voice. At a County
Amateur Concert at Norwich, in the presence of the Mayor—'For

the benefit of the families of those who were lost on our coast in
the late gales'—Miss Lawes had the local critic almost breathless
with admiration :

'Meyerbeer's song, "Adieu mon doux rivage", from the new opera
L'Africaine, was a bold and ambitious attempt, and like most of this
composer's songs, it is full of showy contrasts both in expressive
and executive difficulties. But we do Miss LAWES only bare justice
in saying that the success was worthy the attempt. With a naturally
fine organ the quality, particularly in the middle part of her voice,
being very rich, and with a feeling for the art which at once stamps
an impress upon this lady's attempts, and a strength of will to
succeed which almost ensures superiority, and we may add, inheriting
a family taste for music, it was not unnatural that the Romanza not
a little surprised the audience by its beautiful and varied expression,
executive difficulties, and the vigorous animation and feeling which
marked its complete success. The reception was most enthusiastic.
It was encored, the audience, as is but too frequently the case,
forgetting in their own pleasure, the exhaustion which such a song
creates. Miss LAWES, however, sang a very charming French air,
which showed that her really fine powers were capable of the most
refined and delicate expression, as of the claims of agility. Again,
"Sing, Birdie, Sing", a most winning air, won Miss LAWES still higher
praise for its exquisite delicacy and feeling, which was also encored.'

Her engagement to Walter was announced during the summer.
Among the letters of congratulation, written 'crossways' so that
they are almost indecipherable, is a 'Dear Skye' which ends :

'Of course I have great pleasure in congratulating you. Up to
the present you have passed a life of uninterrupted pleasure and I
hope that when you are married which is the most important event
of your life you will continue to be the cheerful and entertaining
woman that you are now.'

A relative of Walter's, writing to him on notepaper diestamped
with the family crest of a corncrake and the motto 'A Vie La Verité',
adopts the moral line :

'May God prosper and bless you ... most truly do I hope it may
be as you wish. You have my earnest prayers for your happiness
here and hereafter.'

Walter's mother wrote to the bride on her honeymoon. If I
read her aright—she herself apologises for her old pen and cannot
make the new nib work either—it was spent on the Wiltshire Downs :

'Thanks many, my dear Ina—no—Caroline ! for so kindly think-

ing of me. It was a great satisfaction to hear you are both safe &
quiet after the turmoil of the last month. Now pray keep *quiet*
and if you find yourselves *being dull!!* go and see Warwick
Castle ...'

Skye's father, writing from his office at 59 Mark Lane, reminds
them both, on their return, that they must show themselves to the
members of the Allotment Club at Rothamsted on the occasion of the
members' celebratory outing to the Crystal Palace. Beyond that the
record of the Creyke's early married life is as quiet as Walter's mother
could have wished. During Skye's long life a lot of papers were
mislaid. There were also the losses which are the inevitable con-
comitant of large families.

On his medical record, none might have expected that Walter
would have been a sexually vigorous husband; but congenital invalids
are often characterised by an energy which, when they are on an
upward curve, is remarkable. On top of his form, Walter could
shoot and hunt six days a week. During nine years, from 1871 to
1880 his wife presented him with four daughters and twin sons.

They lived in a mansion at 3 Seamore Place in May Fair, the back
of it overlooking Park Lane and Hyde Park, in a style appropriate to
their social station. They had the usual retinue of servants, butler and
footmen, cook and parlourmaids, children's nurses, coachmen and
undercoachmen, and lesser domestics who served the superior ones.
The Creykes arranged their lives, between accouchements, in the
strict routine that fashion demanded. They followed the calendar
of the London Season. They gave the required sequence of dinner
parties, balls and musical evenings on those days when they were not
attending somebody else's. They went to the opera and fashionable
shows in the theatre. She painted in her studio, he read in his library.
They exchanged cards with suitable neighbours, and wrote innumerable letters. They ate too much, and gossiped interminably. On
Sundays, after church, they paraded on foot—it was not done to
ride in a carriage or on horseback on Sundays—to greet their friends
and acquaintances at the Achilles Statue in Hyde Park. It was a closed
stuffy world in which leisure was a full-time occupation. Skye, who
loved it all, was thought an oddity because she wrote articles about
it.

Not for money. She simply added up the cheques she was paid
for her journalistic work as the measure of her literary success.
Both of them had all they needed and throughout their lives, their
money attracted more. The will of Walter's elder brother, Alfred,
(personal estate £180,000) provided £24,000 in equal shares to his

four daughters, £12,000 to his son Launcelot. There is letter after letter from members of the Creyke and Lawes families sending five pounds to each of the children in commemoration of a death or in celebration of a wedding or an anniversary. Jewellery and silver was regularly passed on from one generation to the next one.

But Walter had married a restless wife. As early as 1878, in between the birth of her youngest daughter and her twin sons, Skye went off to the Paris exhibition without him. More and more, sometimes with the children, sometimes without them, she went to Ardchattan Priory or Dalmally, Rothamsted, Narford in Norfolk, where her mother's family came from, and Bolton Percy to her in-laws. She was also a regular traveller to the fashionable continental resorts.

In declining health, Walter could not keep up the pace. Increasingly, she encouraged him to go on his own on holidays to Dalmally and Rothamsted. She persuaded him in the autumn of 1874 to go away with her father and her brother to join a house party at the Duke of Sutherland's. His letters on that occasion reveal his dependence on her, and his increasing inability to cope with the usual misfortunes of a guest in a stately home. This letter was written over several days:

'Dunrobin Castle.

We have had a truly auspicious journey here and I will put it in the simplest and the best sense: 7.30 a.m. Stirling Station. Charles (Skye's brother) forgets to call me so bread and butter and tea. I ask: "Why is not the clerk here? The train is due." Porter: "It's but seldom that a passenger comes for this one—and the train is seldom here before the expreſs." True enough, we waited three-quarters of an hour, then up comes the Mail—we were fasting. Porter: 7 minutes to get tickets, change baggage *and breakfast*. I gulp a scone —but comfort myself that I will have a real good lunch at Inverneſs. At Inverneſs—three quarters of an hour late, station crammed with tourists. We can just get round to the train—and there is a free fight between an aged minister and his wife versus an offensive Glasgy person for a seat. The Glasgy man having removed the shepherds coats and occupied *his* seat, a polite young man cedes to the Lady, but a war of words goes on till I rebuke the Glasgy man— wolves are clawing at my entrails but I get no food. We stop at 4 stations, drop and pick up shrieking tourists and excursionists, but no food. At Golspie Charles informs us we have to get out and our baggage goes on ! A man hails me from carriage that we go on *with* our luggage to Dunrobin. We arrive, I like the Spartan boy, at something past eight. Charles has out all the baggage, *he says*, and especially the Lawes portmanteau and has put it in the Duke's brake—under piles of luggage—your father doubtful but we submit as the train is in motion, and wont stop tho I shriek and wave hands. Arrived at Castle, dinner in 3 minutes! I peal the bell and wait for my portmanteau. In come J.B.L. (Skye's father). "I knew it" he says "my portmanteau is nowhere." I try consolation but in a moment require it as neither is mine, so I hastily dreſs again in my bedraggled garments and we send a message to the Duke. Servant says a dog cart will go to Golspie at once—no doubt they were put out at that station. Charles departs in dog cart. Absolutely fainting I ask a motherly housemaid to get me a biscuit—and at nine o'clock we get some dinner in the smoking room. 10 p.m.: Servant says Charlie has returned with both portmanteaus—but we think it too late to dreſs so remain where we ate. Duke very civil and brings the Duchess. Then others arrive and a long talk begins at 12. We retire, find "a" portmanteau labelled S. B. Cunningham in J.B.L.'s room and all S. B. Cunningham's things spread out by the valet. Send for Charlie who is in bed. At 1 o'clock we rouse him, but he is so hazy we can make nothing of him. I borrow a tooth brush and razor from Fred Marshall (another house guest) and select a shooting coat for J.B.L. who has to start at 7.20 with the Duke. I draw up a telegram to dispatch to various quarters in search, and at nearly two get to bed. This morning I discover Charles has left my ivory hairbrush in the train and slippers at Stirling. He saw the name S. B. Cunningham on portmanteau but it never occurred to him but that it was J.B.L. The Fred Marshalls are here, Sir Augustus and Lady Paget, Edward Lascelles, Oliver Montagu, Lady John Scott, and one or two more are staying in the house. There was a cricket match in which they were very anxious I should play—but I was exhausted, and stood umpire all day in the heat which was nearly as bad. Dunrobin beaten in one innings, and Fred Marshall says it's rather my doing as I could have bowled the other side out. 6 o'clock. A late train just arrived from Inverneſs reports "Lawes portmanteau will come 4.30 train tomorrow." Your father didn't get back from pulling up trees and leaping over rocks with a plough till past 8—so I lent him my dreſs coat. I had to button his suit and made a neat bow to his white tie. My coat fitted him beautifully, and he wore my black socks and Charles' pumps! I shall appear in my velvet jacket at dinner. There is a drop of about 300 feet from the drawing room windows on to a terraced garden—washing the wall of which is the broad sea. My slippers just arrived. I presume you sent them from Stirling? I am utterly worn out so shall lie down till dinner. Kiſs the chicks for me. We leave on Monday. There is no shooting here, disease. They have killed 3 stags. I am very very tired.'

He subscribes himself in all his letters to her as 'Yr. very affec. boy, W.' Surprisingly, he addresses her as 'Dearest Monkey'. I can only suppose that he called her 'Monkey' because she was indeed a handful. Her letters to him, which dutifully give him all the news of her own travels begin briefly 'Dear Walter' or just 'Dear W', ending, as often as not 'Yours afft. cc.' His own letters to her are frequently appealing. His constant complaint is that he is 'dull'. 'Make sure', he writes 'that you are pleased to see me!' 'I long to hunt rabbits with you on the crags.' 'Kiſs the chicks for me, I miss them so much!'

In happier days, when he was in better health, they had taken lodgings together in the shires for the hunting season. They were regular followers of the then Hertfordshire Hunt, now amalgamated with the Old Berkeley and South Oxfordshire to form the Vale of Aylesbury.

Together they had cultivated the arts, singing duets at the piano after dinner, talking about painting, and entertaining their theatrical and operatic friends. Latterly, he found it increasingly more of a physical strain to keep up with his wife's exuberant energy, her unquenchable enthusiasms. She writes to him from Paris: 'I have been enquiring how much it would cost to go up in a *Balloon libre*' (she later went up); from Ardchattan: 'I have just come in from a delicious bathe off the launch, but when I wanted to get in again, neither the engineer nor the children together could pull me up the side, and I had to swim to the pier and get into a boat and be rowed out to dress in the cabin of the launch.' From Bolton Percy: 'Don't buy another horse for me. I don't feel inclined to hunt except very rarely. What a brute that other animal is, and how vulgar. I will paint V. (Archdeacon Stephen Creyke) for you at Bolton if you like.' From Seamore Place: 'I hope that *you* are not very dull; I have had no time to be dull, even if I wished it, for all my spare time has been filled up in trying to make that black striped dress fit on the shoulders. Why can I never be fitted when other people with pillow and bolster figures can be made to look so nice?' From somewhere on the Continent: 'I have ruined you in my dreſs. I saw one on a mannequin with a most beautiful figure, and not for an instant supposing it would fit me, I said I would try on the corsage.

It was simply perfection, not a crease, not a fold. I never had such a beautiful fit, so of course I no longer hesitated but ordered up the skirt—equally perfect and so tight that I was afraid to sit down *précisément comme dans ma selle.* Now for the price *trois cents soixante quinze*,* not a farthing less. I know that you will say it is worth it for the style and fit and that moreover you will also say that I am only to wear it with you—but remember that you can have no more children until it is worn out!'

In her crowded days she often writes to him in such impatient haste that her handwriting is illegible. She has so much to fit in. She is for ever admonishing him not to be 'dull':

'Two letters from you. I am so *very* sorry that you are alone in London, you will be so dull. Do look up all your friends and go to the club for dinner sometimes.'

'Goodbye, and mind you take care not to get a fresh cold.'

'We were very glad to find you better when I came home. We are enjoying ourselves so much but Oh! if you could have seen your Uncle Edward. He had oysters and champagne and every luxury at Bob's dinner, but he says it was the tomatoes which made him sick for two nights. He *will* have champagne tonight, so of course I can't say anything. How is your neuralgia, I hope better?

'I cannot read your letter of Sunday, it would take too long. The cook can make ices and everything. Do take care of yourself and don't be dull. Don't get fresh cold for anybody or anything.'

'Why don't you go to Cannes for six months? I am sure that it will make you feel much better.'

He didn't go to Cannes, but she persuaded him to take some of the children to Dalmally:

'Dearest Monkey. This is your birthday and I am wishing you all good wishes and shall drink an extra glaʃs of champagne tonight when I hope we shall be regaling on my snipe. I can't help feeling very sorry that you are not here to enjoy the glorious weather, the perfectly clear sky and transparent mountains, one day more beautiful than another.'

They had drawn more and more apart. When his child-getting years were over, the invalid years were pressing on him. Most of his pleasure now was in his children; she was seeking hers elsewhere. Look at their world through the awakening eyes of Everilda (born June 6, 1871), Lilian (June 11, 1872), Diana, called Diane (December

---

* The gold exchange rate at that time made the cost of the dress £14-9-4¾d.; equivalent in today's currency to about £150.

16, 1873), Sylvia (December 7, 1877), Walter Launcelot, the surviving
twin (December 6, 1880) before their Papa died, after a lingering
illness at Rothamsted at the age of sixty-four, in 1892. Skye was then
forty-six.

VII

HER CHILDREN

ROM the Highlands, Skye to Walter in September, 1884:
'.... I am really disgusted with these children. They have everything they want done for them and will not take the slightest trouble in return. Lilian has had constant picnics and I hear left all the spoons and everything out on the hills & has finally lost a fork altogether, & Diane dragged her hat behind the boat, dropped it in the river in the shallows, never took the trouble to fish it out & went home & got another & said nothing about it. After this autumn I will have nothing more to do with them.... I hope you are better today ...'

Later in the month:

'Dear Walter,

I had to give up our expedition today as the children did not know their collects. I left them with the order that they were not to be read to by Gogo (Lady Lawes) till they had written to you and learnt their collects. When I came in two hours later they had all finished their reading & not one knew their collects. How glad I shall be to hand over the whole boiling to a governess! I am quite sick of finding incessant fault, and punishing ... children are making such a row I can't write any more....

Yours aff. C.C.'

In due course one of her children answered back. In her old age, Mrs. Charles Maurice, the youngest of her four daughters (Sylvia, born 1877, died 1970) wrote this in a school exercise book she addressed to her own grandchild, Belinda:

'It's a pity the Maurice memoirs got lost when I was ill as really I am not going to enjoy writing about my side of the family. Being a fourth daughter was not much fun. In the first place my mother never cared for children & my father who did, died, after being ill for a year at Harpenden, when I was thirteen. I don't think I can have been an easy child as what I can remember most was either being put into a dark very big cupboard, or being put to bed—or having my ears boxed which seemed to be the mode of punishment my mother administered. I went to bed so often that, in Scotland, I used to save up all my plum and fruit stones & hide them away in a box & then use them as armies to fight once I was in bed.

'I spent most of my existence being frightened. Late at night, or so it seemed to me, the paper boys going through Seamore Place, used to cry their wares: "ANOTHER HORRIBLE MURDER. JACK THE RIPPER CUTS OFF HIS VICTIM'S EARS." The nursery was five flights up & the French nurses used to go down to their supper & I was alone. To this day I don't like the dark in the house though I am quite happy to be out in it.

'I was often frightened. Once I saw a riot going on in the Park.* A crowd collected and two ladies in a barouche who did not turn back had the traces of their horses cut ... Another of my great fears was fire. Actually it was the only thing that my mother was also afraid of. To cure herself, she went to see any big fires nearby. I remember her taking me to see the Japanese Village in flames (it was somewhere near where Harrods is now). Sir Eyre Shaw, head of the Fire Brigade, was a great friend & we used to go and see his practices ... I remember Whiteleys being burnt & from our house on the side overlooking the Park you could see the flames leaping up ... when I was in Paris, aged nineteen, the *Bazaar de Charité* caught fire & nearly everyone in it was burnt ... My husband in the far future from which I am writing knew my fear & when we were married took rooms in the first floor of the hotel with a balcony.

'My father did not like schools but, as the rest of the family were grown up, there seemed nothing else to do but to send me to one when he died & take the rest of the family abroad. Up till now all the lessons I had done were in French & I even thought in French. English history we did do in English (Charles Dickens' History which followed Mr. Markham's). I don't remember disliking my first school. In fact I think I rather liked it. It was near Watford. One night I heard a noise in the garden and looking out of the window I saw a lot of men digging. I heard afterwards that the drains were all wrong. The headmistress got typhoid & all the boarders but myself (because my mother was abroad) were sent home, & I was told to be very quiet. The only thing I remember of that time was walking on a black beetle with bare feet & squashing it & being rather proud of myself that I had not screamed.

'When my mother came home I went to another school at Hampstead where, disliking it all the time, I remained until I was

---

* In 1885, roused by John Burns at a meeting in Trafalgar Square, militant unemployed ran riot in the West End.

seventeen. After that I went to the Ladies' College in Cheltenham. I loved the games but did not understand how to work, though I managed French all right after having gone to my housemistress & said I could not understand French being taught in English, so I was allowed to go into the top French class ... Cheltenham is a stuffy place & it seemed to me as if I was always being ill.... Nowadays parents seem to come down and see their children pretty frequently in the term but in my day it was not done.... My favourite sister Lilian never failed to write to me, so that I got a letter on Sunday which was the day we could really enjoy them. We could choose our partners for breakfast, sit where we liked and make our own toast ... I left Cheltenham at nineteen ...

'One thing before that I have forgotten. I must have been about five years when with the others I was taken to Lord Dudley's children's party. It was held in the big ballroom overlooking Park Lane. The Princess of Wales (later on Queen Alexandra) always came & brought her children with her, who danced with any of the guests. I got tired, could not dance, so went up to the Princess (she was very beautiful so I suppose attracted me) and said : "Take me up. I am tired." Which she did & I sat on her knee & she showed me a fan her mother had painted. My father on the other side of the room saw what had happened, rushed across & took me away.

'I cannot say I was a pleasant child. I was sallow with a large nose, good eyes but no other good point ... greedy to a degree. We were not exactly an affectionate family, but anyway we were very loyal & we were up in arms if anyone outside criticised. My chief companion was my brother but he was three years younger & delicate so that he had to be sent to Rothamsted to live with my grandparents, there or in Scotland. We did most things together. At Rothamsted we collected all the dead birds we could find and buried them under my grandfather's study window. In Scotland, we used to play all day by a stream which ran into Loch Etive. We collected all the broken china we could find and made houses which, when we left for the south, we covered with stones & hoped to find intact the next year.

'When I left Cheltenham I was to come out in the winter and be presented in the Spring. It must have been pretty hard for my mother to have to start again taking out a daughter to dances. My next sister Diane was four years older. She did not care for dancing, but she painted, sang & was clever & amusing & dressed well, whereas I could not do my hair, had no flair for clothes, thought powder and hair pads etc. immoral, was keen on dancing; but, above all, loved hockey which made me slouch. I had my own team in Hertfordshire where I generally played twice a week. I belonged to the Old Cheltenham team and having had to walk in crock (crocodile) for the last five years of my life was terrified at going about in London alone & did not know what to do with myself. I also had an ice hockey team of ladies at Prince's Skating Rink, a club to which my mother belonged.

'When I was seventeen my grandfather and grandmother celebrated their golden wedding with a ball. I simply longed to go but did not think there would be a chance. However, I counted seven stars seven nights running, & I got my wish.... "Now" said my mother, "mind you don't dance with your cousins all the evening." There were no programmes and we arranged everything beforehand. One of my cousins was two years older than I was and the other, in the navy, was four years older. I practically divided the evening between them & we returned in the early hours holding hands and shouting at the top of our voices *After the ball is over*. My mother had a dress made for me which I think now was most unsuitable for a seventeen-year-old. It was pale yellow cotton satin & over that yellow net with a gold tinsel thread running through it & I had a bunch of purple violets (artificial) at my waist. I pinned a bit of the material to the written out programme & only destroyed it when I went out to S. Africa to be married.

'Scotland was always pure bliss. I went often to Ardchattan, but I think I only went to Dalmally in the last year when I was 5½. I caught a trout on a bent pin and wrote to my father in London in French. The trout was so small that I carried it back to the lodge in the tin pail in which I used to make mud pies by the river, but my father was so pleased he sent me up a rod from London.... My mother was very keen on deerstalking & I can remember us all rushing from the breakfast table to see the stag she had shot the day before which had just been brought in.... I don't know how old I was at Ardchattan when the routine was to visit the kitchen after breakfast & ask Mrs. Stratton, the cook, for what sandwiches we wanted for the day. I always chose scones with cheese in them and cold plum pudding. Then we were free to go where we liked, even in the old fishing boat as long as we never stood up in it, & we did not reappear until High Tea in the morning room with boiled eggs and unlimited food....

'I came out at a dance where there was royalty (I have forgotten who).... My mother, however bored she was at having to take out a fourth daughter, always did the right thing. Shortly afterwards she said that as I had never been abroad, would I like to go to Rome for Easter? ... W.K., who was a great friend of the family and who lived in Italy most of his days, came to us. We travelled straight through to Milan, & W.K., who had been very train sick, retired to bed without wanting food or anything. "Such a pity," said my mother. It was the one day they had soup with whole frogs' legs in it. If you are interested in what happened to W.K., he was put in prison as a spy in Spain during the war. He was a most attractive man who took me out to breakfast at all the little cafés in Rome as my mother never got up until later. In the *Café Grices* (Café Greco now, still the most famous café in Rome) I saw a bust of my father who, when he was a young man, was often in Italy ... I wrote to some friends who had both been converted to Roman Catholicism. My mother said I could go out with them "but mind, Sylvia, if they try and convert you, you are to take a fiacre and drive straight back to the hotel!" Needless to say they did nothing of the kind, though I did feel a bit awkward when they fell on their knees each side of me as I stood in front of the High Altar in St. Peter's. I was given a coin, which I still have on a bangle, which is supposed to shield you from all evil. I caught scarlet fever on the way back. I also had a crucifix blessed by the Pope. I thought I should give it to our R.C. housemaid who would really appreciate it ...

'Oh yes, we lunched at the Embassy one day and Lord Abinger, who of course my mother knew, took us to the opera and then to the Coliseum at 1 a.m. It was lovely there in the bright moonlight with all the nightingales singing ...'

The nightingales sang for all her children, except perhaps for Walter Launcelot, Skye's youngest and only surviving twin son. Three of the girls had a yearning for music, poetry and painting; Sylvia the youngest, none. Although they enjoyed every creature comfort, they each believed that they were on their own. Sylvia felt that she was left behind, orphaned by the death of her beloved father, dominated by a mother who was bored with introducing another daughter into society. All her children knew that Skye was fed up with their company. After delivering them into the world, after boxing their ears in preparation for it, after presenting them at Court, she was satisfied that her job was done. After that the less she saw of them, in the adventure of her own life, the better.

With the unmistakable streak of Skye in all of them, sharpened with a sensitivity undoubtedly inherited from their father—a sort of belief that they were being put upon—it seems remarkable that her four daughters should have come into the world as level as the buttons on their Sunday boots. In childhood they are almost indistinguishable. As sentimental as Victorians were, they made a fetish, as Victorians did, of a good illness. Their letters, written under pressure as children's letters are, tell it all. This is Everilda, the eldest, at the age of eleven :

'My dear Grandpapa (Sir John Lawes),
Papa was ill all day yesterday and did not get up till the afternoon. He is very weak this morning and cannot swallow, but he is a little better. He got your article for the "Agricultural Gassettee", and there will be no delay in sending it ... Diana is not very well this morning, so she has not gone to school. I am very well thank you. Yours aff. Everilda.
P.S. I have now got two shillings for writing this letter, and I hope to get some more money.'

Beyond, it barely matters which one wrote which letter. In mood, they are all in the same voice. In part it may be attributed to the upper class discipline to which they were subjected. In part it shows that they all enjoyed much the same tastes as their remarkable mother. Mostly, unless they were feeling very naughty, their letters are written with copybook precision. Never mind whether it was Everilda, Diane, Lilian or Sylvia, they are all revealed.

'Darling Mammy,
I am so very, very sorry that I was so naughty on Sunday, after you had been so kind to me, and given me such a lot of treats. Please answer this, and do let me come in to your (?). It is so nasty, and I will try to be good.'

'Darling Sweet (To Skye in 1887)
Thank you very much for your two nice letters. My throat is nearly well so I did not put on a cold compress last night, but I have got rather a cold and Gogo says it is no use coming down to the country to be cured if I go away before I *am* cured, and as I *must* see you in your court dress, *please* darling sweet do let me come up for the day tomorrow (from Rothamsted). I will pay for myself and can go and come back with Grandpapa. I am sure that you will let me as you are such an angel, and I must see you, so *do*. If you don't get this letter in time to answer it tonight, please send a telegraph ... Diane's cough is not bad but she was only allowed out one day as it made her worse. I hope you will enjoy your hunting, and not tire yourself for tomorrow.'

'Darling Mummy,

I am so glad to hear that dear little Launcelot is getting well ... My cough is worse today and I have been sick twice, but Diane's and Sylvia are much better. Please when you come here will you bring me my flower-book, work-box and my desk?'

'Dear Grandpapa,

Thank you very much for sending me my allowance. I shall not break into it at present as I have still more than seven pounds left of last year's. I have not been able to enjoy the snow at all as I have had a cold all the week and have not been able to go out.'

'Dear Papa,

I meant to have written to you on Sunday, but found that I had absolutely nothing to say....'

'Dear Grandpapa,

.... I am horribly tired of London, and everyone is very cross, especially Diane who ought not to be. Hope the wagtails will have begun to build when I arrive.'

'Dear Mama,

I hope you are enjoying yourself as much as I am. I have not been dull one minute and the time only passes too quickly. Gogo sent me two tickets for the private view of the Royal Exhibition of Watercolours. I went with Madame (an au pair girl today) and liked it very much though there were only four pictures by our Mr. Fripp.* Papa's leg is a little better today.'

'Dear Mama,

Have just seen your letter to Lilian, plead guilty about the air cushion which is down here, but know nothing about the belt. Everilda used to wear it years after I did, but of course if you will have a waist smaller than ours and then lend us your belts you must expect them to bust.'

'Dear Grandpapa,

Can you tell me if the trout will be up in the burns in the months of April and May, also if they be in good condition, and a respectable size, or only young fish of last winter's spawn.'

'Dear Mama,

I wish I had brought decent clothes, everyone is so smart. Mrs. Gribbell came down to dinner in grey crepe de chine and silver, the effect however rather spoiled by a huge hole in the heel of her stocking. Mrs. Gabrielli in a white satin stamped with brown velvet decolté in front and a high Medici collar outlined with brown wooden beads; terracotta silk gloves to the elbow with ten little nails peeping

* George Fripp, the water colourist.

playfully out through the ends of the fingers, and a row of yellow glass beads to complete her costume....'

'Dear Grandpapa,

... Papa is not very well and wants a breath of fresh air so he may come down with me (to Rothamsted) ... I am so pining for the country. It is fearfully hot here, and Diane and I have to go to the dentists' every day as we have to wear horrid plates in our mouths to get our teeth in order. We are all going to the Crystal Palace fireworks this evening which should be great fun.... Is there any sign of the Purple Emperor yet?' (a rare butterfly).

'Darling Papa,

I hope dear little Launcelot will get better, and that you will soon be able to come to Scotland ... It has not rained once this week, and the hay is mostly all got in. I have been getting lots of nice ferns. and planting them in the garden.'

'Dear Grandpapa,

It has been the summit of my ambition for years past to have a book with illustrations of every British bird in it ... and now you have given me one ...'

'Darling Sweet,

I hope you enjoyed your hunting yesterday, tho' I am afraid you did not, as papa said Banglar (?) was very fresh, and you only pottered from wood to wood. My sore throat is much better, but I am still a little hoarse, and Diana's cough is also better, but Gogo says that Diane has got bronchitis, so she is not allowed to go out, and has a fire in her bedroom morning and evening ... I am sending you the first violets of the year which have just come out under the dining room window.'

'Darling,

This is a very nice house (Ardchattan) with a ghost and a lady walled up, and there are two ruined churches with very old church-yards. There are three lovely gardens, and a lot of greenhouses, and a gardener who is very nice ... There are lots of lovely seabirds here, plovers, gulls, sandpipers, divers, oyster catchers, and two pairs of herons. There are also plenty of seals. It is also supposed to be a very good place for moths.'

'My Darling Mama,

Last Friday afternoon nurse and me went out to pick flowers and found one cowslip and some anemaneys (sic).'

'My own darling Mama,

Gogo asked me to write to you to say that she wants to have Launcelot's long hair cut right off, because Cousin Emma says that long hair takes away a delicate child's strength, so will you give your permission for it to be done at once?'

Gogo (Lady Lawes) was a matriarch. Although she was a good water colourist, her hand writing is nearly impossible to read. But her orders, written this time on the back of one of the children's letters, are peremptory:

'Dear Ina,
Will you bring a supply of *strengthening* medicine from Everilda's doctor. She ought to be taking it every day. She constantly flags about nothing, comes over in flush heats at night when she is sitting quite still ...'

They were all hypochondriacs, never happier than when they had a bottle of coloured water from a quack. Such is the psychology of feeling that you are being cared for that many of them, in spite of the worst endeavours of the doctors of the day, lived to remarkable old age.

Everilda, the daughter who 'came over in flush heats at night', died at eighty-five. Skye's eldest, she was the only one of her daughters who had no children. 'Bilda', as the family called her, was hereditarily almost an exact split between her father and her mother. Her father had an unusual degree of femininity in him, her mother an unusual degree of the masculine. I think that Bilda was never quite sure which sex she belonged to. She exploded with enthusiasms which led her to become a member of the London, Natural History Society, Royal Society for the Protection of Birds, the National Trust, the International Union for the Protection of Nature, the R.S.P.C.A., the Association of Bird Watcher's, and Wardens, the Society for the Promotion of Nature Preserves and the Norfolk Naturalists' Trust. She had a list of special charities among which were Friends of the Clergy and the Clergy Orphan Corporations, London Hospital Amenities Fund, the Life Boats, the Blind, Shipwrecked Mariners and John Groom's Crippleage.

She wrote poetry, not as good as her mother's. She presented bird baths to Kensington Gardens and associated herself with appeals for 'our dumb friends'. Her life attitude was clearly born out of a challenge with her mother. When she died, leaving £100,000, her bereaved husband published a privately printed tribute to her of a kind which ought not to be published. The only memorable thing in it, apart from a good oil painting by her mother showing Everilda going out for a walk at the age of twelve, is an extract from an obituary letter written by one of her innumerable cousins:

'A vivid picture keeps recurring, of a boat full of children, a lovely sunny day on Loch Awe, and a gull floating down and settling on the still calm water, quite a long distance from the boat, and cousin "Skye" aiming with her rifle. Then Everilda (about fourteen though to me quite grown up) indignantly pleading with mama not to shoot. I can almost hear her voice now after all these long years, pleading for the life of that beautiful bird. Victor, Sylvia, and I had been playing at Kilchurn whilst the elders fished or shot. I know the rifle "pinged", but the result has faded into the mists of time.'

In the mists of time, Everilda hadn't much love for the memory of her mother. Her mother, it appears, had a little more time for her. At least she took care to preserve a letter from a suitor, lined in mourning black edges for Heaven-knows-who (it could have been his late wife) addressed to Walter in the high summer of 1889. It is a touching example, albeit a pathetic one, of the courtship dance which was the form in the Victorian era:

'New Atheneum Club.
Pall Mall, July 31/89

Sir,

Having for some time past been deeply impressed with the beauty and grace of your daughter, and the sweet simplicity of character that seems to me revealed in her countenance, I have waited only for this month to close, on account of the death of my wife a year ago, before writing to you, as I have now the honour to do.

I need hardly say, I have sought no kind of communication with Miſs Creyke or the young lady's mother, for I did not think it right to do so till I had made known to you my vocation as a Novelist and Dramatist, and something of my position in both capacities by sending the enclosed printed pages, issued by a Publisher in one of my books.

As there is a good future for true dramatists, I have been quietly preparing for such a career. I have now ready three plays, two of which have been successfully tried. The third is an entirely new and original English comedy, after the higher French School, in its mingling of serious interest with the lighter parts that justify its name—Comedy.

I may mention, as a work probably known to you—"Arkwright's Wife", played at the Globe to capital houses through an entire season under the joint management of Tom Taylor and John Saunders.

If what I have here said should interest you sufficiently to go

further, I shall be glad to meet you when and where you please, and
answer with entire frankness any question you may wish to put.

Allow me to subscribe myself

Sir,

Your obedient servant

Jn. Saunders.

As we have so often met, for years past in and about the Row, and
as I generally prefer the part above the Achilles Statue, for my daily
walk between ½p 12 and ½p 1, there can be no doubt, I hope and
believe about my personality.'

Skye was characteristically ruthless about the poor fellow's letter
seeking so much above his station. She made a sketch of him, 'through
my stalking telescope', in which he appears in a pot hat with a beer-
stained moustache, nickelled spectacles and thinning hair. She was
almost certainly unfair to him. As Austin Dobson, a contemporary
poet wrote: 'Apollo, you see, in practical matters, a goose is.'
Everilda was unimpressed. Not long after, she left home. She had
fallen in love with a young man who had little time to live, probably
a victim of 'galloping consumption'; or at any rate one of the diseases
which in Victorian times medicine did not know how to control.
When I reflect whether I would have liked to have lived in a period
other than our own I am constantly reminded of the mortality that
disease brought before doctors in our own time got it on the run.
Tuberculosis, pneumonia, cholera, typhoid, even whooping cough,
were all killers. The people who lived were the toughest. Everilda
was among them.

It is important to point out that the Victorians, even in domestic
bliss, even the most well breeched of them, were not gay people.
They enjoyed a melancholia inherited from the gardens of sadness
and the follies of the eighteenth century. Upper class children were
not supposed to enjoy their childhood. Children, as children, had
yet to be discovered. They were treated as undeveloped grown-ups.

Everilda married late; but when she did, it was a wedding in the
most solemn iced-sugar almond-paste three-tier way. The social pages
of the newspapers made a meal of it:

At St. George's, Hanover Square, Mr. Donald A. MacAlister, of
H.M. Geological Survey, son of Mr. J. Y. W. MacAlister, representative of the hereditary keepers of Tarbert Castle, and nephew of
Principal Sir Donald MacAlister, of the University of Glasgow, was
married to Miss Everilda Creyke, daughter of Mrs. Walter Creyke,
and grand-daughter of the late Sir John B. Lawes, of Rothamsted.

The church was handsomely decorated ... Commander C. A. Fountaine, R.N., was the best man. The bride, who was given away by her mother, wore a charmeuse of ivory satin, embroidered with pearls and crystals, with a heavy fringe of pearls and diamanté at the foot of the skirt, and an old Brussels lace veil, the gift of her mother, over a wreath of orange blossoms. Her bouquet was composed of orange blossom, white heather, gardenias, and lilies of the valley, and she wore the diamond necklace left her by her grandmother, Lady Lawes.

She was attended by four little nieces, wearing white frilled frocks with pale blue sashes with chaplets of pink rosebuds in their hair. White shoes and socks, and wreaths of pink roses and shaded picotees. Each of them had a blue enamel pearl pendant, the gift of the bridegroom. While the register was being signed favours of white gardenias and heather were distributed. The reception was held at Mrs. Creyke's residence, 3 Seamore Place, May Fair. Mrs. Donald MacAlister travelled in a gown of powder blue, with heavy embroidery, worn with a beautiful cape, the gift of her mother.

It is sad to tell that Everilda was childless. She didn't marry her first choice for a husband.

Only Sylvia, the youngest was sent away to boarding school; and that only because of the death of her father. All the others were educated at home, at dame's schools and then by French governesses. Diane, Skye's third daughter, became a Christian Scientist and subsequently contributed regularly to *The Monitor*. She wrote in 1927, quoting memories of her mother during schooldays at Rothamsted. The closed world of private education cannot have been much different for her and her sisters.

'... Why, only to think of my schoolroom makes me thankful to be out of it, even today. Nothing to look at but tapestry the whole way round the room. Even the doors were made of it, so that when they were shut you could hardly find your way out. The wide oak planks of the floor were so uneven and sloping, you had to acquire a special walk to cross the room with dignity. To be sure there was a lovely view from the windows, but they were of such bad glass and in such small leaded panes that everything you looked at seemed crooked.

'My bedroom was a nightmare. I had to climb up a little ladder to get into the four post bed. It used to creak and crack, and if the room was at all hot from the log fire, the carved roof of my bed would make noises in the night like a pistol going off ... The bathroom wasn't a bathroom at all, just another tapestry with a polished dark oak floor and a large bath put into it, because my father thought that we ought to march with the times without disturbing the character of the house. We had to hang our towels on a huge Chippendale settee which had been brought down from the Long Gallery where it had been hidden away as it was far too modern for the house. My grandfather thought that it might do for the bathroom because visitors wouldn't trouble about things being in the right period so early in morning.

'Our dining room was just nothing but old ancestors by Holbein, Van Dyck and Sir Godfrey Kneller looking down on me when I ate my porridge and boiled egg ... At night, it looked much more cheerful, I always enjoyed eating the crystallised fruit, almonds and raisins, glacé cherries and macaroons when I was allowed to come in after dinner.'

None of the children, it seems, got much fun until they found their way among the adults after dinner. There they stuffed themselves with sugary things which, in our generation, are supposed to be all the teeth-rotting food a child can eat. I am sure that their mother was impatient every moment when they were present. It is evident that she never got on with any of them, or them with her.

Lilian, her second daughter (born in the summer of 1872), had three second cousins who wanted to marry her. Her mother was opposed to all of them on the grounds of consanguinity. But, writes one of Skye's grandchildren, 'I think a contributing factor was the fact, as far as I can remember, that my mother (Sylvia) told me that Lilian had been delicate ever since she fell out of a boat and got ill (I think it may have been a bit more than that).

There is no question that all of Skye's four girls, in their own right, were unusually personable people. They all, with the exception of Sylvia, had the distinctive artistic tastes of their mother.* With the exception of Lilian, who died of cancer in 1916, they inherited her longevity. With the exception of Everilda, they were all philoprogenitive. Their progeny flourish in all directions today.

Walter Launcelot, her surviving twin son (born 1880), seems in the photographs of him and on all the evidence of the family papers, to have been no character. Three of his sisters were determined people with strong artistic learnings which measured with their own formidable mother. Lance, as he was called, was sent, as might be expected, to Eton and, unsurprisingly, ran away. Subsequently, in the Kaiser's War, he joined up; and it is said refused a commission. It

---

* Sylvia had the agricultural tastes of her grandfather. When she married, the stud bull at Manton Grange, Marlborough, was named 'J.B.L.'.

is believed that he got through two fortunes largely spent on girl friends he collected at stage doors. He died in an accident in the Underground in the London Blitz in 1942. He may well have felt that he had nothing more to live for.

Barbara Ker-Seymer, one of the grandchildren of Skye, writes a sad obituary of Lance: 'I hope that you are not going to ignore the existence of poor Lance. I never cared for him myself; but all the others liked him very much, and thought him most charming and gentle. I suppose that, although he looked like grandmamma, he was the most like Walter in character. I don't remember him ever sitting in the room with grandmamma. He sat alone, by the hour, in the tiny little back room overlooking dull and sunless Seamore Place (now Curzon Place) with his library which, unlike Walter's that consisted of elegantly bound volumes of French and Italian novels, was littered entirely with rather battered 6d. paperbacks. It is strange, since so many mothers transfer their love to their growing sons, particularly only sons, that grandmamma showed no interest in Lance. He appeared to be used solely as an unpaid servant.'

Lance had been a delicate child, hardly expected to live. His father, when he buried his twin brother, had little hope that Lance would live as long as in fact he did. Skye had no comment. In after years she was to say: 'My husband is dead. My children are launched. And now I can do what I like. I am going on a World Tour.'

But, in the meantime, she had a full life staring invitingly in front of her.

VIII

HERSELF

NA asked me in the train if I should mind her not coming to the church.'

The occasion—'a cold gusty day and drizzling with rain'—was the funeral at Rothamsted of her twin son who died with whooping cough in his first year. Skye, known by so many names even to her husband, counted the ceremony as an interruption in her life. She had produced for Walter, against her own will, six children. She had almost certainly suffered a miscarriage as well. She was not inclined to mourn for one less. Her husband, in continually failing health, was no longer 'one of the most handsome men in England'. As an escort she had no further use for him.

Fragments exist of Walter's diary kept over the years. One of the children in her old age chopped passages out of it (apparently with nail scissors) which she counted interesting. One of them is Walter's reflections on the death of his son. It is Dickens at his sentimental worst:

'The brougham has just driven off with the little white coffin with a beautiful white wreath sent by Dick, and a cross of pink and white flowers, which the wet nurse and Matilda asked that they might give, and a wreath of sweet white flowers of our own at the foot ... Sylvia said "Pinky can't go to Heaven without his baskeynet. Perhaps he has got it in his box." The next day she said to her mother: "Pinky has got wings now—he has gone up into the sky— I looked for him there but I couldn't see him. Perhaps he was behind the clouds. I looked for God in the sky, but I couldn't see Him! ... I have been reading and explaining to Lilian and Diane some of the burial service. They will go into the nursery and read what I explained aloud to Alice the wet nurse and the hospital nurse, just when we are standing by son Pinkey's grave ... I have been to see little Launcelot whom Bilda hopes will soon get better. I hope too, but ... He was in the wet nurse Alice's arms but looking very sad and suffering. He generally laughs and holds out his hands to me but he only looked with inscrutable big blue eyes, as if asking why he suffered so ... At the service we found his little white coffin with all the flowers, and poor Bilda's little crushed wild flowers the most overcoming to look at. Two men carried the coffin and John Lawes, who is always kind in all practical matters, walked with me. I thought of our children at home reading the service at the same moment that I was in church. Mrs. Vaughan had made a cross with her own hands and put it on the coffin. Going under a tree in the churchyard this was swept off, but I picked it up and put it on the coffin when we got to the grave. I could not see when they lowered him into the earth.'

Walter, inclined to tears, emotional and shy, ineffective and undemanding, was no man to manage Skye. He accepted her edict when she declared that she was not going to her son's funeral service. It is possible that he could not understand why. Skye knew. Throughout her life she was consistent in her insistence that motherhood was an unpleasant experience, something that had to be put up with in the interests of good form. Yet such a nubile and vigorous woman, with a husband who can scarcely have awakened her deepest emotions, surely needed men. In her circle she was surrounded by the most desirable men of her times. There is no doubt that she was courted. It is reasonable to guess that, with a strong man who brought a stick to her, she might have fallen passionately in love.

Her grandchildren, who are convinced that Skye never knew any man other than Walter, tell of her that, when she was expecting a visit from Lord Dudley's second wife, Georgina, she made the arch remark that she must hide the brooch given to her by Dudley. I like it that way. The grandchildren, I fancy, underestimate their grandmama. Knowing her only when she was old, they overlook 'the mistakes' which we are all prone to when we are young.

It could be, although it wouldn't have been like her, that she refrained from going to her infant son's funeral in the fear that, in her affliction, she might lose her composure. It is true that, in Victorian times, 'the weaker sex' were often excused from mournful events. It could be, in the tight-lipped upper crust of her period, that Skye was totally unaware of any sexual deviation in her husband's life. It could be that she was so self-contained that she was never tempted to yield to masculine advances surrounded though she was by the gifted, attentive and most attractive men of her day. But, in the balance of probabilities, it does not add that she funked a funeral, that she was ignorant of homosexuality, and that she was disinterested in relationships with men other than her husband. The pattern of her whole life, from childhood in the Highlands to maturity, denies it.

In the scraps of Walter's diary which are left, he writes jealously about Gustave Doré. It was perhaps not without reason. It was 1879, the same year in which Doré made his portrait of her :

'Doré and others dined and stayed until 1 o'clock. His manner is not very pleasant but glad to know him as a man of great genius. Ina got on with him well and he admired her singing very much. He looks about 40 with brown hair and a small moustache. He gave himself no trouble to please but I suppose enjoyed it because he stayed so late. After dinner, when Ina sang, he stood by her, talked to her if alone, and walked about the room if she spoke to anyone else! In despair I retired before Ina sent him off at last.'

Nigel Gosling, in his biography of Doré, describes him as a favourite guest at wealthy society parties. 'Not everybody fell under his charm. The Goncourts (who later relented) describe him at this period as "fat, fresh and baby-faced with an expression like the moon in a magic lantern and the complexion of a choirboy, an ageless look bearing no trace of his terrifying labours; to sum up, he displeases me with his air of an infant prodigy in the body of a grown-up".' Like Walter's, Doré's own sexuality was mysterious.

I wonder whether Walter said anything to Skye about Doré when, in the small hours of the morning, they lay together in their great four poster bed? I doubt it. Such a witty and highly intelligent woman would have laughed him to sleep. As journalist and artist in a period when women in her class were not supposed to exercise their minds she was aware of what made people tick, and surely knew how to use them to her advantage? What she had was discretion. I am convinced that there was nothing which surprised her. In our own time she might well have had a reputation for a series of 'shocking' books. In hers she played the game, no different from ours, with the restraint which was then socially respectable. I question, even when she was 'at home', that she showed her cards to her women friends. She was Skye, always amusing and wise, only intolerant of an acquaintance who presumed to criticise anyone in her immediate circle, most of all her husband, a woman who sparkled in self-confidence and well-being.

Behind the outward image she could have been unhappy. After the fairyland picture of marriage to a handsome prince of men, she can have had little joy in her physically failing husband. She was exasperated by her children. She adored her father, and I cannot help feeling that it was a lifelong disappointment for her that other men didn't fulfil her as he did. The touch of his hand, his paternal kiss, was the best thing that happened in her life. He was her only master.

Maybe her grand-daughters are right. Within themselves, they must know better than any biographer the subleties of her sexuality. Skye loved the attentions of men, but it may be the truth that she preferred them at the dinner table to bed. It is unusual for a woman, full of father love, to be frigid. But the tremendous energy that she displayed in her outward life may well have been an outlet for the disappointment she had in her secret one. She might not have called it disappointment. Perhaps she really detested physical contact; although, in her poetry, she is romantic to a fault. The wealthy Lord Dudley, the gifted artist Gustave Doré, even the Prince of Wales, were just a few who showered attentions on her.

Women, all women, love to be wooed. Some, perhaps Skye was one of them, are reluctant to be conquered. It could be that Skye never had the luck to meet the man that she really wanted. In posterity another man can never know.

One of her grandchildren, Barbara, wrote to me: 'My reason for thinking that grandmamma did not have extra-marital sexual affairs was that she was far too formidable. Only the most lion-hearted creature would have dared to make a pass at her. Loving, affectionate, warm hearted person that she was, she disliked physical demonstrations. I do not ever remember her putting her arms around me, giving me a hug and a kiss other than the duty peck on the cheek on arriving and leaving. I was a very affectionate child; but I would never have dared take her hand, or hang on to her arm when going for walks.'

Yet she doted on pretty feminine clothes. She was above average height, 5 feet 7″ or 8″, she had beautiful hands with long fingers; and even in great old age, she retained the delicate complexion which is the glory of English women. She carried her figure, straight as a rod, even in her nineties, in the way a 'clothes-horse' should. Her grandchild, Griselda Blakiston, has the skirt of one of her balldresses designed to take away anyone's breath. It came from Paris where most of her great gowns were made. Griselda has sent me a mouthwatering description of it, dating it between 1905 and 1907: 'The skirt is black chiffon, with insertions of Valenciennes lace, mounted on an underskirt of cream taffeta. It is hand-gathered at the waist and there are bands of cream silk, wasp-printed in pink and apple green, arranged in an undulating "V" formation at just below the knee level, and at the hemline. The underskirt has finely pleated frills at the lower edge, also ruffled bands with "pinked" edges, all of which expand the hemline and support the sheer fabric of the upper garment. Both upper and underskirts are "trained" at the back. I am sorry that I no longer have the skirt of rose-coloured velvet embroidered with dark red silk and crystal beads which she wore at the Duke of Clarence's ball in the eighties or nineties. In both cases the bodices have not survived, but I presume that they were boned, and for the chiffon skirt would have had a V-shaped point at the waist, a low oval neckline and important sleeves or epaulettes, probably in Valenciennes lace trimmed with bands of silk.'

The Paris couturiers must have loved her.

It is sometimes said that such was society in her time that the opportunities for clandestine intrigue were not there. 'Teddy' disproved that. In a period when any woman alone with a man for a few minutes was counted to be at risk, Skye was alone a lot of the time. Walter was too poorly in health to accompany her. In Walter's favour, Barbara Ker-Seymer wrote to me: 'It is true that the women in our family are the dominating ones. But Walter had a strong family tree—as all the girls "favoured" him, and not one of them looked in the least like grandmamma. They all had Walter's features.' But all the grandchildren whom I have met inherit Skye's energy and ebullient temperament. Genes are a strange subject to unravel. Like sex.

The emotional cycle of Skye's life is revealed by the dates in it. From 1870, when she married Walter, to 1880, when she had the twins, she was constantly childbearing. In the late eighties, looking back to her childhood with her father, she wrote her *Sporting Sketches*, the same period in which her girlhood friend, Gustave Doré, made his affectionate drawings of her. Her first article as a journalist, called 'Violet's Revenge', was published in *Fashion and Sport* in July, 1890, two years before her husband's lingering death. It is significant that she had engraved in gold on her first album of cuttings the title *Nuits Blanches*, a French phrase for restless sleepless nights.

It was the time, I think, in which she wrote much of her poetry—verses like this one:

A *Summer Idyll*

He led me forth into the silent night,
Beside the river where the moonbeams play.
There was no song of bird, nor insect hum,
For all were resting from the long, hot day.

The scented woodbine hung about our path,
And sweet, pale orchids—scattered here and there—
While, in the gloom, some startled, dusky form
In noiseless flight sped through the summer air.

The dragonfly's melodious wing was still,
But sometimes came a sound of cooling breeze
Over the meadows, like a perfumed sigh
Stirring tall rushes; and the sleeping trees
Thro' which it quivered, murm'ring plaintively,
Woke, as tho' troubled by some restless dream;
And, falling thro' the green, a withered leaf
Touched the smooth surface of the tranquil stream.

Long stood we silently; or hand in hand
Wandered within the dark, mysterious glade
With light gleams white as snow. Then, suddenly
Some cloudlet hid the moon; and in the shade
His eyes shone down into mine eyes, like stars.
No word he spoke, but, kneeling at my side
His trembling lips sought mine that trembled not
For love was yet unborn that summer tide.

I felt but wonder, since I knew not love,
And burning hands my cold hands clasped in vain;
Till, at the last, my troubled senses woke
Beneath his kiss—woke slowly, and in pain.
O summer night I ne'er shall feel again
Thy peace and purity; for that embrace
Which wakened love, left its sad mark on me
As, in the dew, our footsteps left their trace.

INA

She is haunted with regret for the past.

> 'Ah! would I could dream till a summer sun
> Shall have melted my frozen tears,
> And, would I could sleep till gentle time
> shall have healed the sorrow of years!'

She signed that, published in the *Pall Mall Magazine* in April, 1894,
unusually as Caroline Creyke. Perhaps she wanted to tell her friends
something. Elsewhere as I.N.A., she yearns for the magic of her
childhood by the sea:

Alone by The Sea

Where are the white waves that beat on the rocks, the white
    spray that dashed up on high?
Where are the seagulls that whirled round in flocks, the dark
    clouds that coursed o'er the sky?
Where is the girl with the eyes and the hair—the girl who was
    with me that day—
Who laughed as the lightning flashed past overhead, the breakers
    swept into the bay?

In her youth, in her beauty, she stood, like a statue erect on
    the peak;
The wind tossed her tresses, and tumbled her gown, and kiss'd
    the red rose of her cheek.
And I—I was young, and I shrank from her eye, and the sight
    of her wind-embraced form;
But I treasured the flow'r she crushed in her palm, and held
    to her lips in the storm.
And I treasure it sacredly still; 'tis my one withered link with
    the past,
As I wander alone on the hill, and recall the weird wail of the
    blast.

It is still, it is tame, it is warm, and the sea is one equable green;
It is silent, and sunny, and calm, and the sapphire blue sky is
    serene;
The daisies have sprinkled the grass, newly grown, where the
    young lambkins play;
The nightingale sings of the Spring, and the lark warbles over
    the bay.
It is pleasant to lie on the cliff, and to dream in the sea-scented
    air—
But I long for the wild winter gale, and the girl with the
    tempest-toss'd hair!

                                  INA

It may not be great poetry; but it is not bad. What is remarkable
is that it was written at all. Skye was a woman of what used to be
called gentle breeding, and of considerable affluence, in a society in
which she was not called upon to prove anything. She painted, at
a time when it was fashionable to paint, and did it better than most
of her contemporaries. She sang and played the piano, with skill and
understanding. She concerned herself with elocution:
The following is a list of common words with their usual pro-

nunciation and their pronunciation by well-bred people, for which reference to a dictionary is for obvious reasons, useless:

gurl	= gairl	see-rious	= serious	ars	= ours
pore	= poor	qu-rious	= kiorious (curious)	binn	= been
ideel	= ide-al	few-rious	= fiorius (furious)	gonn	= gone
reel	= re-al	ar'll	= I'll (I will)	agenn	= again
reely	} = re-ally	there'll	= they will	wur	= were
rarely		your'll	= you'll (you will)	wear	= we are
ordeel	= orde-al	your	= you are		

Her interest in the theatre, and music, was passionate. She wrote gushing short plays, which were never performed, and even wrote the music for six songs which were published. One of her professional friends told her that they were no good. But nothing could quell the flow of her creative energy. In the *Nineteenth Century Magazine*, she lays down the law at length, on amateur singing, the craze of her times:

'It is not good for the throat to practise in a cold unaired room, or a room in which there is a wood fire, if any of the smokes escapes into the room, as wood smoke irritates the throat. The strong smell of flowers is also bad for the voice, as well as painting in oils and inhaling the smell of turpentine. Nor is singing immediately after taking violent exercise good for the voice. A strong person with a strong voice will not trouble about these details, but as a rule amateurs cannot be too careful if they wish to make a good impression, as no one but a professional will make any allowances for the deficiencies of an amateur singer. When practising the amateur should never use the whole power of the voice, and even when singing before an audience it is better to begin with a quiet song to warm the throat than to burst forth into a loud operatic scena.'

And that, from Skye, was that. She was confident that she knew all about singing, and correct speaking. She tells how, in her double drawing room, she and Mrs. Patrick Campbell tested the penetration of their voices across the length of it in their softest tones. Those who knew her in her old age tell that she still spoke with musical precision.

She never, so far as I know, wrote about her painting. Her work was erratic. In keeping with her mood she could be bad, or very good. Some of her oil portraits are remarkable. Most of her sketching is mediocre. But it is her measure that she had a bash at poetry and journalism, music and painting, and brought up five children as well.

Memorable in none of these arts, she cannot be dismissed in any.

She was one of those remarkable people, of large and varied gifts, who are never quite good enough in any one of them to leave a lasting mark. Intellectually, she was fully rounded. She has not been remembered because she never really mastered any of the attainments which appealed to her. But she made for herself a good time.

Her personality was formidable. Her physique was unquenchable. She took it out of life in athletic exercise in a period when exercising for women was largely limited to the hunting field. Walter records in his diary, oddly enough, that she was a shy horsewoman. It may be that she was bored. In the middle fifties she joined in the new cult of bicycling, inspired no doubt by her brother. Characteristically, she laid down the law about it in the *Nineteenth Century Magazine* in 1897:

'Fancy Cycling for Ladies
Cycling as a fashionable craze is played out. Girls no longer go for a spin down to the Tower Bridge in the cool of the evening, when the City streets are almost deserted, before they dress for a ball; nor do they race round the square in their ball gowns at 4 a.m. on a summer morning before retiring to bed. But we question if cycling as a convenient means of locomotion will ever entirely be dispensed with. For country visiting, when carriages are not available, or for shopping in London for those to whom the dangers of the traffic have no terrors and are only looked upon as a pleasurable excitement, cycles will always hold their own; especially as the long-talked-of motor car seems likely to end in smoke—and a bad smell.

There is also another form of cycling which appears to find favour with the young and active, and requires considerably greater skill even than dodging in and out among cabs and omnibuses. I refer to what is called trick riding, and the execution of an endless variety of military rides to the accompaniment of music.'

Irrepressibly, Skye concerned herself with everything which happened about her. *The Hub*, a periodical devoted to the sport of bicycling, had a picture of her with her brother.

She made herself a mistress of ice skating at the artificial rink at Prince's Club in Piccadilly. Walter wrote admiringly: 'She executed figures with long sweeps to the admiration of a crowd who left the space clear for her.' At seventy she took her grandchildren to the Serpentine when it was frozen, and executed perfect figures of eight while they were pushing chairs over the ice.

She played croquet, that formidable game, at Roehampton, Ranelagh and Hurlingham. She presented cups to them for competition. In her nineties she was waving her umbrella imperiously to stop the bus for Roehampton. It stopped at a 'Request Stop' in Park Lane which she had imperiously had moved because the noise of the buses disturbed her when she was playing the piano.

I think of her when she was young. As her biographer I have developed a sort of love-hate relationship with Skye, the thought that, if I could cross the passage of the years, I should have liked to have been a guest at her house, 3 Seamore Place, May Fair.

IX

SEAMORE PLACE, MAY FAIR

T was a big house in a small world. By our reckoning it was then a small London numbering a population in the middle sixties of about three million. While it is statistically impossible to prove it, it is probable that nearly a million Londoners at that time were existing below what we should regard as the breadline. Of the remaining two-thirds the larger number were professional people, and clerks of small means, tightening their belts in the name of respectability, and those who were engaged in trade. The few, and the very few, enjoyed the riches of what was then the wealthiest capital in the world. It is a mere guess, but not far out, that less than ten thousand people commanded all that golden London had to offer. Mr. and Mrs. Walter Creyke, of 3 Seamore Place, May Fair, were among them.

I am sure that, in their heyday, they didn't think about it. They were too early in social history to have an awakening conscience. It was normal for a large household of their sort to have a dozen and more servants. Although the domestic staff were paid, by our standards, abominably, the fringe benefits, as we should call them now, were considerable. A skivvy was better off inside a mansion than she would have been outside it. Outside, London teemed with the derelicts of a growing city and an increasingly industrialised one. Enveloping Seamore Place, the winter fogs, induced by coal-burning, were 'London particulars'. The greatest problem in the hygiene of the streets was horse manure. Crossing sweepers, poor little urchins or broken down old men hired for the job, had to clear the way for the pedestrians. The sweet smell of manure, healthier than oil but just as pervasive filled the air. Electricity was a newcomer. It was still a gaslight city.

Walter and Skye occupied their cul-de-sac in the centre of it in the certainty that they belonged to a class which had been created to rule all that they surveyed. It is cautionary to add that they themselves lived in a discomfort which would be intolerable, at the present time, to any suburban housewife. With their horde of servants—children's nurses and wet nurse, foreign valets and footmen, cooks and parlourmaids—they had no central heating, no refrigerators, no vacuum cleaners or modern cooking devices. Their lighting was unreliable. Their only transport was horse-drawn. They couldn't conceive air travel, as we know it; although Skye, characteristically, made a daring ascent in 1891 in one of Mr. Percival Spencer's balloons.

Three Seamore Place would have been unmanageable as a home today. It had five floors. The attics were for children and servants, the basement for servants and children, the middle floors for grown-ups. The dining-room was on the ground floor. The drawing-room, overlooking Park Lane and Hyde Park, was on the first. The principal bedroom, in which Skye and Walter slept in their vast four poster bed, was on the second. To our taste the house was ponderously, almost oppressively, equipped. It was loaded with velvet curtains, gilt looking glasses, boule and Italian furniture, and yellowing oil paintings in heavy frames. The effects which were sold by auction in 1946, after Skye's death, make pathetic reading. Undoubtedly, the dealers who bid for the stuff to a total of £1886-2-0 made a killing, especially in this age when we are all nostalgic for the period which has gone away. But there are mothballs in the lots which were offered for auction : 'sixty-seven lace table mats, d'oyleys etc.', 'a mahogany nest of open bookshelves with centre mirror', 'an ebonised and boule inlaid wardrobe with bevelled mirrored door and ormolu mounts', 'a mother o'pearl and painted fan, an ivory and lace ditto', an 'ornamental green-painted and gilt Italian 4-poster bedstead, with terminals of vases of flowers, urns, eagles etc. 5 ft. 10 inches wide'. A pastel by Caroline Creyke, 'Geisha' in a gilt frame, with six other water colours, fetched £2.

It was the stuff of Skye's golden years. May Fair, which had long been a slum, had only in her own time become an enclave of the rich. It was a period when, in the evening, throughout Park Lane or Piccadilly, there was nobody on the pavements but gentlemen in opera cloaks, wearing crush hats and white waistcoats, and ladies teetering in egret feathers, lappets and overweighted ball gowns. It was the age of orchids in the buttonhole, random ravages of ladies of easy virtue in hansom cabs, secret suppers in gilded restaurants, and a confidence in the future, anyhow for the privileged, which we have lost.

It was a little world which revolved about St. James's almost within gunshot of Buckingham Palace. There, Victoria reigned over a fifth of the world in serene sovereignty. Skye had what is called 'the entrée', the privilege of entry to the Court. In due course she presented all her four daughters at the drawing-rooms in the great Queen's time, and later. Their heads decked in ostrich plumes, in which they had to sit very straight in their carriages (often with the cushions taken out to make sure they didn't bend the feathers), the debutantes waited for hours to make their curtsey to the Queen. None has written about it better than Mr. Rush, Minister from the United States during Canning's administration. He wrote in an earlier period than Victoria's; but, in hers, nothing had changed except that the occasion in the Throne Room at Buckingham Palace was more grandiose than it had ever been before:

'You saw a thousand ladies richly dressed. . . . No lady was without her plume, the whole was a waving field of feathers; some were blue, some tinged with red; here you saw violet and yellow, there shades of green, but most were like tufts of snow; the diamonds encircling them caught the sun and threw dazzling beams around. Then the hoops, I cannot describe these; they should be seen; to see one is nothing; but to see a thousand, and their wearers. I afterwards sat in the ambassador's box at the coronation, but that sight faded before this. Each lady seemed to rise out of a gilded little barricade, or one of silvery texture. This, topped by her plumes, and the face divine interposing, gave to the whole an effect so unique, so fraught with feminine grace and grandeur, it seemed as if a curtain had risen to show a pageant in another sphere. It was brilliant and joyous; to those even to whom it was not new. They stood at gaze as I did. Canning for one. You saw admiration in the gravest statesmen.'

Such was the world which Skye inherited. She decorated it in her own inimitable way. She wore the plumes of court with the confidence of breeding. She displayed the extravagant clothes of her period on a figure which was unspoilt after carrying six children.* Her house became a centre of high hospitality. Without benefit of telephone she conducted her affairs, like everybody else in her set, in elaborate letters by penny post with deliveries three times a day. She dropped her visiting cards, and received them, in a circle which was largely confined within walking distance of her house on the fashionable south side of Hyde Park. A few letters, all of them with die-stamped addresses, a large number with crests as well, remain. Many are currently illegible, most are undated, they give the day of the month but not the year; but there is enough to interpret the mood in the kingfisher years of Seamore Place:

---

* Some of her dresses are now in the Doris Langley Moore collection in Bath. Some her grandchildren still have. Others were used in theatricals by the boys of Winchester College. Skye would have liked that.

'Cheyne Cottage,
Cheyne Row,
Chelsea.

My dear Mrs. Creyke,

I am so sorry I cannot call today. I have an excruciating headache.
Yours very sincerely....'

Her signature looks like Genie something or another. I wonder
who she was? But there is no doubt about this one. It is from
Mrs. Patrick Campbell:

'48 Ashley Gardens, S.W.

Dear Mrs. Creyke,

I am just delighted with my spoons. Do please tell me where you
got them. I hope my boy was good today. Don't please let him be a
trouble. I know you don't care about children. Many thanks for your
present.
Yours sincerely....'

Stella's signature is as muddled as a wriggle of worms. It is notable
that scarcely anybody at that time, outside the immediate family,
used Christian names, even to close friends. It was surely a better
system of nomenclature than we know now in which the casual use
of Christian names makes it almost impossible to identify who is
who. But it was difficult enough when everybody was writing in
faltering ink. I have done my best to interpret:

'Palazzo Doria, Venice.

Dear Mrs. Creyke,

I feel, since you have a daughter "out", that a thread has snapped
in our relations. I have so little in common with, and interest myself
so little in all that now which, naturally enough, absorbs you. The
other girls, too, who were delightful at the "gamine" age have all,
suddenly, become prim, proper and sophisticated, & have turned into
Everilda's—all of which is very right and proper, and as it should be,
I suppose, but I preferred the bear-garden!

Well, you may like to hear, all the same, that I am thoroughly
enjoying this delicious weather. I bathe every day at the Lido; &
breakfast & dine in some green bower. The Edens have a rose garden
at the Guidecca which is a charming lounge & give you tea & an
occasional "al fresco" under a pergola of vines.

Last night, I went to hear "Faust" and then floated about till
2 a.m. listening to a serenade for some Austrian Duke—in a gondola.

Diane's husband, Walter, appears to have been a sweet and sensitive man whose life was cursed by appalling ill-health. Unlike his wife he adored his children. He called them his 'chicks'. It may be that his Byronesque good looks, perhaps a certain femininity in his nature, undermined his masculine confidence. He was nevertheless a superb horseman, a fair cricketer and a good shot His social connections were impeccable.

Diane was bored with her children, and with her husband. She herself never had a day's ill-health in a hundred years. But she briskly performed her wifely and maternal duties. In her own full life as a journalist, artist and hostess, she presented all her four daughters at court. She had the *entrée*, the right to present her family for a curtsey at the receptions of the sovereign. She is photographed in court dress here.

This is the May Fair where the nightingale sang. No. 3 Seymour Place, May Fair (*right*) is the Creykes' mansion overlooking Park Lane, with the lead caryatids which Diane brought from Italy. The *Punch* cartoons by George du Maurier (*opposite*) recall the years in which she was entertaining Sarah Bernhardt (George du Maurier, too) in a world which has been lost. Here is the fashionable West End of London in the nineteenth century.

MUSIC AT HOME. I.

LAMENTABLE RESULT OF INSISTING ON STRICT SILENCE IN THE MUSIC-ROOM DURING THE PERFORMANCE OF GOOD MUSIC.

OVERDOING IT.

"WHAT? GOING ALREADY? AND IN MACKINTOSHES? SURELY YOU ARE NOT GOING TO WALK!"

"OH, DEAR NO! LORD ARCHIBALD IS GOING TO TAKE US TO A DEAR LITTLE SLUM HE'S FOUND OUT NEAR THE MINORIES—SUCH A FEARFUL PLACE! FOURTEEN POOR THINGS SLEEPING IN ONE BED, AND NO WINDOW!—AND THE MACKINTOSHES ARE TO KEEP OUT INFECTION, YOU KNOW, AND HIDE ONE'S DIAMONDS, AND ALL THAT!"

Throughout his long career, Sir John Bennet Lawes Bt. remained the squire of Rothamsted in Hertfordshire. There, under gables created in Dutch fashion by his ancestors, he transformed agricultural practice, teaching the importance of chemical science. He trod his acres with modest diffidence. He proved that what he had found out was right. He sits here with his daughter Diane, and Gogo, his wife (who painted this watercolour of their home). In her arms is Lance, the grandson who didn't quite come off.

From 1886 to 1896 Sir John Lawes leased Ardchattan Priory in Argyll for the fishing and the shooting. He had a steam yacht on Loch Etive to carry him down the creek to Oban and the outer isles. His wife, ever attached to her dogs, found trouble travelling between Scotland and England. Everybody was relieved when she got safely home. Her Highland house must have been a great burden to her. For her children, and her grandchildren, it was a perpetual delight. All their fantasies came true here.

Certificate of Ascent.

I hereby certify that

Mr. Walter Creyke

made a

Balloon **Ascent**

F. KAPP & CO., PHOTO. CALCUTTA.

in my Balloon, the "City of York" from the
Royal Naval London Exhibition
Chelsea, London.
on Saturday, 15th Aug: 1891

REMARKS.—The "City of York" Balloon is the largest
and most scientifically constructed in the British Empire.
It was manufactured by Messrs. Charles Green Spencer & Sons,
Aëronauts and Balloon Manufacturers, 14, Ringcroft Street,
Holloway, London N. It made its first ascent, with 8 passengers
in the car in June 1889 at the celebrated York Gala, upon which
occasion it was named the "City of York" by the Lady Mayoress.

Percival Spencer

Aëronaut.

Diane: in early womanhood　　　　　　In middle age

On the Continent　　　　　　On her hundredth birthday

She was indestructible until she fell asleep, after a cup of tea, in her one hundred and second year. She had defied time as few people do. She had ornamented her age, and survived to the next one. It was characteristic of her that she was a pioneer astronaut. Even in her nineties, with her rifle at her side, she promised that if the Germans invaded London she would shoot Hitler through the ear at two hundred yards.

In her nineties, Diane travelled on the bus to Roehampton and Hurling-ham, playing croquet with a mallet of her own design, politely insisting that she should be handicapped with the seventies. She always reckoned that she was better than her juniors. She had changed a bus stop in Park Lane because it interfered with her piano playing. To her end she was indomitable.

My old friend "the Count"* is here, looking far better than his letters had led me to expect.

I shall not be able to tear myself away till the heat burns me out, & then shall return to London Society, *à contre coeur*, just staying long enough in Paris to see the Salon and *Exhbn*. The peace and quiet of this place after a long incarceration in town is indescribable....'

Who the lady was who wrote such a good letter I cannot guess because the last part of it is missing. So much is inevitably missing. Among the heap of letters, carrying postage stamps which I suppose that a philatelist would say are valuable now, I found one from her son's housemaster at Eton. It does not compare with the better schoolmaster's report which concluded 'He rows across the curriculum rather than with it.' It is limited to the sort of comment which, in the after event, was clearly untrue: 'His verses are, I think, the best part of his work, and he is able to combine speed with accuracy, and at the same time shows no small appreciation of the Latin language. He is in every way an admirable boy to deal with, & I have not the slightest fault to find with his punctuality, attention and behaviour.'

As if Skye cared. As Mrs. Patrick Campbell wrote, she was disinterested in all her children. But she always fulfilled her maternal duty. She and Walter called on Mrs. Thackeray, the wife of the novelist, to be the godmother of I don't know which one of her progeny.

'8 Southwell Gardens.
My dear Mrs. Creyke,
I am so touched by your kind thought. I thought that I was too unorthodox ever to be a godmother again.'

The letters which still exist are largely replies to invitations to parties. Mary Anderson was then at the top of the theatrical bill:

'My dear Mrs. Creyke,
I was so sorry not to be able to come to your tea yesterday, but my voice was so weak I was afraid I might be tempted to talk too much and not be fit for my night's work. I hear your daughter's dress was charming! I must beg her to show it to me some other day. What a pleasant lunch you gave us on Sunday. Yours sincerely
Mary Anderson.'

'I have been so ill ever since "La Tosca" & everything has been a

* Lord Carlisle.

trouble to me, or I should have written to thank you for the kind card you sent me which I daresay you have forgotten all about. Believe me, sincerely yours,

F. Bernard-Beere.' (*She was Fanny, called the poor man's Sarah Bernhardt*).

'3 Holland Park Road,
Kensington W.

Dear Mrs. Creyke,

I feel I must refuse myself the pleasure you are so kind to offer on Tuesday. I have had of late a very fatiguing time in various ways and I feel that the late hours involved in accepting your tempting invitation would be wholly incompatible at the moment with easel next day. Please accept regrets, and believe me, yours sincerely

Frederick Leighton'

'It will be of much pleasure to be of your party Monday night— J. Forbes Robertson.' 'It was very kind of you to afford us the opportunity of such a charming evening—Charles Wyndham.' 'Thank you for your kind reminder about the 26th. I shall look forward to lunching with you on that day at 2 o'clock—Mary Moore.' 'Mrs. Bancroft has run down to Westgate for a few days, so you will forgive my writing on her behalf. The demand for seats for "Diplomacy" is so extraordinary that it is out of our power to help you—S. B. Bancroft.' 'Thanks, the warmest, my dear Mrs. Creyke, for your most kind congratulations. I must admit to having experienced a delightful sensation on learning that a son had been given us—a fine little fellow too—a strong infant giving promise of being able to hold his own in the struggle before him—Tweedale.' 'Criterion Theatre. Dear Mrs. Creyke, Will you give me the pleasure of your company at supper (11.30 p.m.) on Tuesday next, and confer a great delight on yours sincerely—Charles Wyndham.' 'My dear Mrs. Creyke, I am sure you would like to see the lovely embroideries that Mr. Steinhart is selling dirt cheap—Stella Campbell.' 'I want to have a good look at Doré's drawings. They are very beautiful and I had no time to look at them—Elcho.' 'Dear Mrs. Creyke, I put your request to the Queen and Her Majesty says she will be pleased to accept a copy of your book—Mary F. Hughes.' 'A thousand thanks for your book which will find a place of honour on the shelves of my library —Dufferin and Ava.' 'Apsley House. My dear Mrs. Creyke. You never condoled with me when you heard of it so I don't know whether you pitied me or not under the inflictions of *Good Society*, the *best* people (that is not you and I) who went to see the Prince of

Wales off last evening. The arrangements beat everything in badness that I have ever seen in England ... many great ladies without their male encumbrances all struggling in a dense mass.... The poor prince looked bored and not well but he plunged into the sea of hands and shook a good percentage of them. He couldn't tell which hands belonged to which people. He agitated somebody's flipper instead of the German Ambassador, and mistook H.E. for the Duchess of Manchester ...'

The letter, from Lord John Hay, was not irrelevant. Skye already had a reputation for breaking the rules of 'Good Society'. She delighted in Bohemian company. The letters show how she filled Seamore Place with actors and actresses, musicians and painters. In 1879 she had actually given a dinner party for the notorious French actress, Madame Sarah Bernhardt. Lofty eyebrows were raised when it was learnt what she was up to. 'In those days', she wrote herself, 'there was a great gulf fixed between the stage and society, which few women cared to bridge over.' Her friend, Lord Dudley, tried to dissuade her when she asked him to arrange an introduction. She was undeterred. She took 'the divine Sarah' into her charge, challenging all society to ostracise her.

On the occasion of Sarah Bernhardt's first triumphant appearance in London, she wondered whether anybody who was anybody would come to a dinner in her honour. In fact, all her friends accepted. She was embarrassed by the eagerness with which they welcomed her invitation. Arthur Boucher, the actor manager who was so snobbish that he could not give a curtain speech without telling that he was educated 'at a little known public school called Eton', begged to be invited. When he learnt that the table was full, he offered to appear in the capacity of the butler. In the end, a place was found for him :

'Garrick Club.

Dear Mrs. Creyke,

I shall be charmed to come on Tuesday next—but please don't put me too near Mme. Bernhardt, as my French, or better the infinitesimal amount I know of it—is of the very worst ! !'

'77 Sloane Street, S.W.

My dear Mrs. Creyke,

Pray forgive me for suggesting it to you—but Mons. Richepin is here & is, I know, disappointed not to have met Sarah in London.... He is deploring that he hasn't seen Sarah yet.... Yours ever sincerely, Maud Tree.'

'48 Ashley Gardens

Dear Mrs. Creyke,

I am afraid Madam Bernhardt will find it dull without anyone who speaks her language fluently, but....'

Society crowded in on the scene. Cornelia Otis Skinner in her biography *Madame Sarah* refers to it:

'She (Sarah) was rather mystified that some of the invitations should have come from titled individuals. In France at that time no theatre people were socially accepted by the Upper Crust. The English attitude was becoming less strict but conservative aristocracy still regarded players as "rogues and vagabonds", and now to find the doors of London's élite opening out for an actress, and a French one at that, struck her as pleasant but odd until she found out the reason. Her old friend Marshal Canrobert, who as a former diplomat knew most of the international *beau monde*, had written to Lord Dudley asking him and his wife to look out for the young artist. More powerful influence came from the Heir Apparent, who asked the Rothschilds to extend their hospitality, and see that she met amusing people. Word had got about that Sarah Bernhardt was to be received by Society, and May Fair was agog.'*

Skye almost certainly inspired the change of social attitude twenty years before Henry Irving was dubbed the first theatrical knight. Not everybody welcomed the 'divine Sarah' into society. At the time, Lady Frederick Cavendish wrote:

'London has gone made over the principal actress in the Comédie Française who are here; Sarah Bernhardt, a woman of notorious character. Not content with being run after on the stage, this woman is asked to respectable people's houses to act, and even to luncheon and dinner and all the world goes. It is an outrageous scandal!'

Skye couldn't have cared less. Outrageous she might be, but she was rich and independent, and she liked the company of people who interested her. She was certainly far ahead of her times, times in which she was destined to outlive them all. She exchanged warm letters with Mario, the Italian tenor, who wrote to her 'Bienchese Dame'. She cultivated the company of all the leading artists; in the world of theatre, Patti the opera singer, the Grossmiths, Mrs. Patrick Campbell, Charles Wyndham, Forbes Robertson and Dion Boucicault. She was friends with the foremost painters of her day. When Donald MacAlister, a second choice, became engaged to her eldest daughter he was overwhelmed:

* See Appendix 2.

'For a while I was lionised. I was full of the zest of life and high spirits, and sang to the accompaniment of her mother or a sister, good robust songs such as Walter Scott's Border Ballad, Percy French's spirited Irish Songs, and not too bad impersonations of Harry Lauder. It was all a charming experience to meet so many 'literary and artistic people'.

Skye, whose taste was fastidious, would have preferred to do without the music hall stuff, which was emphatically not her world. But in her day she couldn't send the young people off to look at television. I conclude that she was only grateful that one of her daughters was nearly out of her hair. She preferred the company of 'literary and artistic people'.

One of her friends was George du Maurier, the artist. I am certain that the character of a society hostess he created in *Punch*, Mrs. Ponsonby de Tomkyns, was based on Skye with her reputation for associating with unlikely people. Du Maurier was a friend of hers, and a regular guest at Seamore Place. One of his cartoons, dated November 1884, shows her talking with her husband: 'Ponsonby, dearest, the Claimant* is at large, AT LAST! Don't you think we might get him to come and dine, or something? Surely there are still *some* Decent People who would like to meet him!' Another crueller, depicts the parting guests at the end of a musical soirée: 'What? Going already? And in Mackintoshes? Surely you are not going to walk?... Oh, dear no! Lord Archibald is going to take us to a dear little slum he's found out near the Minories—such a fearful place! Fourteen poor things sleeping in one bed, and no window! and the Mackintoshes are to keep out the infection, you know, and hide one's diamonds, and all that!'

I like to think that that was unfair to Skye. But there is no denying that, in her small circle, there was little sympathy for the deprivations of the poor who surrounded them. It was an age in which the rich put spikes on the back axles of their carriages to prevent street arabs jumping a lift. It was supposed, as Disraeli stated, that the world was for the few, and the very few. Skye was brave to break down just a few of the social barriers.

George du Maurier, in what are called his 'social' cartoons extending over a period of about seven years in the seventies, adopted the ploy that 'Mrs. Ponsonby de Tomkyns' was a clever social climber with a somewhat impoverished husband. His conception of a parvenu was artistically acceptable. It greatly increased du Maurier's popularity in *Punch*. That Skye and Walter were neither new to

* The Tichborne Claimant.

society, and least of all impoverished, suggests that he might have been thinking of somebody else. Yet the cartoons, with their ponderous captions, tell again and again of unmistakable incidents which Skye wrote about, under her pseudonym of Diane Chasseresse, more wittily herself.

George du Maurier's biographer, Leonee Ormond, says of Mrs. Ponsonby de Tomkyns that 'she was clever enough to get the right people. She was possessed of a cool judgement and an iron nerve. The key to her success is that in her after dinner performers she contrives, by a variety of balancing tricks, to capture without paying them any fee....'

Du Maurier, fascinated by her beauty and wit, was enchanted by Mrs. P—de—T. She was, writes Leonee Ormond, 'one of the most sharply characterised, endearing and successful of all his cartoons'. He owed her to Mrs. Walter Creyke. There is no doubt in my mind that Skye, whose patronage launched the artist Frank Salisbury on his way, also inspired George du Maurier's best work. His own pretensions to French nobility could not compare with hers as an English milady. But they found a joke in common. They remained friends. She was his Becky Sharp.

Her husband, poor Walter, pottered behind her like a lame spaniel. Even in those early days in Seamore Place he could scarcely rouse the energy to keep up with her. He writes of her, always admiringly, but in weary incompetence. He talks of going to 'the office' but it means simply that his wife's father tried to keep him amused, when he was up to it, by asking him to make a translation of a foreign letter, or put the commas and stops into an article. Judged by the few pages of his diary which remain he wasn't even very good at that. He reveals how he trails behind Skye's twinkling shoes. He himself usually called her Ina. The extracts of the diary which are extant extend from December, 1879, the year in which Sarah Bernhardt conquered London, to Christmas, 1882:

Dec. 4: 1879: Ina's birthday which she spent skating at Prince's, and on her newly sharpened skates exceeded all previous performances.

Dec. 5: To see some pictures. Angelica Kaufman's Sappho* brought her novel to which she has now added some chapters and wanted criticism so read aloud as I reclined before the fire. Ina went with Lady Violet Greville to 'Lohengrin'. A long lone evening as I dined at seven, depressed and chest congested.

* Sappho was almost certainly one of the wealthy and artistically concerned members of the Greek Ionides family of Tulse Hill.

Dec. 6: Sappho took Diane (daughter) to see 'Lucia' at Her Majesty's, a box sent to Ina. Heard she burst into tears when Edgarde stabbed himself and her description of the whole opera was delightful.

Dec. 7: Sylvia's birthday. She dined (luncheoned) downstairs in state, announced she was two and would help herself to apple pudding. Deposited a good deal of apple in her back hair as she took to scratching her head with her spoon. Alex came and brought an umbrella with a silver plate for Ina. A pleasant dinner. Lord and Lady W. Campbell, Lord Chief Justice (Cockburn), the Bancrofts, Colonel Hozier and Sappho. The Lord C. very pleasant. A fight at dinner between Ina and Mrs. B. on the Labouchère–Levy case. Each implored the Lord C. to give the verdict for her man. He took each by the hand and smiled and squeezed. After Ina sang 'Oh for the wings' and two other songs which touched him, and he went off at 12 o'clock saying he had passed a delightful evening.

Dec. 8: Ina went off early to skate with Sappho. In the evening to the long looked for 'Merchant of Venice' which Lilian and Everilda know pretty well by heart. Irving sent his own box and we went with Sappho. I was so prostrate with cold I could not sit up. About the first speech of Irving's 'to smell pork' Lilian irreverently called out 'po-ack', why does he say 'po-ack?' The play well put on but to me the acting was very hopeless. Not even Ellen Terry was endurable with her hoarse enunciation and ungainly attitudes. Ina and Sappho went on to a ball. I brought the children home enchanted to be up till 11.30 and have soda water in my room. Thaw slight only.

July, 1880: To city but home at four. Rode in evening. Ina to Mrs. White's concert but I am still suffering from cramp and chill so did not go. Sappho read some selections of her favourite authors to me while I reclined on the sofa in a languor and I retired to bed very sleepy.

July 11: A brighter day and felt more myself for a quiet night at home. Rode with Miss Blood while Ina and Sappho went to Kempton Park Races. To Eton and Harrow in afternoon, ground soft and no scores. To Mrs. V's concert taking Sappho who looked very well in a white dress half decolté.

July 12: Return of sick cramp. Rain most of the day which I spent on my sofa in my little room. Wretched in the morning but rather better afternoon. To the Ranelagh Club with Ina and Sappho in Hartopp's coach. Cold and wet. A most rowdy party dancing after dinner.

July 14: Office, but back to lunch, sat in one chair and gazed at the other with a headache all afternoon. Dined and to opera 'Mignon' but I deaf and couldn't see so left after first act and took a walk up Park Lane as it was fine, but a shower finished me.

July 15: Heavy morning. Went after lunch to Lord's. Walked up park and part of the way, and enjoyed very much. The flowers and trees are lovely, and I inhaled sweet scents. Play on wet ground impossible. Ina and Sappho came back to dine by Fulham and Clapham in a rattling trap. Shaw dined. Sappho read an Italian novel while the other two talked.

At this point the dates of the torn-out pages of the diary are confused. Much is unreadable. But the mood prevails:

Lady Violet dined, and we went to Comédie Française. 'Les Caprices de Marianne' which I had not seen before. But the whole story is one to read, not act. Very tired, prevented perhaps my enjoying it as much.

Everilda's birthday, eight years old! Presents poured in all day.... Lord Dudley had a species of fainting fit and is still unwell, so the party tonight was put off.... A Miss de — was brought by Mrs. Lowther to dine. She was brought up in Rome and Florence. Tosti who dined seemed much taken with her. Mrs. L. very ill and coughed like 'Marguerite'. Went on to Millais for half-an-hour, a great crowd of beauties, artists etc.

Lady Rivers let me have two stalls for the Sphinx, so I shall see Sarah Bernhardt. Thunderstruck as usual. Ina called yesterday on Sarah, who was utterly miserable and spent her time weeping.... She will dine Sunday next.

To office. J.B.L. telegraphed me to go to Miss Fountaine who is again in extremis. Not a favourable account of Lord Dudley heard yesterday at Lady Molesworth's. He cannot pronounce words.

To 'Rigoletto' taking Miss de la Poer.* She writes for *Temple Bar* and there are no men write so well as some women.

Two Miss de la Poers took us to a very hot theatre, amused at first but very flat at the end. I am too old, I suppose, for young ladies, and I was absorbed in the play. Heard of Miss Fountaine's death.

Wet. Rode in evening. Dined with Lord Chief Justice, Elcho, Lord and Lady Ravensworth, a Mr. Cadogan old and courteous, Spanish Minister & others. Sat between Mr. Cadogan and Mrs. Pereira who regretted that the Comédie Française had ever come to London, it was so bad.

Called on Sarah Bernhardt with Ina to offer Ruby and a mount.

* Frances De La Poer, a cousin of Skye's.

She was just back *pour reception* and slighter than I expected but very pleasant manner.

To see the Dufferins before breakfast. To Sarah Bernhardt private view of her pictures and sculptures in Piccadilly—the sculpture better than the pictures tho' they showed a sense of colour.

To the Sphinx, but too far to hear well, Monsieur — disappointed me. He hadn't the physique, a very hard voice and no charm. Sarah on the contrary, perfect. In the death scene she missed the chair in falling, hit her arm and rolled over. It was a dramatic effect, and probably she hurt herself.

Bernhardt came to dine and was charming. Lord Dufferin sat next to her and we had eleven at dinner. Tosti sang well. Ina sang too, which Sarah in a dramatic pose with her chin resting on her hand, listened to in deep silence. Ina sang well happily, as successful as any evening we have had.

To the office. In the evening, Miss de la Poer, went with me on the river, a lovely night with the stars and electric lights reflected. Went to Greenwich and back to Chelsea—out until 2 o'clock. Feverish from no sleep and two nights up.

In December, 1881, the diary is more coherent again:

December 24: To Dudley House with the four girls for the Xmas tree and child's ball. Lord Dudley perhaps appeared rather feebler, but spoke perfectly sensibly. Evidently his memory is quite a blank and that he forgets all about those he has known best. He asked Ina if Sylvia was her eldest child, and never recognised Bilda whom he was so fond of, or indeed Ina. The tree was splendid reaching nearly to the roof of the big ballroom and 100's of £5 worth of presents on it. In addition old Father Christmas gave special gifts with each child's name printed on them. Bilda had a scissors penknife mounted in mother of pearl. Diane six silver bangles etc., etc. Sylvia was as usual the success. Diane danced best. Came home with an enormous basketful of toys and presents.

December 25: Went to Berkely Chase for service with three chicks. The three chicks who sat up made a tremendous noise, but it is only once a year.

December 26: Went to Rothamsted by 2.15 train with Miss Clarke, 2 French nurses, 4 chicks & Carlo (possibly the Italian foot-man). Ina on a drag to St. Albans. Wrote to Warde, the huntsman, to say poor Martyn (his horse) must go to the kennels, asked him to send a competent man to spare all any pain. The case is hopeless, I know.

December 27: Rode with Lilian morning on Cornucopia who was

fresh but, tho' fidgetty, carried me well. Poor Martyn was shot at 3 o'clock. I never regretted a horse so much.

December 29 : J.B.L. produced a long Italian legal letter for translation, and two more articles. All this I can do well and the work suits me. Tried Cornucopia over several jumps. Frank Forster writes that he will look out for a horse for me but they are dear in Ireland, and the Kildare horses fetch absurd prices.

December 21, 1882 : A bad cold and cough. Dudley House with the children and Ina. The Prince and Princess and all the family there, also Princess Mary Teck and their children. The tree was more beautiful than ever, and the presents also. The Prince as usual very civil—with a large pair of scissors cut presents off the tree for our chicks. Missing Sylvia I found her sitting on the Princess of Wales's lap who was laughing very much. Party lasted from 5 till 9 when the Royal party went....

I hope that I have not misjudged Walter. I interpret him from his own words. It is difficult to entertain his reputation as the fine horseman he so obviously was with the sad creature who wrote that diary. It is evident that, a mere ten years after he married Skye, he could not keep up the pace with his wife. It appears that, when she was at full gallop, she seldom looked over her shoulders at him. My guess is that he was a much nicer person than she was. Their children clearly thought so. In chronic ill health, stuffed with sentimentality, he couldn't cope.

Without professional medical knowledge, I cannot diagnose the reason for his lifelong weariness. Clearly, he was hopelessly neurotic. From early youth he was melancholic, purposeless, and delicate to ineptitude. I find it difficult to think of him laughing, or getting drunk. He may have been asthmatic, although there is no evidence that that hereditary disease has been inherited by any of his descendants. His eldest daughter, Everilda, had a taste for invalid life; but she lived to a good old age. I suppose that the most likely explanation of him was that his personality was split, in recurring migraines, by the devious femininity in his make-up. He was one of those people of whom it is said that they are 'born losers'.

His wife was a born winner. In 1891, encouraged by the critical acclaim for Sporting Sketches, she began her career as a society journalist.

X

PLEASURES OF A CHAPERON

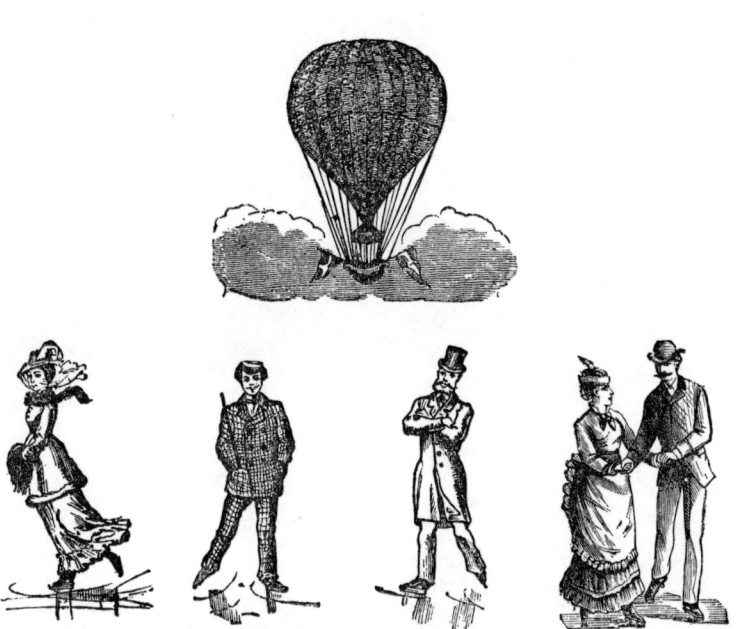

KYE'S articles in *The World*, which she again signed Diane
Chasseresse, extended over a period of ten years from 1891.
The World, a predecessor of glossy magazines like *The Tatler*,
was the society periodical of its day. By our standards, it was
appallingly snobbish, complacent and parochial. It had no pictures,
it originated before the invention of photo engraving, and its typo-
graphy was as forbidding as an early issue of *The Times*. Nevertheless, until it died at the outbreak of war in 1914, *The World* had a
wide following. It also had distinguished contributors. Going through
the file in the British Museum, I noticed that, again and again, Diane
Chasseresse's piece was preceded by a music criticism signed G.B.S.
What is remarkable is that Skye herself poked fun at everything
that the magazine stood for. Yet she became one of its star writers.

The titled feature 'Pleasures of a Chaperon' only emerged after
she had published a number of articles, mostly instructional ones
on such subjects as how to hunt rabbits, how to skate, how to fish,
and how to ride a bicycle. But it wasn't long before the editor discovered she had a larger gift. 'Pleasures of a Chaperon', which
delighted her contemporaries, is a remarkable record of upper class
social life in the nineteenth century. It extends to well over sixty
reminiscences.

At the time she started to write them Walter was fading, waiting
to die in 1892; although, under her pen-name, she pretended that he
lived much longer. When she began the series, her eldest daughter,
Everilda, was twenty. Her surviving son, Lance, was eleven. In the
context of her articles it is amusing to know who was who:

'Agatha' was mainly Everilda.
'Ella' was mainly Lilian.
'Florrie' was mainly Diana.
'Patience' is Sylvia.
'Maud' is a composite.
'Geoffrey' is Lance.
'Thomas' is Walter.
It is also important to note, before I hand the pen to her, that,

writing under her pseudonym, she reveals only half of herself. Her style is to pretend that she is a scatterbrained woman haunting the then fashionable world of Venice, Paris, Rome, Monte Carlo, Cowes, Maidenhead, Homburg, Eton and the races, without much notion what it is all about. All she knows are the right people. She invites comparison with Jeanne de Casalis who, in our own time, invented the character 'Mrs. Feather'. She adopts the attitude that she is quite 'blah'; although, of course, she was certainly not. A pioneer of the conversational form of writing she is often over-effusive; but she never ceases to be entertaining. Out of a hundred thousand words that she wrote I have endeavoured to extract the essence of her:

'*May Fair* (1891)
Heigho! Another ball tonight; no rest for the wicked. Maud and Ella are the two who are going to this one. Maud, of course, put off seeing about her shoes till the last minute, and now says she can't get any to match her dress; that means that she will have to go about in a hansom with her maid from one shop to another all day long, and I shall have to pay more for the cabs than she will for the shoes. What girls are! Now she says she has found a pair at last, but that the toes are so pointed they pinch her, and will I wear them a bit and stretch them? No, my dear, I will not.

Now here comes Ella. What is it she wants? Every pair of gloves split? The shop has changed its make? Yes, they always do change their makers just as you are nicely fitted; but, my dear child, how many times am I to tell you not to put everything off until the last minute? It is always the way—always. And your dress won't meet by two inches? Now you will have to go without your dinner, and drink no tea or coffee, or else wear an old gown. How I do pity girls who go to balls!'

The pattern of her joke is that while she claims she is doing her social round entirely for the sake of her girls, she makes it clear that, as chaperon, she wants all the fun herself. I remember another personable mother wrinkling her nose when she told me that she had been ogled in the street only to discover, belatedly, that the look was not for her, but for one of her daughters.

'*On the Cross-Channel Packet Boat* (1892)
Now what possible objection can you make to my wearing my pink-and-gold bonnet? Loud indeed! It's nothing of the kind; I have only put it on twice—and I know it was admired, because I noticed several people turn round to look at it. Besides, it is the greatest

mistake not to put on your best clothes for travelling; they make the porters and people so much more civil and attentive, especially at hotels abroad, when one doesn't know the language.

Oh! my dears, what an awful day for crossing! It's not the roughness that I mind, but the cold and the wet. Thank goodness we shall have a large boat and plenty of accommodation, so it won't be bad when once we get on board; in fact, I always think a sea-voyage makes rather a pleasant break in a long railway journey. Eh? Yes; please put our things on board; we will sit in the deck saloon. Here, steward, where is the deck saloon? No deck saloon? You surely can't expect us to sit on deck in the pouring rain? A "ladies' cabin below"? What! down there, in amongst those groans and basins? I'd rather die. Do you mean to tell me that in the Calais-Douvres there is no proper saloon where ladies and gentlemen can sit comfortably and enjoy the view? Take a private cabin? No, thank you; why, it costs nearly as much as an opera-box. Here, sailor, bring me one of those deck-chairs—I see other people have them—and put it down by the paddle-box; not there—here. Why, it's all dripping wet! I didn't say I wanted a *bath*-chair, did I? I should be laid up with rheumatism in all my bones long before I got to Calais if I sat on that. Now be so good as to rub it down with a cloth till it's dry—so—and the arms too. What is he waiting for? Surely he can't expect a tip! Certainly not; I shall report you to the manager, and I shall write to the *Times* to complain of the disgraceful want of accommodation on board your steamer.

Now I must munch some biscuits—I always do on a sea voyage; and, Maudie dear, give me my flask with whisky-and-water in it. Oh! Agatha, how ill you look!! Never are sick? No, my dear; but think of that peach-tart last night. Didn't I warn you not to take a second help? but you always will go your own way, and now you are suffering for it; you look worse and worse. Oh, Maud! how can you be so vulgar? She says "*Mais, dépêchez-vous donc*"—*pêche*, peach, don't you see? Why, Agatha has disappeared already; well, she can't expect me to go down and look after her; I like to get as much sea air as I can when I'm aboard ship.'

'Paris (1892)

I don't know what it is, but there's something in a long morning's shopping that always puts me in a good humour. Among other things, I have ordered myself a large grenadine and lace hat at the Louvre—and now, my dears, I am afraid you will say it is rather like a lampshade; and so it is, but one must have something shady for

Italy, and you will soon get used to seeing me in it. And how have you been enjoying yourselves, and what do you think of Notre-Dame? You hate it! and are bored to death at having to wait so long? Why, you have only been here about two hours, after all; just time to look at everything properly—and a funeral going on all the while. So depressing? So interesting, I should say; but it is just like you girls to want to take the cream of everything, and do nothing thoroughly. You should have been thinking of that delightful book of Victor Hugo's, *Notre Dame de Paris*. You have not read it? No, of course not, I don't approve of girls reading French novels; but you will read it some day, when you are married—and think how much more you will appreciate it from having seen the place where it all happened! For my part, I like to take my time about things, and see them leisurely.

Meanwhile, I will tell you my plans. In the first place, we will go to Monte Carlo—I know it is considered a very wicked place; but still, you girls have arrived at an age in which you ought to see a little of life—and as the season is over, there will be nobody there, and, of course, you will not go near the gambling-rooms. And another thing —I know Agatha will laugh at me—but I have a sort of presentiment that we may meet Lord Chesterton somewhere abroad. It was so unfortunate that he had to leave England just as we had made his acquaintance; but still there is such a *sans gêne* abroad, that if we were to meet him, we should become much more intimate than if we saw him in London—people always do. Then, after Monte Carlo, I propose to go to Pisa, and Florence, and Rome.

'*Monte Carlo (1892)*
I think, considering the fuss that is made over it, that Monte Carlo is not so very beautiful, after all. The villas are neat and pretty enough; but there is only one road, and one has to drive there and back again every day, unless one goes up to La Turbie, which is such a very long way off, and costs such a lot of money; and as for the noise the drivers make to their horses—well, it reminds me of crossing the Channel and poor Agatha! If it were not for you girls, I should go and have a look round at the gambling-rooms—not to play, of course, but just to see what is going on; but I don't quite like to leave you all alone. Don't you think that, just for once, you might sit on the bench outside? I could give a franc apiece to those two porters on the steps to look after you. I'll not be long....'

No wonder the children got fed up with her. In her act as the chaperon she was as completely egoistical as she undoubtedly was in real life. Her account of bathing on the Lido is an unmistakable echo of that time in the Highlands when, as a young girl herself, she was happily alarmed that a patch of white skin might attract the indelicate attention of the gillie:

'The Lido (1893)
Now, what do you say, as it is rather warm, to going to the Lido for a bathe? ... Andate al Lido.

Come, girls, get into the tramcar; and do hold your petticoats well up around you, for people have evidently been smoking in it.... Now this I call really pretty; it quite reminds me of England, with the woods on each side ... What! out again already, just as I was beginning to enjoy myself? How tiresome! Oh, Maud and Agatha, the water is alive with men and women. Do look another way. No; don't—there is a man coming out of that box. Do let us go home. Not till you have had your bathe? But you two girls can't bathe all alone. I suppose I shall have to come in too, and look after you. Are those red-and-white stripy things what one has to wear? How shall I ever get into it, and what shall I look like when I am in it?... How hot this dressing-box is! Girls, are you ready to go into the water; and have you got on one of those large straw hats? I have, but my bathing-dress is so fearfully tight I don't know how I shall ever get down that long ladder before all those people. Maud, I insist on your holding up a parasol in front of my face, so that no one may recognise me when I come out.'

She was indeed, as Walter called her, 'a monkey'. She makes no secret that she is herself anxious for the attentions of her imaginary character, Lord Chesterton, the hoped for suitor of one of her daughters. She affects that Walter ('Thomas' in 'Pleasures of a Chaperon') is still alive. He died in 1892:

'May Fair, London (1893)
Maud, my sweet, he has accepted! I am sure that is because I put 'en partie carré' on the invitation. It always gives such an air of mystery to a little dinner. They generally know who three of the people are, but can't imagine who the fourth is to be. In this case the fourth is your papa, who has had to give up a man's dinner at the club to dine at home. I thought it would be better for Lord Chesterton to see us quite en famille the first time he came to the house, and I particularly wanted him to see that your papa and I are on such good terms. It is a great pull for you girls to have a

respectable and presentable father, now that half the married women one meets about can't get their husbands to go anywhere with them, poor things!

And now about the dinner.... Oysters? Why, my dear, they are four shillings a dozen! Do you really think we need to go to such an expense? Well, perhaps we had better have them, as it is the first time Lord Chesterton has been asked to dine with us. We might put three on a plate—only three looks so very little, even when you put bread-and-butter opposite, and a little pot of pepper to fill up the odd corner. Suppose we have four on each plate—and you, my love, can go without.... Fond of oysters? No doubt you are—so are most people. Well, why not buy half a dozen out of your pocket-money? It is only two shillings after all, and you can contribute two of them to Lord Chesterton.... Nonsense, my dear, you always manage to throw away money right and left when you want anything to wear, but you wouldn't buy so much as a biscuit if you were starving. It is just like Agatha when we were abroad; she would insist on saying that the *vin du pays*, or the *vino di Ravola*, or whatever they call it, was 'cheap and nasty', and I had to pay for the most expensive lemonades all over the Continent because she would rather have died of thirst than have paid for them herself! On the whole, I am not sorry to be back to good wholesome champagne and English comforts—and as for that last day in Venice, I shall never forget it. It all came of Maud and Lord Chesterton going out at one door of a church as I was coming in at the other; and I lost them, and lost my way, and when I asked how to get to the 'Grand Hotello', nobody seemed to know what I meant, and they told me to go first to one place, and then to another, till I should have been quite thankful for a four-wheeled cab, of even an omnibus.

House of Commons (1893)

The question is, Agatha, how we are to dress for the Ladies' Gallery. There was a picture of it in last week's *Queen*, and some of the ladies were in evening dress and some were in hats and bonnets, so it is impossible to tell. Suppose we put on bonnets and our smartest opera-cloaks—you might borrow Maud's red one with the large gold suns embroidered on it—how do you think that would do? You don't think it would do at all? Well, for my part, I don't care to go about everywhere in black velveteen, looking a dowdy object; but, of course, it is quite enough for me to say I like a thing for you to say you don't; only if you can't take the trouble to dress nicely, I shall take Maud.

Here we are! Give him a shilling, Agatha, and smile at him. I have often known cabmen to take a shilling without grumbling if a girl smiles at them. The lift? Yes, I certainly should much prefer to go up in the lift. Oh, Agatha, what a bump I had! I had thought the bottom had come out. A short seat? Yes, it is a short seat, and you might have told me so before, my good man, when you saw I was going to sit down upon nothing at all. Is this the Ladies' Gallery? It *is* dark. There are some vacant seats in front, and we had better get them quickly, for we can see nothing from any of the other places. What can all those M.P.s be doing standing up with their backs turned? At prayers? I didn't know it was a church, and I didn't bring a Prayer-Book—not that I could see to read if I had one. It is not in the least what I expected. Waiter! will you please open the grille in front of me? It makes me squint so. I see half Mr. Gladstone with one eye and half Sir William Harcourt with the other, and it is most uncomfortable. Won't open? Then can't we sit on the benches down below? I should hear so much better, and see better too. They belong to the Press, do they? Well, I wish I belonged to the Press. But how they smell of tobacco! Agatha, do take care, or you will drop your opera-glasses on to the Press's heads. How those members keep getting up and sitting down, and fidgeting in and out; they are never still a minute—and some keep their hats on and some take them off.

Gladstone speaking? No, you don't say so! I just missed him; how very tiresome!'

She didn't want to know anything about politics. It was a matter of no importance to her in a world which was so obviously so secure. She had the same attitude to business:

'The City (1893)

How lovely it is, my dears! I feel as if I must go into the country, and spend the day alone with Nature. And I shall write to Lord Chesterton, and asked him to come with me.... Nonsense Agatha! I don't know what you mean by making myself conspicuous. How could one be conspicuous alone with Nature and Lord Chesterton? Besides, you know very well I am only civil to him on account of you girls; as soon as I have made up my mind which of you he likes best, we shall always take whichever of you it is about with us.... Oh! so we did. I had forgotten all about it. We promised to go and see Mr. Palliser's business today; we must go there instead—it will be just as nice, and more instructive. All the young men we know talk about their businesses in the City; but if one asks what their business

is, they never seem able to put it into words, so I am glad of the
opportunity of judging for myself why it is so difficult to get them
to join a party in the daytime. I think, Ella, you shall come with
me—and I would not put on my smartest clothes, if I were you, for
fear they should get spoilt; I shall only put on my second-best
mantle.'

She remained the constant clothes horse. In Paris, her first thought
is to find the most outrageous vogue of the day. Her notion was to
wipe the eye of fashionable London:

'Paris again (1893)
The dress represented Electricity. It was pink satin, embroidered in
green paillettes to look like flashes of lightning ... Yes, I ordered two
dresses—quite quiet, for I think at my time of life one should wear
subdued colours. My little *toilette de ville* is pale yellow shot with
magenta, and two flounces over it of black net embroidered in cream,
with a high ruff, and pelerine all over flounces to match. I know I shall
tumble down stairs in it some day, as I have no neck, and cannot
possibly see over the top; and I was nearly suffocated in it as it was.
But, as of course you know, the *mouvement d'aujourd'hui* is to have
everything bunched up round the neck and shoulders. And, after all,
one does not go to Paris only to come back to London looking exactly
like everybody else, does one? ...'

She was jealous of her daughter's youth. She makes an article of
it; but you can read between the lines:

'May Fair (1893)
Agatha! What are those voices? Are those same young men *still*
here? ... What, both of them? ... Going to stop to dinner? ... Not
both of them? But we've only got cold beef and salad! ... They can
hear every word I say? Well, I can't help it if they can. How should
I know they were in the hall? And what were they doing in the
hall?—lighting their cigars, I suppose, so that all the tobacco-smoke
might go up into the bedrooms ... Going home to dress? I should
not have thought it was worth while to go home and dress for cold
beef and salad. I am not going to dress, and they will have to sit
one on each side of me, of course; and I really don't see how we
are ever to economise if you have young men dropping in to dinner
day after day in this sort of way. I can't give them champagne,
especially as your papa has gone out to dine with the key of the
cellar; they must drink beer—I daresay they would not get anything

better at their clubs. What *do* young men drink at the Bachelors', I wonder! ...

Here they are—back again before one has time even to order their places to be laid.... So glad you were able to stay to dinner, Mr. Cole—Charles! put two extra places at table.—So very pleased you did not mind our being quite *en famille*, Mr. Palliser; and I hope you don't object to *la fortune du pot*, for the fact is I had to take all my four girls to the Home of Rest for Horses ball, and pay a guinea apiece for them, and one for myself besides; and, really, five guineas is such a terrible sum to have to give for one evening's entertainment that we are obliged to economise in every possible way to make up for it, and that is why we are having cold beef and salad tonight. Not but what it is very good beef, you know; and it was not cut hot, so that it might be all juicy cold; so, you see, it is not really such a hardship, after all, when one thinks of the many poor starving creatures there are in the slums—and small-pox on the increase, I fear—only when one is accustomed to quails, and plovers' eggs, and early strawberries, and primeurs—which I suppose you get every night at your club—it seems hard, does it not? ... Was it a good ball, did you say? Well, it was not a very full ball, but it was a beautiful ball-room, and there was a good band ... People one knew there? Oh dear no! not a soul; but that did not matter in the very least, as the girls took their own partners, and one extra to talk to me and take me into supper, as I only had a meat tea at seven o'clock; and so they enjoyed it very much. They only asked young men who ride in steeplechases, and one other poor young fellow who was thrown out of a pony trap on his head and stunned, as they knew they would be sure to be fond of horses, and have so much sympathy with the charity; because, you see, a guinea is a guinea to most young men, who get more invitations to balls than they know what to do with, and yet never dream of passing them on to girls ...

Ascot (1893)
Now, Ella, have you got everything ready? Have you got your opera-glasses, and your dust-cloak, and your parasol, and a dirty pair of gloves for the train, and a clean pair to change to when you get to Ascot, and a pocket-handkerchief, and a powder-puff? And you might bring some smelling-salts and a fan for me, in case I am hot in the train.... Very well, then; order a hansom, for I am not going to take the carriage to be jammed to pieces on Westminster

Bridge.... What a terrible crowd! I don't believe we shall ever get
to the station....

Interjection (1893)

... Oh dear no, Sir John, Agatha is not our only daughter; we have
plenty more.... No, none of of them are married. I always think it is
such a disadvantage to girls to marry young; people immediately
think it is because they are not happy at home; and I am sure my
girls are happy at home.

Interjection (1894)

I mean to wear a knickerbocker suit, Agatha, so it's of no use for you
to say I can't.... Not get one in London? No, perhaps not, but I
telegraphed to Paris directly I heard of Lady Rismore's invitation to
Scotland. I saw plenty of them in the Louvre, they wear them for
bicycling, and nothing could be nicer for the hills than a pair of
homespun knickerbockers and a Norfolk jacket, and who knows but
what we shall have to go all over the moors on bicycles; electric
ones, probably, like electric launches? ... Too fat to wear them?
I? Nonsense, Agatha, there are plenty of women in France much
fatter than I am, and you may be fat yourself some day, then
you will be sorry; and as for its being indecent, why, look at the
tableaux at the Palace! If the Lord Chamberlain allows them, he
will allow anything; and I am not likely to forget what I went
through out deer-stalking last year in a silk petticoat and a mackintosh. One lives and learns. What a pity it is that the 12th is on the
13th this year—so unlucky, you know; or is it lucky—I quite forget
whether thirteen is lucky or unlucky, but I know that the Italian who
dined with us last season disappeared under the table after dinner,
but whether it was because we were thirteen or only because he
drank too much of your Papa's old port on the top of a hot room,
I really don't recollect.

May Fair (1895)

What a beautiful kitten! and how blue its eyes are—just like
forget-me-nots! And what a splendid white tail it has! It was most
kind of Lord Claud to give you his Persian kitten, Florrie; I am sure
we shall all be very fond of it. Now, girls, you see what it is to have
a mother with tact. I left Florrie alone with Lord Claud for hours
and hours yesterday afternoon, and this is the result: today he
sends her his aunt's favourite cat. How pretty it will look when it
dies—for Persian kittens are always delicate—and we can have it
stuffed, and stand it upon the writing-table, holding on to a silver

photograph-frame! Here, pussy, pussy! Why does it not come? It is a very disobedient kitten.... *Stone deaf?* How stupid of Lord Claud to give us a deaf kitten! ... What do you say? *That pure-bred kittens, with white coats and blue eyes, are always deaf?*

Turkish Bath (1895)
I want to have a Turkish bath, and to be attended to by English-women, if you please; and, as I have never had one before, they must take great care that nothing happens to me.... *What! take off my clothes before I go downstairs?* Well, I am quite sure the Society for the Protection of Vice will take you up if they see me walking about the passages without my shoes and stockings. Are you *quite* sure there are no Turks—I mean men—about? ... Why, this room is as hot as an oven; I can't stop here, I shall faint. Open the window; quick! ... But I tell you I am stifling! ... *Put a wet cloth on my head?* No, certainly not; I want the window to be opened, I don't want a booby-trap; I want air.... *Come into the next room?* That I will, gladly. Why, this is hotter than the last. I shall be roasted alive! Look at those women with purple faces; have they been under a shower bath? I only hope I don't look like that. Have not you got a looking-glass? I tell you I am not going to stop here if I am to be gradually turned into a boiled lobster—the girls wouldn't be seen with me anywhere in society.... *Lean back on this easy-chair?* But I tell you I am *melting*; positively melting. There now, the attendant has gone and left me all alone with those four hot females. I don't like it at all. I feel as if I were going to burst. I wonder how much longer she means to be away, and what all that swishing and swashing behind the curtain is. What can be going on there! Oh! here she comes.... *Am I ready for my bath?* Yes, I am; that is if you don't think I am wet enough already.

What are you doing with that hot water? *Throwing it over the marble slab to make it warm enough for me to lie on?* Have I got to lie down on *that?* But I *hate* anything hard and damp! Take off my—! What next, I wonder! Are you *quite sure* no one will come in? What *are* you doing? You hurt me; you are pinching me black and blue, and pulling all my fingers out of joint! Talk of Armenian atrocities! I am sure they weren't half as bad as this. For Heaven's sake, don't scrub me so hard!

The Bicycling Craze (1895)
No, Ella, I don't approve of it at all, and I am very glad you don't ride a bicycle; as for your sisters, they ought to be ashamed of themselves for the way they go about everywhere without me, and

without asking with-your-leave or by-your-leave. Yesterday Florrie went off to Putney with her Uncle, both on bikes—I mean bicycles: you know how I disapprove of vulgar abbreviations—and a hansom pursued Florrie and drove her into an omnibus—bicycle and all, I presume—and then upset your Uncle and broke his machine to pieces. Of course I can understand that hansoms don't like bicycles any more than hotels like tea-baskets, because they lose money by them; but I don't see any reason why young ladies should put themselves into the position of a tea-basket to be knocked down by a hansom cab. Then just look at the way girls walk about the streets, with straps hanging about their legs and short petticoats and gaiters. I wonder their mammas allow them; and as to their costumes at Battersea, I hear they are quite outrageous, and I really think, Ella, we might call a cab and go there this morning. I should so like to see if all the things one hears about it are true.

Ella! Do you hear Lady Maxie Mum has got on a bicycle and gone off? Well, if she can ride, all I can say is I don't see why I should not have a try. Of course it would be very convenient for your sisters to have me as a chaperon in all their little expeditions, so I shall begin to learn at once.... You thought I said it was immodest? My dear child, modesty, like morality, is only a question of climate, and I don't suppose if the Fijis rode bicycles they would wear petticoats over their knickerbockers, even if they wore knickerbockers under their petticoats; so, you see, there is no sort of reason why I should not begin at once.... Yes, if you please, Mr. Humber; I will have a nice quiet bicycle brought to the north gate of Hamilton Square at two o'clock today, so that I can have a ride when people are at lunch.

Maidenhead (1895)

Is it not nice of Lady Wessex to ask us to visit her on her houseboat? I have never been on one in my life, and I do so wonder what it will be like. What do you think about it, girls—will it be hot, or cold, or wet or fine; and will it leak, or be quite dry; and will it be like a barge, where you creep into a hole and all sleep together, or won't it? I think it will be most exciting, but I should like to know what clothes to take. I know one want's plenty of diamonds ... Don't always contradict me, Ella, when you know nothing about it. You did not see *John-o'-Groat* at the Haymarket, and I did, and all the actresses wore heaps and heaps of diamonds on the deck of the yacht, as they always do on the stage, and the stage sets the fashion nowadays, as every one knows, though how they manage not to catch cold in their low dresses when a gale is blowing I can't imagine. Anyhow, you had better be quick and pack, for I mean to take a hamper and lunch on the river bank, and go to the houseboat in time for tea....

What a pleasure it is to get out of London for a bit, and see all the trees and green fields again! Here we are at Maidenhead. Look at all the people on the lawn at the Riverside Club. We will leave our luggage in the cloak-room, but mind we bring our hampers with the lunch down to the boats.... Yes; thank you, that looks a nice roomy punt, and you may put all the hampers in the bows and tie me to a post while you see after the other boats.... Yes, I think that canoe will do nicely for Ella, only she must sit quite still, and wait till the others are ready.... Would I prefer the canoe? No, thank you, Lord Chesterton, I don't want to part with my lunch.... Oh! Ella, a huge rat—it is coming this way; do stab it with your parasol—quick, child, quick! I know it will attack me.... There—now you have gone headlong into the river. How could you be so stupid and tiresome! Don't you know how rickety canoes are? Why couldn't you sit still and be quiet? Here! Lord Chesterton! Somebody! Do jump into the river and drag Ella out! She has her sister's best hat on and my cloak.... Dear, dear, what a nuisance! Do you think she will drown? No—I see her; here she comes bobbing up like a cork, with a red face and no fringe. Pull her out, do! ... No! not into my punt; she will wet me and the lunch too. You must take her to the Riverside, Lord Chesterton, and give her some hot whisky and water, and put her to bed till her clothes are dry, and then pack her off to London, and I think the best thing for me to do will be to sit here and eat my lunch, for there is no use in wasting all this good food; I shall be quite safe tied to a post, and Heaven only knows what we shall get to eat on the *Vagabond*, probably nothing but the fish they catch out of the windows.... Lady WESSEX! Lady Wessex! Is *anybody* on board? Mr. Barnett! Do get up out of your bunk and let me in! ... Yes, it is me; back again like a bad ha'penny. I am very sorry to have to call you up in the middle of the night, Lady Wessex, but it was all Lord Chesterton's fault. He pitched me head-first into a train for Reading, and there left me, and I might have broken my neck for anything he cared; and I am quite sure he would lose his place at Court if the Queen were to hear of it. I had to take a return train and walk from the station.

The Exhibition (1895)
How charming of you to have thought of bringing me to the

Exhibition, Mr. Gatling; for, what between bicycling and the river, we poor chaperons get left out of almost everything nowadays. This Indian Court is really lovely. Look how blue the sky is against all those white buildings and palm-trees. I don't know which is sham and which is real, it is so well done; and those white bridges and electric barges are too delightful. I always think it so much nicer to have India and Constantinople brought to us, instead of having to go such long journeys to see them. It is just like the Queen having the opera taken to Windsor, instead of Windsor having to go to London for the opera ... No, Mr. Gatling, I really don't think I dare go up in the Wheel; and what should we do if it were to stick as it did the other day, and we were left up there together all night? And how do you know we shan't have to hang head downwards when we get to the top? Somebody told me we did, and I wish now I had put on my bicycle dress.... Dear, dear, how you hurry me along? No, no, I really can't, it is too bad of you! ... No, I am not at all comfortable do let me get out—I shall be frightened to death—just look how the car rocks every time the passengers cross over from side to side! It is evidently hung on that bar, and swings about. But it does, I assure you. Try crossing over and leaning out of that window.... You don't want to part with your *what*? ... Oh, your lunch! But why did not you lunch before you started, as I did? Have you got sandwiches in your pocket? Pray keep them in case we stick. Oh! how dreadful; we are really going up! Do ring that electric bell ... Isn't it a bell? Then how are we to get the stewardess? I don't like it at all.... There is St. Paul's, and the Crystal Palace, and the Thames. There, now, we *have* stuck! I told you we should, and now we have. What are we to do? Is not it lucky you have sandwiches? ... *You haven't*? Then why did you say you had? ... Plenty of automatic cigarettes and an opera-glass? No, thank you, I feel quite bad enough without cigarettes. Why don't they have a penny-in-the-slot with brandy in it? They always seem to have things that nobody wants in those machines, and even if you do want them, the penny sticks and you don't get them. Do open the door and let us get out; there must be a platform somewhere....

Brighton (1895)

That reminds me, Mrs. Boulter, that I have bought a new French bathing-gown, and I must use it. It is geranium colour, and trimmed with white lace; and the cap, instead of being like a sponge-bag, as other people's caps are, is a blue-and-red plaid, with a bow in front, most *chic*. What do you think I could wear it with the greatest

effect? ... Much too rough, and the breakers full of pebbles? But I
see one woman bathing; at least, she is standing in the sea up to her
ankles, holding on to a rope, and oh! do look, Mrs. Boulter, *she has
got a tail*! She actually has; I see it wagging in the wind. How
extraordinary! I never saw a woman with a tail before. Do you think
she can have come out of a show? No wonder all those people are
staring so.... Yes, certainly I will go on to Brill's Baths; perhaps I can
use my new costume there, for it would be quite wasted in a mud
bath at Homburg.... What a noise, and what a lot of people, and
how the children scream! Look at that old lady scouring away at her
purple face as if she expected to get the colour off! No, I don't think
I should care to bathe here. I am afraid I shall have to reserve my
bathing-gown for Scotland, and use it to bicycle in.

Slumming (1896)   ,
Oh, please, I should certainly like to do the Shelter, as I have come
so far; I suppose it is close by? ... Miles and miles away? You must
be joking, Captain Boulter; I had no idea London was so long; we
must have driven quite fifteen miles straight on end. And just think
what it will cost in cabs! ... What a nice-looking man, and *such* a
clean collar! Surely he could have afforded to pay 4d for a bed in
the Doss-house, without coming all this way to sleep free, especially
as he must have spent quite fourpence in trains and buses ... That is
the man who looks after everything? I understand, now, you pay
him to look after the Shelter, and the Shelter is free to every one else.
That is really most charitable of you.... Yes, I should like to see
round; but what are all those wooden coffins for? Is this a mortuary
or a morgue? Anyhow I am glad there are no dead bodies in them ...
What? Those things *beds?* I never saw anything so narrow; surely
people can't fit their shoulders into them. And what is that black
heap against the wall? ... Mattresses and coverlets? ... You say the
mattresses are made of coconut matting covered with American
cloth, and the coverlets made of skins and washed every day? How
clean people seem to be down here! We don't wash our counterpanes
every day, or even every week, in the West End....

Venice (1896)
What thousands and thousands of gondolas! How shall we ever
get through them in time to meet the Emperor! And look at those
lovely *bissone*—gold, and silver, and green, and crimson, and orange
—and that mermaid sitting on a silver wheel in the stern, and the
man in the top-hat sitting all alone under the canopy in the bows.
Surely he must be the King of Italy! ... No? Then he must be

somebody else. And look at all those gondoliers in lovely velvets and satins, with wigs, and two different coloured legs. There! Florrie, do you see the *Hohenzollern* just coming round the *Maison des Fous*? It is like an enormous white street steaming along the lagunes; and there is the Emperor*, in full uniform, with his hand on his sword, ready to fight; and the Empress, in white serge painted to match the steamer, like people and their bicycles in London. Now they are playing with the fire-hose on all the people in the boats, to make a passage for the King of Italy's launch—though how they can be expected to get out of the way when there is not a drop of water visible between the river dei Schiavoni and the Orfano Canal, I can't imagine.... Do you hear, Florrie, that no one ever fishes in the Orfano, because that is where they used to take people out in sacks and drown them some years ago? ... Oh, look what a rush of boats round the *Hohenzollern*, and all the Venetian noble ladies in them—one all in white, and one with a little orange velvet cape, and another with orange hair! How interesting it all is!

Interjection (1896)
Goodness gracious, girls, what do you think has happened? I have just had a letter from a lawyer to say the cook has summoned me for sending her off without her wages.

Eton (1896)
Yes, dear Mrs. Hamden, I think your plan of taking an electric launch from Walton to Eton is most delightful—so much nicer than a stuffy train; and I think it so wise and right of you to keep all the young people together, for you know backwaters and backstairs are my abomination; not but what at one ball the backstairs were empty the whole evening because all the men had gone to a prize fight—such bad taste to prefer a prize fight to dancing with my daughters.

Why, here we are at Windsor, and Geoffrey is waiting on the bridge, and I never found out we had moved; and to think that I shall have to eat another lunch in less than an hour! I am sure I don't know how I shall manage it.

Yes, I should certainly like to see your room, Geoffrey, but how can I go up strange stairs in the pitch dark? Why don't you light a match or a cigarette or something? ... The other boys will hear me? Well, I'm sure I hope they will then, perhaps, they will bring a light and save me breaking my neck. Pray, do all the boys' *people*, as you call them, have to grope about on all-fours in the dark when they come to the Fourth of June? Is that part of the ceremony?

* The Kaiser.

Oh, here we are at last, and you seem to have quite a nice little room with these pictures stuck about it and the trees outside; but I really should bury all those meat tins in the garden below, if I were you. And whereabouts do you sleep? In a dormitory all together, or do they bring in a bunk or a hammock at night-time? ... What! That little square box, your bed? Why, you must have to crumple yourself up into a ball to get into that! No wonder you are so short. I call it quite disgraceful. It is worse than giving gin to jockeys, and pinching Chinese feet. Someone ought to speak to the Head Master about it ...

Interjection (1896)
No, no balls tonight; only a dinner and the Opera, and a party or two, which the dear girls do so enjoy!

Homburg (1896)
You will find Homburg sadly spoilt this season; the Germans have quite crowded out the English, and they speak such bad German they hardly understand a word I say. Only the other day I went into Louisenstrasse to buy a cushion because the seats are so hard, and I asked the shopman to give me *ein kleinen Kuss*, and he actually burst out laughing in my face. Then I said I wanted *ein kleinen Kuss von Pferdes haar*, and he was quite impertinent, though I really pronounce very well; but I suppose he must have been tipsy. It is a thousand pities there are so many Germans about.... A German town? Oh, no, Lord Chesterton; it is an *English* town; it belongs to *us*, and I suppose that is the reason the Prince comes here every year ... But I assure you I have had letters from Homburg with the English stamp on them—or is it Heligoland I am thinking of? Anyway, I am quite sure it began with an H.... Are you taking the waters? I am, so you might escort me to my bath ... No, not *into* it, Lord Chesterton, I did not say that; not but what it is a perfectly decent bath, for I always go in in my bonnet and veil to save trouble, and really, after they have poured in the bottle of ink—I mean pine—one might as well have wooden legs for anything anyone would know to the contrary.

A Skating Carnival (1897)
At last I have found you, my dear Lady Arthur! What a magnificent dress you have! I am sure all that gold embroidery must have cost a fortune; and everything so correct too; purple and red, and what lovely diamonds! Do you see Mrs. Langtry in rose colour and spangled black and the man with the evening papers. Oh dear, what

a bad fall he had, poor man! If I could skate I should come as a large fur muff, then I should not mind tumbling about. Do you see Curtan in plain clothes, and those other plain men from Prince's skating with three pink dominos and a Polish costume? Take care, Lady Arthur, there is that waiter man coming into your box. I suppose people think they may take any liberties they please at a carnival ... Lord Arthur's uncle did you say? How can Lord Arthur's uncle be a waiter? Not but what I heard that a member of the aristocracy once drove a cab—but that was a hansom cab—and Florrie once knew a man who had acted as a footman in a London theatre. Why, he is talking to the Duke of Teddington! Surely I can't have made another mistake, and that he was the man we met at dinner the other night; and such an eligible *parti* too; and he did get on so well with poor dear Agatha, who is really getting quite passée; but I don't see how one can be expected to remember everybody. I must really get a new Peerage at once. Now, Lady Arthur, you must go down and skate; they are playing the March from *Tannhauser*, and Mr. Adams is waiting for you in white and silver. Do look, Lord Arthur; they have put Mrs. Langtry first and your wife second in the procession. Now the judges have sent Sir William to stop one of them. Yes, it is Lady Arthur who is being led up to receive the first prize. I am so glad; and John Bull has got the first prize for men, and the organ-grinder the second, and the sweep the third. I do hope the third prize will be some Pears' soap and a scrubbing-brush, as I am sure there is not a cab in London that would take him home in it.'

While Skye was writing the series, 'One of Her Four Daughters' wrote a letter to the editor of *The World*. I have little doubt that it was Diane. The content is revealing:

'There are four of us out. We have all been brought up precisely according to the rules laid down by "Materfamilias" with regard to her own daughters; we are all more or less good looking; and, thanks to having a mother, we are none of us married, or even engaged. Now for the reason of this sad state of affairs. In all the books we have been allowed to read the mother of a grown-up girl is fat, and has white hair and a homely face. Our mother, unfortunately, is tall and slim, and has not a grey hair in her head, and when we have been spending hours putting on the most expensive new dresses, she runs up at the last minute and appears arrayed in some French-pattern frock she has picked up cheap at a sale, and cuts us all out. She says it is because she is old and has had such long experience, and knows how to wear her clothes. She is always flinging her age at our heads. When young men call, mamma leaves us alone with any who are rich, and eldest sons; but as these are generally plain and stupid we don't care about them. Then when the good-looking and amusing detrimentals appear, she comes gliding in after them, and suggests that they should come into her room for a minute to see a book or a picture, or to be consulted about something purely imaginary (for she never was yet known to take anyone's advice), and she gives them a comfortable chair and a cigarette, and they never come back to us the whole afternoon; and we don't think it at all fair. It is always a difficult matter to know who the young men are calling on, whether they come to see us or only mamma; and they write long letters to her which she won't show us, and she reads all their short notes to us, which quite takes the cream off them. Then, when we have little dances at home, if we don't keep her at the piano, she dances the whole evening. I once saw her dance right through *five valses running* with the best dancer in the room, and no one man has ever even asked one of us to dance five times running with him—and we should not if he did; but mamma says that "exercise is so good for her liver", and that "at her age what does it matter?" but we think it matters a great deal. She says we just think what a long time we shall have to wait! A few nights ago we got another chaperon, and went, a nice cheery party, to a play; but, for some reason or another, we managed all to sit next to the wrong partners, and the men were cross, and we did not enjoy ourselves a bit. Then we came home to supper; mamma did not appear, saying she had a headache (she *never* has headaches, we sometimes wish she had!), and the supper was very flat, in spite of any amount of champagne, and all the young men, one after another, asked if they might not go up and sit with her in her boudoir. Afterwards we discovered that she had our pet young man to dine all alone with her, and he had said he could not come with us because he was going into the country! Mamma does not care for her contemporaries because they are old fogeys and have nothing in common with her; and she says she only encourages young men to come to the house for our sakes, as, naturally, they don't amuse her in the least. If we venture to complain, she turns upon us reproachfully and says, "You surely cannot be jealous of your poor old mother!" '

XI

THE MIDDLE-AGED MOTHER

KYE was an incorrigible snob, without a flicker of conscience for anyone who was not as well booted as herself. She was also jealous, in their flowering, of her daughters. She exposes herself, unwittingly perhaps, in an article in *The World* (1892) written, not as Diane Chasseresse but as I.N.A. It was titled 'The Middle-Aged Mother':

'The position of a middle-aged mother living in London and going much into society is one from which many women would gladly escape. True it is that some mothers have never been so happy as during the time in which they are taking out a daughter. It is the Indian summer of their lives, the last brilliant gleam of light that comes before sunset. They feel for the first time the benefit of having a constant companion at whom no evil tongue can cavil; and they have never before been so well or so animated, nor have they appeared to so much advantage. But to others—to those, for instance, whose chief interest in life lies in the pursuit of literature, painting, or music—it is a terrible wrench to be obliged to put away books and easels, in order to write and answer invitations, do endless shopping, and leave useless cards.

The woman who has a grown-up daughter has arrived at a time of life when, as a rule, she likes to spend her evenings in a comfortable armchair au *coin du feu*. She has had enough of London seasons, with their round of balls, parties, dinners, and fêtes. She has had her hours of weakness and her moments of passion, her illusions and her disenchantments. She is past her first youth, and feels she is no longer in great request, and she has just settled down with quiet resignation into the enjoyment of a peaceful life, when the moment arrives in which she is obliged to appear before the world again with a grown-up daughter at her heels. And the world in which she has to reappear is not even the same which she so lately left—a world of cheery dinners and parties, from which the guests disperse at midnight; for she has to begin a new life in a turmoil of balls and late hours. Her limbs have lost the elasticity of youth.

and long for rest; but, instead of retiring early, she has, at a late hour, to make an elaborate and lengthy toilette, and to go to perhaps some second-rate dance, where she knows neither the hostess nor the greater part of the guests, and where she must sit for hours in some corner with no one to speak to—frumps to the right of her, frumps to the left of her—while her daughter, who imports her own partners with her, is enjoying herself hugely. And for this sacrifice of her sleep and, indirectly, of her health she gets no credit, for she is only doing what other mothers have to do whether they like it or not, whether they are ill, or tired, or sad, or only bored.

To some mothers, who live for society only, it is a great trial to have to bring out a daughter, and it is generally they who have what is called "kept their figures" who feel it the most. They like to dance and flirt and be admired, and do not appreciate the attention bestowed on what is perhaps, a younger and fresher edition of themselves. They are generally a long time before they can be made to understand that men do sometimes prefer the *beauté du diable* of their girls to their own maturer charms. . . .

The truly happy middle-aged mother is she who is wholly unselfish. The mother who is self-denying and not naturally unselfish, however much she may give up to her children, cannot help sometimes feeling bored or tired, or filled with an occasional longing to be young and admired and loved. It is, therefore, all the more to her credit that she suppresses herself, and, in apparent contentment, keeps herself always as a background to her children. A woman of this sort is probably more capable of understanding and entering into the feelings of her girls—she is, in fact, more truly sympathetic than the unselfish mother who has no *arrière-pensées*, and it is therefore she who has the greatest influence over her daughters, and to whose judgement they would defer in all cases of doubt or difficulty.'

Her latter 'Pleasures of a Chaperon', more skilfully written than the earlier ones, and just as pleasurable, are tinged with a certain bitterness. Diana ('Florrie'), in an article she contributed to *The World* in 1897, underlines the antagonism which existed between Skye and her four daughters.

Homburg (1897)
'We have most of us kicked at going abroad with mamma. Even "poor dear Patience", as she calls her, said she couldn't stand it twice in a year, so she went to Ireland, and Maud has gone to Scotland to avoid going with us, but I really don't mind going to Homburg with her, because one is so delightfully independent there. Lots of people

don't even know I've got a mother with me, I keep her so carefully concealed. When she comes to the tennis-courts I go for a walk in the woods, and it doesn't matter how long I am away, for when once she has paid her mark to go in, she will be certain to take her money's worth out of the armchair and footstool. If she wants me to bike with her, I wait till she is dressed, and then say that a court has been kept for me, so that I can't come with her. Not that she ever *rides*, but she dresses up and walks solemnly beside her Columbia, and makes a fool of herself. I am sorry to have to say it of one's own mother, but she *does* make a fool of herself; and it is very hard on us girls.'

Within a month or two, almost as if she was writing in reply, Skye's fifty-ninth 'Pleasures of a Chaperon' began this way :

'*May Fair (1897)*
So charming of you to take me with you, Lord William. How few young men ever think of doing anything for the mothers of their friends; though, nine times out of ten, the mothers are far more agreeable than their girls, because they have had so much more experience. But, oh dear, no, they come to one's house and sit and talk to the girls, and eat and drink and smoke till the whole place smells like a vulgar pothouse, and never even say "Thank you". Not that I object to a little smoke, because it keeps the moths away; and really one's woollen things do get so—eh? ... Are we going to walk to Prince's Restaurant, up Piccadilly? Then I am afraid you must wait while I put on another dress and my sables, as I know how much young men object to walk up Piccadilly with a bicycling skirt; not but what mine is a very nice bicycling skirt, though it is not "braided all over", as they described it in the papers; because I shouldn't think of having any braid where it could possibly catch in the pedals in front of an omnibus; and I am sure your mother wouldn't either, would she, Lord Billy? You don't mind my calling you Lord Billy instead of Lord William when we are quite alone, do you? It seems so much less formal; and of course one always does it behind your back. And really I don't like the principle of abusing people behind their backs and being servile to their faces; not that calling you "Lord Billy" is abuse, only it seems more familiar; and familiarity breeds contempt, you know.

You always have the same table when you lunch at Princes? ... It certainly is in a very good position, as we can see who comes in and goes out so well.... Yes, do move your chair nearer to mine; we can talk ever so much better, and you don't know what a relief it is to me to be able to talk freely, and not to be snubbed by the girls every time I open my lips! I am sure you must feel it too, Lord Billy. Doesn't Florrie snub you as she does me? ... Not at all? Now that is very odd, but perhaps you let her do all the talking, which is very diplomatic of you.... No, thanks, I won't begin with a sardine, because I so often have sardines at home. In fact, we always have a tin handy, to supplement the food when young men drop in to lunch unexpectedly....

I do hope I haven't done the wrong thing in coming to Prince's alone with you in an ordinary bonnet. Anyhow, I am glad I wore my sables when everyone else is so smart in transparent blouses and diamonds and a north-east wind. What nice little ices in leaves, and how nice the leaves are to scrunch, Lord Billy! ... Please; I should like both coffee and liqueurs, for I'm sure I couldn't keep awake through a classical concert without them.

Yes, let us walk up the Burlington Arcade and take a cab to the Queen's Hall at the other end. How I love the smell that comes up from underneath those scent shops! Why, they have taken away all the photographs from that window; I wonder why. Do let us stop and look at these jewels—I am so fond of jewellery—and those silver-spangled fans on the opposite side; but you mustn't think, dear Lord Billy, that I expect you to buy all the things I admire, for I really don't; though, of course, there are heaps and heaps of things I should like; a diamond muff-chain, for instance; and oh, do look at that diamond bow with the emerald drops—that really strikes me as not being at all out of the way in price! ... What? we must hurry on or we shall be late for the concert? Oh dear, what a pity, for I am so fond of shops, and I am sure the concert will be deadly dull; not but what I dare say I shall enjoy it very much with you, Lord Billy, you talk so amusingly always.'

Walter was right when he addressed her as 'Dear Monkey'. Although she would have been disgusted with the comparison, she was in so many ways a monkey on a stick. She was spoilt, arrogant, self-centred; and, in her love of finery, perhaps more jackdaw than peacock. It is possible to believe, as her grandchildren do, that she had no lovers. Yet masculine attention was profoundly important to her. She resented it when her children took it away. It is exasperating, in many respects, to meet the person she reveals in her writings; but she defies disinterest. In her favour, she was always able to laugh at herself which is the surest definition of a sense of humour. I wasn't far wrong when I first looked at Doré's drawing of her, and concluded that she was someone on whom no man had ever put a bit. She had a nimbleness of wit which matched the nimbleness of her figure. She was the sort of woman whom another man, other than Walter, might have tamed. As it was, in her middle years, she became the matriarch:

'In a Motor-cart (1897)
I wonder at what time the motor-cart will be here, and whether one rides *on* it or drives *in* it; and whether a bicycle dress or a riding habit will be the most suitable for the occasion. Anyhow, I think I had better put on a divided skirt in case I should have to sit astride. I know people always wear yachting caps on motor-carts, because I have seen them in the illustrated papers.... Yes, Agatha, I really think it would be a good plan for you to escort me on your bicycle.

I am quite comfortable, thanks, and the rug is tucked well in; but why am I to sit on the right side? You surely don't expect me to drive. Why, I can't drive in London with horses and reins, and I certainly couldn't without.... Oh, I see; the long handle is for you to steer with, and you prefer to hold it in your right hand.... Yes, I do feel a little bobbley if I lean back, but not at all if I sit up. Oh! do take care round the corners; you make me so nervous! I had no idea you were going to twirl round so quickly. Agatha! don't come so near with your bike, you might run into us.... I like the Park much better than the streets, as the traffic frightened me so.... Yes, I really think I might manage to drive it a little, by the Serpentine. Why, it is stopping! ... Oh! I am to lean on the handle to keep it going, and turn it to the right or left. There now, the horrid thing would have run into the Serpentine if you had not caught hold of the tiller. It is just like steering a yacht; if you want it to go one way it is sure to go the other.... Now, do tell me what you call this. Is it a *cart* or a *car*? ... You call it a *waggon* in the States? ... Agatha! Do you hear? Why don't you keep alongside, here, where there is plenty of room, instead of riding in the smell? ... Do take care; those horses are frightened to death.

Interjection (1897)
I don't know what girls are coming to, I'm sure; they certainly are of no use to me....

Coming Out (1897)
Yes, indeed they have; they altered the arrangements for the Drawing Rooms as there were so many disappointed debutantes, and Patience is going to be presented after all. Not that it is a good

thing for a girl to be presented in a Jubilee year, because everyone knows her age by it; and in ten years' time, when poor dear Patience will be an old maid of twenty-seven, every one in London will remember how old she is.... Looking forward to it? Yes, she is, very much; not to the Drawing Room, because I am afraid she will look like a tallow candle in her satin and pearls (though Lord Chesterton has promised to escort her in his togs), but to the Drawing Room tea afterwards, because our cook does make such delicious petits fours, and she has asked all her skating partners to come to it, and I shall hang my dress on a stand with its back to the company. Because I don't like people tumbling about over my train, and upsetting tea and coffee over it, and I am sure no one will be any the wiser.... Yes, we are going abroad immediately. I am taking Patience to a purer atmosphere for Easter.... Oh no, Mr. Trevor; I don't mean smoke and fog; I mean *morally* purer—I want to get away from all those abandoned women who valse on the ice all through Lent, Fridays and Sundays and weekdays as well; as though there were no such thing as religion in the world. I am taking her straight to Rome, where she will see the dear Pope and hear the silver trumpets before she begins the frivolities of her little London life.

Rome (1897)

Hungry already, child? Why, you had a complete tea this morning.... So sick, you couldn't finish it? Then, why don't you read your *Walks in Rome* and your Bacon? When you are reading Hare think of currant-jelly, and when you are reading Bacon, think of fried eggs, and if that doesn't take away your appetite after thirty-two hours in the train I am sure I don't know what will.... Only fancy, Mr. Carone, Patience never slept in an hotel in her life till last night in Milan, and I suppose that is the reason she slept eleven hours at a stretch to make up for lost time.... Oh, no; I wasn't a bit tired, and went out to dinner at Virgiglio Savini's, and had delicious soup with frogs swimming about in it.... No, child; not *live* frogs, of course; but cooked ones, full of little bones and rice, and they only have it once a year in the restaurant. Now, Patience, look out of the window and you will see Florence down below; and don't be awkward and tumble over that old gentleman's toes, which reminds me that both my shoes have disappeared under the opposite seat; do fish them out with your stick, Mr. Carone. There now, Patience, you have just missed the moon by going to sleep again! I can't think how you can like to waste so much time in sleep on such a pleasant journey.

So this is Rome! What crowds of people and what a noise! I do wish there were some canals and gondolas here as there are in Venice. I am tired to death already and have been nowhere. Let us take a fiacre and go to St. Peter's. How hideous that embankment is; and I thought there was always a sunset behind Saint Angelo! There certainly is in pictures. I shall never get up all those steps, Mr. Carone; do buy me a camp stool, and don't let me go anywhere without it ever again. Now, plant me in the middle of St. Peter's and there leave me, and you and Patience can go and poke about while I sit—oh! Patience, Patience, look at those people kissing St. Peter's toe and touching it with their foreheads! They have made it quite shiny and polished. I did hope we should have seen the Pope in here, but there are nothing but Cook's excursionists wherever we go, so suppose we leave this and do the Vatican.... Shut, is it? Well, I think Rome is a stupid place.... Very well, we will go and lunch somewhere out of doors, and then do the 'halo of pink parasols' on the Pincio that Patience was reading about in her Hare. Now what shall we have to eat? ... Some *cappretto* and *lingue di Passaro*? What on earth is that, Mr. Carone? *Goat* and *sparrows' tongues*? What a mixture! I do hope the goat won't taste as strong as it smells; and let us have some of that delicious *ricotta* cream cheese for Patience....

What a mean little staircase up to the Sistine Chapel! ... No, thank you, I prefer to keep my parasol, as I'm a little lame. Look at that man lying on his back in the middle of the chapel reading a book; is he stuffed, or dead, or doing penance, or what? And lots of people are looking at themselves in looking-glasses. I never saw anything so odd. Why, I do believe they are looking at the painted ceiling up above them and I might have gone away and never seen it. I do think you might have told me, Patience. What is the use of your reading everything up if you know nothing about anything at the end?

Now, this is a really quiet, nice spot you have brought me to, Mr. Carone. I should not mind being buried here, if I had to be buried anywhere, I mean. I like all those weeping willows and yellow roses, and the violets on those other graves; but I don't see what there was left of Shelley to put under that stone. If Mr. Trelawney had his heart and the rest of him was cremated, what do you suppose there is here? Anyhow, it is very romantic; and such a comfort to be away from the incessant babble of that child. I am so glad she was able to hire a bicycle and go off with Mr. Greenock. I hope she will go a long way and be thoroughly tired out, and go to bed when she gets— Why, *surely that is not Patience and Mr. Greenock pursuing us to the Protestant cemetery?* I call that too bad; I did think we should have got away from them here; especially as Mr. Greenock is not a Protestant; and who on earth has Patience picked up? Surely it must be that Mr. Fisher who was such a friend of that young man who used to tell all those pre-Adamite stories? What can he be doing in Rome? I thought he was a Benedictine monk. Surely they are not allowed to go out with girls bicycling!

That Lord Chesterton (1897)

No, Captain Boulter, no news. We get more begging letters than invitations, and I haven't heard any news except that Lord Chesterton has had another proposal.... You didn't know girls ever proposed to men? That was because you married so young. Why, Lord Chesterton has as many offers as if he were a Mormon! I can't think what the girls see in him. Anyhow, he only had one flower sent him for the flower ball, and that he took for an advertisement from a shop till Maudie told him he was expected to go to the flower ball and dance with the girl who was dressed like the flower; but it might have been her mother for anything he knew, and I am sure he would have been just as happy, for he actually wanted me to ride down St. James's Street with him on a tandem! ... Will I dine with you at the Bath Club, Captain Boulter? Of course I will, with great pleasure; and it will remind me of when I was a girl, and we went to Leucherbad, where all the people had skin diseases.

Church Parade (1897)

I don't care whether you miss your train or not; to Church you must go. Why, it wouldn't feel like Sunday if we didn't go to Church.... You say you can't go to Church in river clothes and haven't time to change them afterwards? And why not, pray? You told me I was to wear my smartest gown for the river when I wanted to go in a coat and skirt and a nice jaunty little hat because you said Maidenhead on Sundays was like Ascot; so why on earth can't you go in the same clothes you wear at Church? ... Now, don't let me hear any more nonsense, but come along directly.

No; we won't sit in the front pew, because I ordered lunch at half-past twelve; and if the sermon is too long.... Yes, this pew will do nicely; but, can you see the clock from here, Florrie? I don't like to see people taking out their watches all through a service just to find how much longer it is going to last; it looks so irreverent.

Maidenhead (1897)

No, thank you, I will go in the punt.... But I don't at all see why I should go in a rickety little boat, when I prefer to spread myself out at the bottom of a punt, with two men to pole me along.... Well, Florrie, I think it extremely selfish of you to take Captain Bootles away from me. Why can't you punt yourself and the dinner, and leave the two men to row me? Anyhow, I insist on your joining us at the Riverside at tea-time; and I wonder if we can get a poached egg and some ham there, for I don't much fancy a cold dinner on an island, especially as the cold dinner is going in the punt and I am going in the boat.

But I assure you, this is the Riverside, Mr. Carone. I must know it better than you, as I have been here before and you haven't; and don't you see what a lot of smart people there are on the Club lawn? We will have our tea out here, and you must give Captain Bootles' name if they ask if you are a member.... No, I certainly won't wait for the others. I know what Florrie is when once she gets away from me with a young man; she never comes back, and pretends her watch has gone wrong or leaves it behind on purpose, or something. I know it isn't Captain Bootles' fault, for he is always punctual when he comes to tea with us in Eaton Place and seldom goes away till dinner-time; but I suppose he is weak and easily led astray.... Actresses? Oh no, I assure you they are not allowed here. Those are some of our smartest Society people. Just look at their clothes.... You say you know one of them, and that she acts at the Victorian Theatre? But I tell you they are not allowed here—you don't think I can have made a mistake, and that we have come to the Riviera and not the Riverside at all, do you? Oh dear, how tiresome! That is because they both begin with an R I V and I am so short-sighted, and now you will have to pay for our tea instead of Captain Bootles.

Which island did she say? I haven't the slightest idea. You must go on rowing round all the islands till you find them. I know it wasn't Formosa; and it wasn't any of the places where "Loiterers will be prosecuted" is written up; and it wasn't under an alder tree, because I know what comes of sitting under alder trees in Scotland and I refused to dine under one. You must go alongside of all the punts that are moored by the edge of the stream and peep into them.... You would rather die, Mr. Carone? But I insist on your finding my dinner—I mean my daughter. There is a punt right in the thick of the rushes, with a parasol up and a shirt-sleeve; do you think that is them? ... But they must be somewhere, unless they went down in the lock; and even then the hamper would float, wouldn't it? I am getting so hungry with all this tossing about; and there are so many punts with apparently nothing in them but a parasol and a shirt-sleeve—though what people can want with a parasol at this time of night I can't imagine.

Homburg (1897)

What a delightful spot! And we are evidently to sit on those benches by the tables covered with flowers, in the middle of the wood; and there is the Duke of Cambridge just arriving, and Mr. Beit. What a pity it is the poor, dear Prince has had to go to Marienbad this season! ... You wonder I did not go to Marienbad, instead of coming to Homburg? But I should have gone there, dear Lady Carseam, only once before when the papers said the Prince was going to Marienbad he came here instead, and I went all that long journey with Maud and Agatha and poor dear Patience for nothing.

Seamore Place (1897)

It is nonsense for you to say Lord Chesterton has not been here, Maud, when I know that he has. Do you suppose I can't tell the difference between the smell of a cigar and the smell of a cigarette? And if it was your New Zealand cousin, as you say, who only smokes pipes, and only stayed here ten minutes, pray what are these two large cigar-ends doing at the bottom of my Oriental pot-pourri pot? It is always the way if I go off to skate or try to have a little amusement, I come back to find a coat and hat in the hall and a strong smell of tobacco in the boudoir; or else I find a horrid patch on the looking-glass behind the sofa, and know that Lord Billy has been lolling against it with his brilliantined head.... Oh, it's no use for you to say it's the cat; cats don't use brilliantine, though I did hear that a poodle was onduled by a French coiffeur for the dog show, and it took a prize too; but that has nothing whatever to do with cats, and, if you must have men in the house when I am not here to look after the furniture, why can't you keep some caps in the hall, and make them put them on before they come into the drawing-rooms? or why can't you be satisfied with old men with bald heads? For my part, I much prefer bald old men to brilliantined boys.

My dear Duc (1897)

I don't at all see why poor dear Patience shouldn't have a little birthday party if she likes; just one or two of her intimate friends and a few dancing men to make it go off well. At this time of year people will be glad of anything to amuse them, but I really don't care to entertain on a large scale in the London season; every one is so ungrateful ... What? No, my dear, I never have; but other people have, and just look how they get abused if the music doesn't arrive, or there aren't enough quails. The hostess gets no thanks, and the men don't even know which the girls of the house are; and as for introducing partners to them, why, there isn't one hostess in a hundred who dare do such a thing. No; we will just have a few people we know very well, and can depend on; and, Florrie, you had better write at once and secure the *Duc de Gaetano*, whom you met last Monday.... You say you have only just been introduced to him, and couldn't think of doing such a thing? And pray how could you ask him if you *hadn't* been introduced to him, I should like to know? Write to him instantly; foreigners will go anywhere in a strange country, and I am not at all sure he isn't related to the King of Sicily; and think what an advantage that would be if we ever went to Rome again ! ... Well, if you won't, I shall write to him myself. He can't possibly tell which of us was presented to him, especially if I begin "*My dear Duc*," ... I don't know his address? What *does* that matter? I shall send it to the Foreign Office, and they can find it out free of charge. They always do things free of charge at the Foreign Office and General Post Office.

The Social Whirl (1898)

But what are we going to Hengler's for? I am sure I can't think why you girls couldn't have been created with several mothers apiece to take you about, instead of having only one mother among the whole lot of you! I am getting quite worn out with all the work I have to do just before Lent; one day broiled alive at a ball and the next frozen to death on the ice. And I should like to know how I am to go out to two different lunch parties with two different girls on the same day! And goodness only knows what the two are up to at home when they are not asked out! And, talking of clairvoyants and the German who cured Lord Billy's sister of insomnia by telling her in a letter to rub herself all over with hot vinegar, I am sure I would gladly give a piece of my hair and a guinea to anyone who would keep an eye on you girls; or give me a crystal ball, so that I could sit at home in a comfortable armchair, and look into it, and see everything that is going on.... You say I hate being left at home, and always want to go everywhere? Nothing of the sort, Florrie. It is most ungrateful of you to say such a thing. You know I only go about because I have to do my duty by you—by the way, if Mrs. Black does not ask me to her drum with Maud on Thursday, I shall scratch her off my list for Patience's Drawing-room tea, and I particularly want her to come, to see how much smarter my friends are than hers.... No, my dear, indeed they were not. She sent a list of the people she had *invited*, to the papers; not a list of the people who came to her house—and that just makes all the difference. Now, I should never stoop to do anything so low as that! But, as I said before, I should like very much to know *why* I am perched up here, with a bad cough and cigarette smoke blowing into my face, and *what* I have come to see at Hengler's. Is it the man who walks up a ladder and vanishes, or is it the man who bicycles on the ice, or is it a carnaval, or what? ... The World's Championship in Figure Skating? That will be most interesting, I am sure, and I hope, Florrie, you will take a lesson and improve your style.

Do you see, Patience? That is the Prince who has just come into the box opposite. Mind you have a good look at him now, so that you will know who to curtsey to on Friday; and mind you don't begin curtseying to the Lord Chamberlain before you get to the Royalties, for I heard of a girl once who was so nervous she turned her back on the dear Queen, and made her curtseys to all the gentlemen-ushers and people about the Court who stand in a row to shovel the trains along. And you mustn't stop to speak to Lord Chesterton when he gives you your train, as if you didn't care a bit, because boldness in a debutante is worse than shyness. I only tell you all this while I am reminded of it, so that you may not be nervous at the crisis. The Prince, I see, has two Americans and two English ladies with him, and a large cigar, and a lot of men behind.

A Charity Matinee (1898)
... Have I got a ticket, did you say? Yes, thank you; Lord Chesterton gave me one, because he used to go behind the scenes at the *Gaiety*. Very improper of him, I call it; but, then, I didn't know him in those days, and I do hope I have influenced him for good since I have been thrown so much with him. You know all my dear girls have been presented with him, and he has spread out all their trains and tucked them under their arms when it was all over; and beautifully he folded my black velvet one, this time; quite like a professional dressmaker; and I was very grateful to him too, because I had borrowed it from a friend who did not want it till the last Drawing Room; so I took the edge off it, so to speak, at the first, and I don't suppose for a moment that the royalties recognised it, especially as there were only three of them there, and it was all black and shovelled behind, quite out of sight. Still, of course, I

should have felt responsible if it had got creased in any way. But, as I was saying, dear Lord Chesterton gave me a ticket—a roving one—so I can just wander in and out of all the best boxes and stalls as one does at the Eton and Harrow at Lord's; and I shouldn't wonder if I found myself in the Royal box, unless there are any royalties there, and then I certainly shouldn't force myself upon them.... You say I must go in old clothes? Of course I must; but one has plenty of them just before Easter, and the spring fashions not yet in. Not but what it is a great advantage to take care of one's old clothes just now. It is so very economical to put a plain old top on to a brocaded old bottom! coming up in a flounce at the back, so that one really ought to be careful what gowns one takes to hack at an afternoon performance. Anyhow, I shall certainly take a pint bottle of champagne, for one doesn't know how many hours one may not be without food and drink, so order me a few egg sandwiches, Maud, and put them in my black reticule with my opera glasses and smelling salts and a fan.

A Ball on Ice (1898)
Florrie! Come back directly. I don't have you go off and sit in the proposal corner when I want to talk to you! Don't they do this quadrille quite beautifully? Every one is in perfect time, and when they all go to meet each other in the middle, and do a *Mohawk* back, it looks just as if they must all run up against one another, only they don't. That tall lady in white satin is the sister of the one who bicycles so beautifully in the Park. She stands still without touching the handle-bars and rides backwards, and stands still backwards without holding on. It is quite wonderful! Now they are all valsing, and the man dressed up as Bacchus is evidently quite tipsy, though he can't have had supper, as it is not ready. I wonder they allowed him to skate in the quadrille; and doesn't the girl with the pig-tail look nice in a fair wig and long petticoats, and doesn't she skate prettily? Florrie! Florrie! where have you got to? I am sure it is time for supper, and I can't be left here all alone. Have you seen my daughter, Admiral? ... Surely not in the proposal corner? Then I beg you will have it bricked up before another season, or I really cannot allow my girls to come here.'

Skye writes 'Diane Chasseresse' as an imagined character; but writers are always themselves. She was less careful than most to conceal her image. At her worst as a person, she was not very nice.

At her best, she was witty and wise, and vulnerable.

My thoughts about her are mixed. She was so obviously an exceptional woman. She was full of the love of life, although disinterested in the lives of other people, including her own children. She had that quality, common among artists, and she was a wishful artist, of shutting out anybody who distracted her from what she was determined to do.

Her writing, even after the sub-editorial slashing I have given it here, is lacking in discipline and wasteful of words. But Skye, in her blooming, belonged to a period in which there was no television, no radio, no popular newspapers. It was still an age in which relatively few people could read. Those who could had time to digest words in a leisure comparable with their enormous meals. The greatest novelists of the nineteenth century could be cut, to our taste, by half. It doesn't make them wrong that they wrote in the way they did. It doesn't make the twentieth century right that we are increasingly seeking information by turning an electronic knob.

The surprising thing about Skye is that she survived, without losing her own vital interest for nearly another half century—and into our own times.

XII
HER LATER DECADES

N the spring of 1909, the year in which Everilda, the eldest of her daughters, was the last of them to be betrothed, Skye, who was then in her sixty-fifth year, might have been expected to withdraw into a lavender and old lace retirement, fragrant in the potpourri of her memories, blessed with welcoming her grandchildren into the world. She did nothing of the sort. She rejoiced, without a tear of regret, that she had got 'the whole boiling of them' out of the way. She prepared, at the turn of a new century, to make a new life, free from the encumbrance of four daughters and their men friends, free from running a large household, free at last to do what she jolly well liked.

She was back where she had started in her girlhood in Scotland. She was again without dependants and out on her own. She decided to move house from her mansion at 3, Seamore Place, to a smaller one, but a mansion which was still big by contemporary standards, at No. 6 which was almost next door. She insisted that the four huge lead caryatides, which had distinguished the façade of No. 3 overlooking Park Lane, should move with her. To the dismay of her children, but not to their surprise, she planned a World Tour.

With over three decades of her life still to run, she made the most of them. I am sure that the secret of her longevity is that she never looked back. She never lost her enthusiasm even when she was a left-over from another age. Unlike her husband, poor Walter, there were never enough hours in her day to be 'dull'. She admittedly had a constitution in which she scarcely knew a moment of ill-health throughout her long life. But health is in the mind. People who make the most of living do not die young. 'Those whom the Gods love' is a poetic fallacy. Those who challenge the Gods, those who deny the weaknesses of old age, last the longest. People who retire, die. People who don't, people who feel that they are not yet fulfilled, are the ones who keep the Gods waiting. Skye was one who kept them waiting.

She was not going to give in because she felt that there was so much more that she had to put in before her time was out. A survivor of the nineteenth century, she came into a period in which all she knew was past. She married off her eldest daughter in 1910 on the brink of the cataclysm of the First World War, still at a time in which she and her generation believed that everything was as safe as the gold in their purses. When so much was destroyed, she remained undeterred.

There is a naïvety in the diary of her World Tour. A few parts of it remain. That the whole of it does not exist is no loss to posterity. In the age of package tours nothing that she has to say is unfamiliar. What she saw isn't changed. All the sparkle of 'Pleasures of a Chaperon' vanished. She undoubtedly hoped that it would be published because she breaks it into chapters. But it represents no more than the account of a brave old lady, travelling alone in a larger world which was beyond her compass.

'As, I hope, this simple account of my journey may be of some use to others who, like myself, long to see distant lands yet do not know how to get to them, I must be pardoned if I put in a few dull details. For instance, it is needless to buy deckchairs in London and send them all the way round by sea, when you can get them on the quay at Marseilles. It is also a great, and useless expense, to pay for a whole cabin to yourself all the way to Colombo when the boat is half empty after Port Said or, certainly, after Aden....'

When the notion of a World Tour got into her head she could scarcely sleep:

'The next day was Sunday, excellent for thinking, useless for doing. On Monday morning, early, I rushed off to Cook's office in Piccadilly. Cook's seemed to think that it was not such an unheard of thing as I had supposed of an elderly female, who hated travelling, to start off suddenly on a long voyage to Ceylon. The only obstacle seemed to be that there were hardly any vacant cabins....'

She was asked to come back a day or two later. After her return visit, she walked home with a round-the-world ticket in her purse.

'I almost danced along Piccadilly so elated did I feel at the bare possibility of seeing Japan, though I never expected to get so far! But the simplicity of all the arrangements was astounding; and the price of the tickets seemed a mere bagatelle, as I had always supposed that a trip round the world meant, at least, a thousand pounds, taken out of capital, and six months in which to prepare for the journey.

'The plan that Cook suggested was this. I was to return to England from Ceylon in another P. & O. boat, if the climate did not suit me, or if I did not like going further, alone. Otherwise, I could stay on here for a fortnight, or a month, & then take another P. & O. boat to Hong Kong. At Hong Kong I still had the chance of returning home by the same route; but if I decided to continue my journey I was to stay in China for eight days, seeing Hong Kong, Canton and Macao, and then go on in a Canadian Pacific boat to Japan and to Vancouver, and come back to England through the Rocky Mountains and Canada. I confided to Cook how very much I disliked travelling and that I did not want to go a yard out of my way, even to see Honolulu, but there was one thing I insisted on, and that was that I should see Niagara.

'Well, my preparations were soon made. I bought four new dresses, all of which I left behind because they were too good to take. I ordered a large green and white sun umbrella, several green and blue veils, a blue silk bag to sleep in, in case I was away from European hotels, some Eliman's Embrocation for the same reason, three yards of dark thin silk for curtain to pin along the berth in my cabin, when it was too hot to have the door shut, and several untrimmed white felt hats, & most important of all, a quantity of films in tin boxes for my Kodak. I took two cabin trunks and a small box for the hold; a hat box instead of a dressing bag, as it is less likely to be stolen, & a hold-all for pillows, wraps, dressing gowns etc. Unfortunately, just before starting it was found that none of my hats would go into the shallow trays of my boxes, so I had to take them in a common carton. From first to last those hats gave me no end of trouble till I gradually shed them all, and finally came home in the one I started in six months before.'

She writes in simple charm of Colombo, Macao, Canton, and Arabia. In the souks, and among the sampans, she traded for presents for her grandchildren. She wielded her Kodak and her sketchbook with the authority she imagined was England's own for ever. In dark corners she watched the ceremony of Arab marriages. In rickshaws, she penetrated the East. It certainly never occurred to her that she was looking into a world which, a generation later, would be largely closed to the West. She was one who believed in an Empire 'on which the sun would never set'.

She came home, loaded with bric-à-brac to decorate her new house. She was a compulsive collector. On a table at the end of her rococo four poster bed, doubtless with memories of Sarah Bernhardt and her coffin, she displayed a human skull. It was a child's skull that she had brought from Italy on an earlier tour. In her drawing room, with its grand piano and gold-leafed desk, she treasured half a gondola. She had two easels for her painting. She traded feverishly for others' pictures. When there was no space on the walls, she piled them against the wainscoting of her rooms.

Her grandchildren tell that, when she took up occupation of 6, Seamore Place, (after an interlude during the move from No. 3 in which she lived in the Hyde Park Hotel), she climbed a step ladder like a Michelangelo in the Sistine Chapel, to paint a plaster moulding of vine leaves and grapes which she thought would look better in full colour. They expected her to break her neck. She was made of sterner material. She got hold of a portrait of an unknown woman, reputably by Sir Peter Lely, and ruthlessly proceeded to improve the eyes because the woman had a squint. No woman should be left with a squint, she declared. Her energy, on the edge of seventy, was breathless.

When in August, 1914, the war, which was supposed only to last six months, was declared with King Edward's cousin the Kaiser, she was singing to convalescent soldiers. Not ragtime. The old lady treated them to, 'Where my Caravan Has Rested', 'O Sole Mio', and 'Roses are Blooming in Picardy'. Her voice can scarcely have been what it was in her youth. The young men, stale from Flanders, might well have wished to go without it. Instead they loved it. With a lifetime's experience as a hostess, Skye knew how to entertain.

She was undismayed when she welcomed a party of wounded men whom she asked, conventionally, whether they would like 'a wash and brush up'. One of them answered: 'No, ma'am, we've had one behind a tree in the park coming here.' Her parties, although she herself belonged to an older generation, brought up on anthems like 'Soldiers of the Queen', were as splendid as anything that Seamore Place had known when Sarah Bernhardt was the guest of honour.

Barbara Ker-Seymer evokes the mood of them: 'I remember them well as I had to hand round the teas, and got my bottom well pinched in the process. Grandmamma did sing one or two request numbers to break the ice: but the soldiers brought their own sixpenny sheet music for her to play, and she was very game. I wondered how the huge inlaid Bechstein grand felt about it! Her rings were removed to the top of the piano and, settling her specs firmly on the tip of her nose she would pound out in a rather staccato manner "Tipperary" and "Carry Me Back to Dear Old Blighty".

'When the tea was well under way, Grandmamma would tactfully disappear with us, and the maids were sent for (a very popular move) to do the rest of her entertaining. The matron of St. George's Hospital said that the men preferred Grandmamma's parties to any of the others.'

In person, Skye was austere and quiet. Her children rolled their 'R's'. She herself spoke with modulated exactness. She was always critical of anyone whose use of voice did not match her own standards. Not excepting Charles Dickens. In her old age, in a handwriting which I recognise belongs to it, she records: 'I was taken as a great treat to hear Charles Dickens read in St. James's Hall. Frankly, his reading was a disappointment, and it was acknowledged by competent critics that his reading was quite unworthy of the author of so many good books.'

All her life she was obsessed with fires. She followed fires, whenever she heard of them, like a courtesan. She had in the past even made friends with Captain Sir Eyre Shaw of the London Fire Brigade. It is a common sexual perversion. I have known women go mad in the excitement of the annual fireworks orgy at Lewes in Sussex. It may explain something of her own enigmatic love life.

Another passion of hers, so surprising in such an energetic woman, was chairs. In 'Pleasures of a Chaperon' she was always demanding one, or complaining about the absence of one. I cannot conceive of any psychiatric reason for that.

Undoubtedly, there was a certain sadism in her. She showed it in her treatment of her children; and perhaps her husband. She showed it, although she loved animals, in her thoughtless treatment of poor Trots the otter (see appendix 1).

Perhaps, as I contemplated when I first looked at the sketch of her by Gustave Doré, she was just a supreme egoist—spoilt, exclusively self-concerned and selfishly proud. Against that, she had a strong sense of family duty. She had courage and the kind of mind which distinguishes if not their way of life, the work of writers, poets, musicians and painters. She had resolution. She has left a puzzle without resolution.

Late in years she lost her hair. She adopted, like Queen Elizabeth the first, a ginger wig. She never lost her sharp intelligence or her percipience of what was going on about her. Her grandchildren were awestruck in the presence of their grandmamma (see appendix 3). Her oculist, when she complained of failing sight, wrote apologetically, even abjectly, from a holiday retreat that on his return he would see what he could do. To the very end, she wasn't going to accept oblivion without a fight.

Thus Skye.

Between the two World Wars, she bent her knee in devotion at the Church of Holy Trinity in Dover Street as she had ever since she had attended the Sunday Church Parade with Walter at the Achilles Statue in Hyde Park. She collected about her a new generation of artists. Ronald Squire, a successor of actors like Charles Hawtrey and Charles Wyndham, was among them. She took into her house her daughter Diane, and her grand-daughter, Barbara, when her father, who described himself on Barbara's birth certificate as 'A Gentleman of Leisure', then lost their nice house in Ovington Square, Kensington, 'in one hand of poker at White's'.

In her eighties, she watched the looming of the Second World War. With a trembling hand, influenced no doubt by the silly pre-war debate in the Oxford Union in which the young men voted that they would not fight for King and country, she made her own comment. I quote just a little of it, the far voice of a gallant old lady wondering what had happened to the England she had grown up in. She called it 'England's Sons':

'Can they fight, these young idlers in luxury bred,
White-handed, soft-hearted, effeminate led,
Like slaves to the bidding of each passing whim—
Can they fight? Can they ride? Can they shoot? Can they swim?
Can we trust untried youngsters—an unruly host,
Can we trust them with honour, with all we prize most?
Will they fight, all these idlers, to save our great name?
Our rights and our prestige, our country's fair fame?'

The old Victorian need not have worried what England's sons would do. In her sunset, her youngest daughter, Sylvia, took her out of London, when the bombs began to fall, to Manton Grange, in Marlborough. She loathed it. Surprisingly, she had no patience with country life. Rothamsted, Scotland, all that, she had put behind her. She needed to go back to May Fair and so she did.

She offered her leaden caryatids to the country, when the country was raking every stretch of iron railing for metal, and was disgusted when she was told that it would be much too difficult to remove them. So she took the war into her own drawing room. In her nineties, she got out her stalking rifle, loaded it, and announced that, if Hitler ever got to London, she would guarantee to shoot him through the ear from her window at two hundred yards.

She sat in her mansion with a blag pug dog called ''Arry', 'a drunken Irish cook in the basement, and a State Registered Nurse looking after her'. Her eyes were giving her trouble. She had a contempt for the oculist. She selected her own glasses from the counters of Woolworths.

She attributed her continuing active life to her pursuit of croquet. She regularly travelled to Roehampton, Ranelagh and Hurlingham on the bus from Park Lane, waving her umbrella to bring it to a stop. In her eighties she designed her own mallet to play with. In her nineties she insisted on being handicapped with the seventy-year-olds. One of her grandsons-in-law tells that, when he asked her how she was managing her game, she replied : 'I tend to push my long shots too far to the left.'

At 85, she was surprising reporters of the London evening news-papers who discovered her, without a clue what her background was, and wrote the usual ephemeral nonsense about her opinion of 'the modern girl'. They had found her playing croquet at Hurlingham from ten in the morning until seven in the evening. To the reporter's questions she sensibly answered 'Nothing wonderful in playing croquet at 85. Next week I am in a tournament at Roehampton— and I hope to give a good account of myself. Age is no handicap when you have lived long all your life. My friends tease me because I become rather jubilant between strokes. I can still skip with delight....'

At 91, she was interviewed again in Seamore Place; 'I wouldn't live anywhere else in the world than London,' she said. 'The fas-cination of it increases; it does not diminish. It is a city of memories for me now, but I cannot honestly say that I prefer it better to the London of the old days. But what I am most grateful for now is that I still have the health and strength to get about—and play croquet.'

At 94—'oh dear no, not 94, just ninety-three and a quarter'— she ordered the reporter to be quiet, pushed her Woolworth spectacles firmly on her nose, while she watched a tournament at Roehampton. She suggested that the young woman from the *Evening News* should come back to see her playing in another tournament on Monday; 'or, if that won't suit you, come to Ranelagh on Tuesday and see me play in a tournament there'.

At her 101st birthday party she put on a wine-coloured velvet dress and black lace mittens. Then, sitting bolt upright in her drawing room, she offered tea and chocolate cake to her friends and the press photographers about her. To one of the photographers she insisted, courteously but firmly: 'That light you used was very bright, young man. I shall appear with no eyes. But you need not worry. Paint some in. I have often painted eyes on photographs.'

She kept command of all her faculties to the last months of her life. When she was 90, the *Daily Express* noticed, reviewing an amateur arts exhibition, that the most outstanding work was a flower study of hers 'painted with brilliant precision and delicacy of colouring'. At the age of 97, she wrote a letter to her youngest daughter, Sylvia, in a hand steadier than many she wrote when she was in the pride of motherhood:

Dear Sylvia,
So very glad to get your long letter from the Highlands!! and I feel sure you are really appreciating my beloved Scotland which used to be my only holiday in the governess time. I am sure you ought to have such a complete change after all you have done in England; but all the modern restrictions sound very dull to me who never had any restrictions of any kind—probably because one knew from childhood what could be done, & what couldn't!!

Scotland, for me, was a great relief from the governess & lessons; & later on, I had my brother's little rifle, & anything I could shoot with it!!! Three months of happiness in the autumn & a fortnight of salmon-fishing in the spring when I was older ... BUT, OH!!! how I *hated* being wet through till—late in life, my aunt and cousins appeared in nice waterproof jackets, in colours that matched the ground, and were almost invisible. I am leading a deadly dull life now; but am never wet through! I can't spell, never could, and have no dictionary, so please excuse faults. I never could spell, & no writing of a word (forty times over in my playtime) could teach me to spell right. Please excuse this stupid letter, & again thanks very much for taking the trouble to write me. Yrs. afft.
                    Caroline Creyke

It was only in her late nineties, when she could no longer play croquet, that she admitted that she was having 'a really hopelessly dull time' with failing sight and hearing. She wrote to Sylvia during the war:
'I don't hear any bombs and I don't see anything that goes on. I go out all night in air raids because I can only hear the "all clear" if the window is open.... The only joy I have is a kitten, & I have never had one before who deliberately went several yards away from the table to get the strength to jump up & sweep the whole cloth with itself & silver & flowers all on it on to the ground; I am

writing in the dark as all the blinds & curtains are drawn in the blazing sun.

'In case of accidents I carry in my handbag a paper to say I have got my grave at Harpenden paid for, & that is really all I have to look forward to. The cat has appeared, so no more....'

In her last years she was able to manage walks in Hamilton Gardens, the private square behind Hamilton Terrace at Hyde Park Corner, at the time when the royal princesses, Elizabeth and Margaret, used to be taken there by their nurse to play. I was just a little disappointed, although not surprised, to learn that the Queen has no recollection of the remarkable old lady, the acquaintance and contemporary of her great-grandfather, who passed her by.

She left her estate, £83,839, in exemplary order. She gave £500 to her servant, Mary Rook, 'for taking care of my house during the air raids'. She bequeathed to the London Museum at Kensington Palace the Charles I relics, including a lock of his hair, given by Queen Henrietta Maria to her husband's ancestor, his page Ralph Creyke; and the pins given by Queen Caroline (the estranged wife of the Prince Regent, later George IV) to Captain Richard Creyke.

After a life in which she had not a moment's noticeable illness she faded away, after a cup of tea, during an afternoon in the autumn of 1946. She is buried, according to the instructions in her handbag, at the Parish Church of St. Nicholas at Harpenden, beside Walter, her infant son, her brother and her beloved parents. The Manor of Rothamsted is just across the road.

She is reputed to have asserted: 'Never live to a hundred. It is deadly dull.' But, at the same time, she remarked to a press reporter, in her precisely modulated voice: 'Thank you, I have had a very nice life.'

Appendix (1)

'TROTS'

by Diane Chasseresse

I was always very anxious to have a young and tame otter to live with me in London, and to follow me about the garden, and across the Park to the Serpentine.* My favourite pets when I lived in the country had been otters; they are so affectionate, and have such fascinating ways, and can be taught to be as clean as cats. I was sure that if I had one tame enough to let me lift it up by its tail and carry it about in my arms over the street crossings, it would live very happily in London, as I had a large balcony to keep it on.

I was many years unsuccessful in finding an otter, when an advertisement was sent me of one that was supposed to be quite tame and I wrote at once for particulars.

Of course they are many degrees of tameness, and I was not without misgivings when I thought of importing an almost amphibious wild animal into a London house. But when a letter came saying 'It trots up and down stairs like a cat', I decided at once to have it, and all day long I thought of nothing but 'it trots up and down stairs like a cat', till at last we called it 'Trots' in speaking of it.

* One of the most amusing of the *Sporting Sketches* (1890); it was nevertheless unforgivable to introduce a wild water animal as a captive in a May Fair mansion. Yet it must be said that, in a later generation, Gavin Maxwell, the author who claimed to be the champion of otters, did the same himself. I remember him bringing one of his own animals from the Highlands of Scotland to a house in a Chelsea Square. He exercised it in the King's Road and fed it live trout in a tank in the squalid garden.

Trots arrived in an enormous box, large enough to hold a sheep, a great wild full-grown beast tearing at the bars and trying eagerly to catch some drops of water that were being poured over its nose. My heart did sink at the sight, but that was nothing to what I felt when we undid the cage and let the creature out. It dashed all over the room like a mad thing, jumped on to the dressing-table, scrambled on to a high chest of drawers, upsetting everything as it passed, dashed three times up the chimney, and had to be brought down by the tongs, rushed into the large fixed bath, climbed out again dripping over everything, plunged into a round bath we had prepared for it, and then after having drenched everything in the whole room and exhausted itself in trying to find a way of escape, it finally jumped on to the bed, got under the clothes, and tucked itself up to go to sleep.

All day long that stupid otter never moved. We visited it constantly, and ventured to uncover it, and gently and timorously to scratch its nose. We thought it must be very tired after its journey, and left it for the night. In the meantime it had hidden all its bits of fish and meat in out-of-the-way corners, keeping them in reserve for when it should be hungry.

Next morning at about 3 a.m. I was awakened by the most fearful row; bang, bang, bang, scratch, scratch, scratch, at the loose door of the next room! This was Trots trying to get out. I jumped up and went in to see if I could calm it, but I might as well have tried to calm a lion, so I thought I would let it out and see what happened. It rushed past me and on to the landing, and to my horror began to crane its neck through the banisters; every moment I expected to see it fall headlong and be dashed to pieces on the basement floor below. The house was immensely high, and there was nothing to break its fall. It was a most horrible feeling to have brought this poor wild creature all the way from Ireland to run such a dreadful risk, but I did not know what to do, or how to get it back. At last, after leaning out through all the rails, it found the top of the stairs, and began to descend at a gallop. I followed it all the way, and it visited every corner of the landing, and every part of every room that had open doors; and what kept me in an endless fright was that it would stretch out through the bars and sniff at all the glass globes of the gas lamps that hung over the stairs. Every time it did this I expected it to lose its balance and to hear a thud on the flags below. At last, however, it got to the hall, and then it made a rush at the front door to try and get out. Failing in that, it jumped on to the wooden side seats, and then on to the windowsill; finding that this was also shut, it jumped down again, though I saw it was very lame with one foot, which had evidently been caught in a trap at some time in its life. Then it made a tour of inspection round the dining-room, and finally descended to the basement. Here it poked and pried into every corner, and bumped up against the pantry-door, while I was ready to make a bolt upstairs if it should wake the footman who slept there, for, of course, I had not dressed when I started on this very unexpected and prolonged journey of discovery. At length, greatly to my relief, having paid a final visit to the gong hole, it started upstairs; and the upstairs journey was just as protracted as the descent, not one single corner that it visited on the way down did it omit to pay a second visit to on the way back. It was very interesting to watch because if he forgot a corner anywhere he ran back and poked into it directly after; but I was getting rather cold and very sleepy, and I was most thankful when we arrived safe on the bedroom landing, and he lay down panting for breath after so much exertion.

I sat on the top step, longing to take him in my arms and kiss him, but wisely thinking the time had not arrived for such familiarities.

Suddenly he recovered his breath, walked over me, and started off downstairs again. I was obliged to follow to see what he was up to and he did exactly what he had done on the previous voyage of discovery, not omitting the endeavour to kill himself by his curiosity over the gas lamps. He went right down to the basement, then again visited the gong hole and came upstairs; this time, however, he went up the next flight of stairs, and paid a long and exhaustive visit to the schoolroom, after which I got down and hustled him into his bedroom, quite worn out with anxiety, and left him to scratch as much as he liked, while I went to bed.

The next morning he was in great pain from his foot which had gathered; and I was very very sorry for him, so I let him come into my room, and he slept all day on his back on my bed, while I stroked his nose. I also ventured to stroke his back and so did one of the children, but he turned and snapped at us, and we got most frightfully bitten on the arm and hand, so for the future we always took up a fan or a broom to stroke him with.

The following day I decided that we must risk his going on to my balcony, which had a wire netting fastened all round it ready for him, and where he was intended to reside. So we moved his cage there and hoped he would follow it. He, however, preferred to spend the day in the dark, in a little housemaid's cupboard on the landing. We had a box of matches outside, and every one who passed up and down stairs struck a match and peeped in. Sometimes he was asleep, and sometimes he had collected all the candle ends and was lying upon his back playing at ball with them. His foot got better towards evening, and at about 6.30 we managed to stir him up and get him to follow us on to the balcony. There we had great fun giving him his bath. We put a round bath and a jug of water for him, and he jumped into the bath, lay on his back with his fore-paws held up, while we poured the water on to him, then he sprang out for us to fill the jug in the bath, plunged in again, and lay down waiting for the shower of water, repeating this over and over again for an hour. Then he rushed into my room through the open window, jumped on to the red velvet sofa to roll himself dry, then rushed out again into the bath, then up the chimney by way of variety, and on to the bed and all over the furniture, flooding the whole room with water, and *such* dirty water, and finally settling himself down on my bed for the night, at least for his idea of the night, but not for mine, as I never got half a night's rest the whole time he was in the house.

However, the first night he spent in my room I was very soon asleep after so much excitement and anxiety; but every time I moved, the savage brute made a dash at my toes and tried to bite them through the bed-clothes, so I was not altogether happy or at ease, and I expected every moment that it would make a pounce at my face, which I kept well under cover.

Very early the next morning Mr. Trots got off the bed by the chair I had put for him, and began rattling at the shutters as hard as he could, so I had to get up and let him out. Once on the balcony all my troubles and fears began again, for he never rested till he had torn up some of the wire netting and got under it on to a tiny little narrow ledge that ran outside the balcony, on which there was hardly room for a mouse to stand.

I rushed out in light attire with bare feet on the cold leads, and implored him to come back. I knew he could not turn round, there was nothing for his claws to stick into, and it seemed impossible for anything to save him from falling the whole height of the house on to the leads below. However, I suppose he was conscious of his danger, for he very cleverly backed up to the wire, and I held it for him to creep under again. Then I felt easier for the moment, and we went back into my room, and I hoped to get a little rest, but not a bit of it; for an hour or two Trots played games all over the place. He found a large black fan, which I had used for stroking him, on the table, and this he knocked down and began to rush about with and roll over, then he got hold of everything round and noisy that he could find, and banged them all over the room, tearing after them like a mad thing, and it was not until a short while before it was time for me to get up that he came back to bed and we both fell into a sound sleep. When I was called, he was tucked up on my feet, and no one would have supposed we had passed such a tempestuous and anxious night.

My letters are always brought to me in bed, and as soon as they were put down, Trots woke up, and coming beside me lay on his back and took up my envelopes and played at ball with them, tossing them up in the air and catching them in his fore-paws. He was in every way a most fascinating pet, but I felt it would be quite impossible to keep him in London, as he would not let me take him up, or touch anything but his nose. Having been twice bitten, I did not care to stroke his back again, though I was always longing to treat him as I had treated my other otters. He was not an atom afraid of any one, and he would jump on to my lap for his food, but there was something very terrifying in the way he would rush after one's bare feet.

He used to be immensely fond of playing with my hunting-whip. I used to undo the lash and drag it all about the room as fast as I could, over the tables and chairs and bed and sofa, and he would tear after it, jumping on to the furniture and trying to catch it, behaving like the maddest of mad kittens. Then he was devoted to the thing that strikes the gong—the gong-banger we call it—and a large black fan, and a ball. But unlike other otters he would not keep reasonable hours. He slept all day, and woke up for his bath at 6.30 p.m., then began his romps, which frequently included going wet through, up the chimney, and rolling himself on my bed.

One evening after dinner, when I was dressing to go to a party, Trots got my black fan off the table and rushed all about the room with it, rolling over and over, then he threw one of my slippers up into the air as high as the screen, and ran off with it, then jumped on the dressing-table where I was trying to do my hair, and upsetting every bottle on it, went off to the balcony for a dip in his bath, and came dancing back and got in and out of all my clothes to dry himself. I had at last to ring for the maid to keep him amused with the black fan whilst I finished dressing.

When we came home he was sound asleep on my bed, but he woke up again at dawn; however, he went quietly out of the room without first banging open the shutters as he usually did. Then he went up to the top of the house and had a terrific encounter with the cat. No one knows exactly what took place, because the foreign man-servant, who was the only person on that floor, bolted his door and hid under the bed till it was all over, but we presume

Trots got the best of it, as the cat never appeared in our quarters during the rest of his visit. After the fight, the otter came back quietly to bed until I got up, when he jumped in and out of my boiling bath, and fled to his cupboard for the day. He was most fascinating; but when he jumped on to my lap for his whitebait or beef, I never knew if he would not seize my arm or my knee in his teeth, partly in playfulness and partly from being such a savage.

We bought the best of fish for the otter, and most expensive salmon, but he did not really care for anything so much as beef-steak. The cook complained very much of the expense of this extra mouth to feed, but I told her she must smuggle his beef in with the other bills and not say anything to her master about it.

One night poor Trots was sick. We were so sorry for him, and went up to the Zoological Gardens to ask what we were to do; and I got a bundle of long grass, thinking he might take it as medicine. I always offer it to the monkeys when I go there, and they are so fond of it; you see long skinny arms stretched through the bars in all directions till every blade has been seized and eaten.

There were no otters in the Zoo, and no wonder, for how could such particularly clean animals be expected to live in such a dirty place as the one set apart for them. After a long hunt we found the otter man, and he told us we were to starve Trots for twenty-four hours. Poor Trots! We went home and gave him the grass, which he did not seem to fancy, and leaving him without any food, went down to our own dinner.

We had only just begun when we heard an avalanche on the stairs, and the door was pushed open and Trots appeared like a mad thing jumping on to the tables and chairs, and finally on to a high sideboard, in his search for food. Both the servants fled from the room, and to pacify him we were obliged to give him something to eat; then I clapped my hands, and away he went flying up the stairs like a flash of lightning. Our stairs are excessively steep, as the rooms are lofty, and Trots was quite lame with one foot, but nevertheless he could run upstairs much faster than any dog, and he was in all respects far more active and full of tricks than the otters I had been accustomed to. My previous pets also did not turn night into day, as this fiendish creature did.

At the end of ten days I was quite worn out with anxiety and want of sleep, and having settled that dear Trots was to go away from London, I went over to Paris, leaving him in charge of any one and everyone who would take such a heavy responsibility. Every one loved him, so I knew he would be most kindly treated; but it was not how he would be *treated*, but how he would *behave*, that was such a source of worry to me. First he banged at my husband's bedroom door when he woke up early in the morning, and never stopped making a most awful to-do; then the next day he disappeared altogether out of the house. There was, of course, a great fuss, and the whole place was searched. At last he was found on the sofa of a house two doors off, and he had to be enticed back by a servant who wagged a fish's head just in front of his nose and got him safely home. Then came the day when he was to be packed off and sent away. His box was got all ready for him, but how was he to be got in? No one dared touch him, and of course the most tempting food had no attraction for him when he thought of that horrible cage. They had again to have recourse to the Zoo, and the man who used to have charge of the otters was sent for to catch poor Trots. Then began a regular otter hunt, all over the house, in and out the rooms, up and down the stairs, until at last he lay down panting and exhausted, and the man caught him by the tail and dropped him into the box. Just as he did so his nail boots slipped on the marble floor and he fell down, and in a second the otter would have been out again, only every one rushed forward and sat on the lid and hammered it down with large nails, and that was the end of my poor sweet otter's short visit to London.

Appendix (2)

SARAH BERNHARDT

This memoir, from the unmistakable change in the handwriting, was written by Skye in her great old age. She had contributed an article 'Sarah, Quand Meme' to the Globe in 1895. But in keeping with the period it was more reticent, more reluctant to name names. This, so far as I can tell, was never published:

In the Autumn of 1878 I was in Paris for the last weeks of the Great Exhibition. H.R.H. The Prince of Wales—the late King Edward—was there; also the late Lord Dudley and his beautiful wife. One day they informed me that H.R.H. had asked for a special performance at the Comédie Française, in order that he might see Sarah Bernhardt in 'Le Sphinx'; and they invited me to dine at the Café de Paris and go with them to their *avant-scene*. And this was the first occasion on which I saw that wonderful, and fascinating actress.

Very thin, *'souple comme un roseau'*, with a play of features, and a charm that has never since been equalled—such was Sarah Bernhardt, who completely eclipsed the more robust and handsome Malle Croisette, who was taking the leading part. During one of the long entr'acts H.R.H. came into the *loge*. I did not hear what he said to my hosts about the performance, but no one could have criticised such perfect and seductive acting. It was far above criticism. It was entrancing, enthralling, and carried one completely out of oneself. I felt that I must know this wonderful woman, and begged Lord Dudley to get me an introduction. He said it could not be done; and that no actress in Paris was received in Society. I said I did not care for that,—I *must* know her—; and, at last, Lord Dudley, who always took immense trouble to give pleasure, said he would write to her and ask if he might bring me to her studio.

And so the meeting was arranged. A few days later he took me to her splendid apartment; but, instead of being received by the svelte and elegant *Sphinx* in flowing draperies, we were met by a fuzzy-headed boy, in a white jacket and trousers, high heeled white satin shoes, and a large diamond lizard—*le dernier cri* in Parisian jewellery—fastening a bunch of flowers on her coat. This she called *'mon petit costume d'homme'*, which she wore when she was modelling in clay. She not only found time to amuse herself with sculpture, but there were also pictures in oils, on easels, about the studio; and all her work was far above the average, in merit. We did not stay long for fear of interrupting her work, but she most courteously invited me to come again on her 'at home' day. Of course I went, though feeling very much at a disadvantage, as my French was anything but fluent. There were several other people present, but, after giving me a most charming welcome, Madame Bernhardt left them all and took me upstairs, showing me her pictures, and then her bedroom, where we stayed & talked till I went away. This bedroom was large and dark; and at the further end of it gleamed the white bones of a perfect human skeleton! This, she informed me, was the skeleton of a great friend who had taught her all her parts. I regret to say I forget his name. He was standing by, and holding on to a large cheval glass. All the fingers of his free hand were jointed, and I moved them about. Madame Bernhardt was not dressed in her *petit costume d'homme* and, I must say, she looked far nicer clad in white feminine garments. I cannot attempt to describe how charming she was, nor how lovely was the sound of her voice. At the same time that she was talking to me she was holding a conversation with her little son in the room above, through a speaking tube; and sending him kisses—the little, only child, whose hair she always wore in a locket, which, by her express wish, was buried with her.

I did not see the celebrated coffin under her bed, but, when she offered me one of her photographs some time afterwards, I chose the one of her in her coffin. Before I left, after this most delightful and original interview, she told me she was coming to London the following season, and asked me to be kind to her as she knew no one in England.

As my husband was a good linguist and had a real appreciation of talent in any form, whether literary, musical, scientific, or theatrical, he was delighted to welcome the great actress when she came to London in the season of 1879. We asked a few intimate and appropriate friends to meet her at dinner, & had a small party with music afterwards. I do not remember who came but there were the late Lord & Lady Wemyss, the late Lord Dufferin; Lady Dufferin, who had been coming, wrote a most charming letter saying that they had just been appointed to the embassy at St. Petersburg where it would not be considered etiquette to meet an actress; I believe the Archbishop of York & Mrs. Thomson came, as she said to one of my daughters, shortly before her death, that she remembered so well the evening when they met Sarah Bernhardt at our house. We certainly were not more than ten at dinner; just enough people to fit at a round table; so, imagine my feeling when in glided the guest of honour accompanied by her little boy! I did not know what to do, but, fortunately, my husband at once arranged matters so that it should appear as if we had expected the child; and all went well. Sarah Bernhardt captivated everyone by her charm. Her voice was like the cooing of a dove; her manner quite simple and unaffected. She never posed; & no one could have imagined that she was a French actress making her first appearance among wellbred English people. No wonder she conquered us all; no wonder she was such a success in London, and that she had so many invitations she was constantly obliged to throw people over, thereby causing considerable annoyance.

Lady Violet Greville at once invited her to a big lunch party, to which Sarah Bernhardt asked me to bring her. Evidently she had some feeling of shyness, or diffidence, which prevented her from going about alone, for which reason she brought her little boy out to a late dinner when he should have been in bed. At the lunch I sat next to Robert Browning, & there were very many other distinguished guests besides the great actress, who, by the way, was so ashamed of her thin arms that, as she peeled off each long white glove, she hastily slipped on her very costly white lace mittens.

We never bored our distinguished friends by running after them, or exploiting them, and, as Sarah Bernhardt at once became not only the fashion, but the rage, that season, we did not see much of her. She caused a good deal of ill feeling by so often throwing people over. Probably they did not realise how little time she had to waste on Society functions and that part of her success on the stage was caused by the way she transformed herself into whatever part she had to play. I know that in 'La Princess lointaine' she arrived at the theatre at 7.30, though she did not appear till past 9 o'clock, so that she might think quietly about the piece, & absorb herself so completely in her part that, for the time being, she ceased to be herself & became La Princess lointaine. She introduced us to Edmond Rostand behind the scenes, one night, saying he was 'un jeune homme qui promet!'

In this piece all her jewels were real. The toes & straps of her gold shoes were embroidered in jewels. Her manteau de cour was the most magnificent I have ever seen. The collar was composed of masses of jewels veiled with a gold net. The cloak itself was of cloth of gold with a border of white satin embroidered with seraphim. She wore as many rings as she could cram on to her small fingers; but they must always be designed for the part she was playing; & in 'La femme de Claude' she wore no rings at all, because the heroine was poor. She was, at one time, so surrounded by harpies who preyed & lived on her that Gustave Doré, who was in & out of our house, told me she had quarrelled with him because he tried to warn her against her false friends. I think they made it up afterwards, when she found that what he had told her was quite true.

She was extremely fond of her medieval fortress at Bell-Isle (for which she only paid £40) and was absolutely untirable when there, though supposed to be resting from her strenuous life. She was up at 5.30, would, herself, rouse the crowd of friends & relatives with whom she was surrounded, &, in a short white skirt & fisherman's jersey, would climb down the steep rocks to the sea, & there spend hours shrimping in the little pools; after which, they would all go long expeditions by steamer or on foot, & when, towards evening, her exhausted guests were reclining in easy chairs she would appear in English flannels, brandishing a racquet & exclaiming 'au tennis, au tennis!' and play till it was dark. No wonder, when in England, she spent a day with Madame de Falbe at Luton Hoo, she astonished all the guests by starting off in pursuit of a squirrel!

When Mrs. Patrick Campbell was in the height of her fame in 'The Second Mrs. Tanqueray' I got up a little supper party to introduce her to Madame Bernhardt. It was to be an informal affair so I decided we would not go downstairs to supper, but would have it in the small end of the long drawing-room. I was most particular in giving Sarah a card for her coachman with the full address & route on it, because strangers, & particularly foreigners, are constantly taken to some place on the way to Lords which had a similar address. I collected a few suitable friends who all duly arrived, hung about, & waited for their supper, and then left in disgust as neither of the guests of honour put in an appearance. However, in due course, both the *tragediennes* turned up. It was pouring with rain, Sarah's horse fell down; she was obliged to get out of her carriage & into a fourwheeler &, of course, had left the paper with the address with her coachman & the fallen horse, and was taken to the usual wrong house.

Mrs. Campbell was acting at the St. James' Theatre, where there is no covered passage from the street to the stage door, so she had to drive all the way to her own house to change her wet clothes. In one way the rain was a blessing as there were only a few young people left which enabled the two great actresses to be together the whole evening.

But what rather spoilt the success of the party was that everyone refused to sit by Madame Bernhardt, as they would not air their bad French; & she, who always said she could speak English, never did so in my hearing. Even Mrs. Campbell fled to the other end of the table to join some young people & one of my girls, about whom she once wrote—'darling Diane, I don't see her but I always love her'. However, eventually, Sarah & Stella, one in all black & the other in all white, found a tiny ottoman, & there they sat & gazed at each other. They were mutually attracted & I saw Sarah take off one of her rings & give it to Stella. Everyone will remember how the two, subsequently, acted together in French, in 'Pelleas et Melisande'; what a success it was for both, & what a triumph for Mrs. Campbell who had to relearn her part in French, as well as to acquire a French accent sufficiently pure to play with an actress from the Comédie Française.

When in Paris my daughter & I used to go to see Madame Bernhardt in her apartment. We breakfasted with her once, & she gave us a *loge* when she was acting. The last time we went, many years ago, she was in a vast apartment with no furniture except a colossal divan piled up with huge cushions and was engaged in modelling a bust of Coquelin, of which she was very proud.

My looking glass has persistently refused to admit the great and flattering likeness that I was constantly told existed between Sarah and myself. Even in Paris the same resemblance was remarked on. I remember, many years ago, the maid who waited on me in my hotel in the Rue de Rivoli exclaiming: 'O, *Madame, c'est à faire retourner la tête à tout le monde dans les rues de vous voir!*' Before leaving, I asked the maid if there was anything she would like me to give her; she said the one thing she most wanted in the world was to go and see Sarah Bernhardt at the Comédie Française '*sans faire la queue*'; so, of course, I gave her a ticket. Another year I was looking at chiffons in the Louvre and one of my daughters, who was some way behind, saw the shop girls looking after me, & heard one of them say: '*on dirait que c'est Madame Sarah Bernhardt.*' So naturally, when I went to a fancy ball in London, I copied her as Dona Sol, in Ruy Blas; white satin, lace, pearls, a little pearl crown on untidy hair, & a very painted mouth.

There was nothing tragic in her appearance off the stage. Her face was all softness and charm. Her eyes were gentle and far apart; she had a refined, slightly aquiline nose, a small mouth, & very small, even teeth. She had a bush of extremely thick, rather short, untidy hair, which English people, who knew no better, always spoke of as 'Sarah's wig'. She showed me the special hairbrush that was given to her by Ellen Terry, who, I believe, also has very thick hair. She was quite short and her extreme slightness was a most valuable asset in a play like 'La Dame aux Camelias', where the heroine has to die of consumption on the stage. Nothing that she ever did was so pathetic as that last act. The restlessness of the consumptive, the excitability, the momentary feeling of renewed vitality, & then, the final collapse, when the whole audience would weep in sympathy.

Having seen her so often at her very best, I could not bear to be disillusioned, so I hardly ever went to see her on the stage when a little of the charm was gone.

One night when I arrived from abroad I hurried off to see Mrs. Campbell in 'Bella Donna'. After the performance my daughter & I went round to her dressing room to talk to her, & she said we must go across the street to see Sarah, who was acting at the Coliseum. We were accompanied by a quiet & unpretentious man to whom we had not been introduced, & he was left out in the passage with my daughter whilst Mrs. Campbell & I talked to Madame Bernhardt in her tiny, crowded up room. After a time Mrs. Campbell said she would so much like to bring in & present Mr. Robert Hitchens the celebrated author, whose play she was acting! My daughter had no idea of her companion's identity as we had only made his acquaintance through his entrancing books. After we left the Coliseum he took us three to supper at one of his clubs; and we spent a most pleasant evening as Mrs. Campbell was in great form.

Appendix (3)

GRANDMAMMA

Two of Skye's grand-daughters who, so it seems to me, have inherited much of her sprightliness and keen intelligence, have sent me notes about their grandmamma in great old age. To some extent, they echo each other. To some extent, they repeat what I have written in the body of the book. It is, nonetheless, worth reading what her own kin have to say about her. They knew her; and I didn't.

This is what Mrs. Gerald Eastwood, Sylvia's daughter, writes of her girlhood memories at Manton Grange, Marlborough, in Wiltshire :

'My first recollections of Grandmamma must have been when she was in her late sixties and used to come and visit us at Manton. I can see her sitting at the Baby Grand Piano in the drawing room bow window, encouraging us without much success to sing.

During the First World War she used to entertain the wounded convalescents in her house in Seamore Place, and sang to them. During this period, when she was already in her seventies, she "lost" her voice; but some "man" she went to restored it for her.

During her visits to Manton, when we were children, we were expected to play croquet with her on our far from perfect South Lawn. I remember the boredom of standing on the side lines while Grandmamma used one's own ball to take hers right round the field to victory. We had few chances to hit the ball ourselves. Grandmamma played to win, and made no concession to youth or inexperience. With it all I enjoyed her company very much. I remember her as bright and amusing, and ready to be amused; although I was a bit scared of her as well. She had a sharp tongue and was far from tolerant.

I think possibly the relationship between herself and her grandchildren was a good deal happier than that with her daughters, and her son. She had little use for boys.

She was a great bridge player. It was always auction bridge. She never attempted to master contract. In her latter years she took to backgammon instead.

As a child, visits to Seamore Place were rather an awe-inspiring though enjoyable experience; sometimes staying with my sister, sleeping or not sleeping in an enormous all enveloping feather bed on the fourth floor. To get to this we had to pass my Grandmother's third floor bedroom, with its enormous fourposter bed, and the child's skull she had brought from Italy sitting on the large tall boy near the door. It filled me with superstitious fear. There was also a marble effigy of a baby on a side table, which I think was Launcelot's dead twin brother.

In my early teens dances were held at 6 Seamore Place, given mainly for an older cousin who lived with Grandmamma at that time. I think the original dances were held in the first floor drawing room, but the floor was considered unsafe for this purpose. They were then arranged in the dining room downstairs. It was on this occasion that Grandmamma had a violent attack of cramp, the only time I can ever remember her showing any physical distress. She was as strong as a horse and until near her end I never remember her ill.

Grandmamma was not lacking in a sense of duty to her family or to her church. She made a rule of Sunday attendance at Holy Trinity in Dover Street. To her the Divine Right of Kings was unquestionable; though this did not include a duty to curtsey to commoners who married royalty. She could be generous and showed concern and help, especially where her family was concerned.

I stayed with her to attend Chelsea Polytechnic when I was nineteen. My time at Seamore Place was a very happy one. There were no restrictions on my coming and going. I was given a latch key to wear round my neck when I went out in the evening with strict instructions not to lose it, as that meant changing the lock on the door. My escort was always received very graciously. Although already over 80 Grandmamma enjoyed the presence and attention of young men; especially the goodlooking ones.

Dinners were excellent, usually starting with soup served in Chinese bowls, sipped out of china spoons bought on her world tour, and possibly ending with her favourite "brie coulant". In a rabbit warren of a basement, a friendly cook played "The Merry Widow" waltz on an accordion.

In the drawing room of Seamore Place there were enlarged coloured photographs of her world tour on a ledge all round the right hand wall. The grand piano had a bowl of coloured gourds, or a vase of rhododendron leaves with most realistic artificial paper flowers, which pleased her very much. Her enormous flat topped desk was covered for tidiness with a sheet of brocade. Her arm chair was surrounded by a glass draught screen. The large china figure of the Chinese god of Happiness, Hoptoi (?), was on the mantelpiece. There were pictures everywhere on easels or stacked against the walls. She bought and sold at Sotheby's and elsewhere, and though her Kneller may not have been a true Kneller, I believe she really did acquire a Romney. Earlier it was of course a 'Rembrandt' that she discovered in the butler's pantry at Rothamsted, where it was used for target practice by the pantry boy with an airgun.

She used make-up—rouge and eyeshadow I think. She wore a lace cap, generally black, on the top of her head, a long dress with a sort of beaded over-mantle. She liked gay colours and had a passion for clothes. She bought her spectacles—which actually I seldom remember her wearing—at Woolworth's—6d each lens, and sixpence for the frame—and said they suited her perfectly. She also bought jewellery there, replacing her own rubies and emeralds, though she usually wore the yellow diamond Creyke family engagement ring. As I first recall her she was tall—straight-backed in old age—and always trying new interests.

During the Second World War when many of the houses round her had been bombed to ruins she was persuaded for a time to come down to live with my mother. It was not a success. Grandmamma got bored with her daily walk of over a mile to Marlborough. She was then in her mid nineties. While she was feeding the ducks with liquorice allsorts for the amusement of her great-grandchildren, she was worried too about what was happening to her possessions in London.

By some means my mother managed to raise a hired car for her, and I accompanied her to London, where she spent most of the day sorting and packing her collection of clothes. She then said that she was tired and wished to leave, refusing to bother about her more valuable possessions. On the return journey we stopped at Skindles at Maidenhead for tea—which she enjoyed enormously; and when we arrived back at Marlborough in the late evening, she was as bright as a button. I was the one who had a splitting headache.

She returned to London before the war finished. She refused all efforts to persuade her to go to a nice country house nursing home and lived in Seamore Place with a wild elderly Irish cook, whose stamina seemed equal to her own.

She used to talk for effect with her head thrown back and her eyes closed. On one occasion, when I was living with her, a small packet containing a small seed pearl necklace which I had had restrung was stolen from the hall table. Grandmamma insisted on calling in a detective to investigate. She then informed him that the Devil had taken it. She knew he had because he always took her spectacles. It was a whimsy which the poor official hardly knew how to take.

I remember she thoroughly enjoyed her 100th birthday, for which Barbara had given her, at a time of rationing, a precious flagon of whisky. "What, all these presents—and only ONE BOTTLE" was her comment.'

This is what Barbara Ker-Seymer, Diane's daughter, who lived in

London, and shared her grandmamma's house for a time when her
father lost his own 'in one hand of poker at White's', has to say:

'I can see Grandmamma clearly as she used to be when I visited her
for Sunday lunch. She would be sitting bolt upright wearing a lace
cap which, by then, replaced the red wig. On the end of her nose
was a pair of Woolworth wire-framed spectacles which she chose from
a sixpenny tray after her sight began to fail for reading. She would
be reading the paper and on her lap a horrid little black mongrel which
she found as a stray. She called him "Little 'Arry", talked baby talk to
him and lavished more love and affection on him than she ever did
to any member of her family.

She was a formidable character and we were rather in awe of her.
She had no love for children but she was very kind and we were all
devoted to her. I remember when I was quite small, Mother had to
go away and I was sent to stay with Grandmamma. I was very upset,
but Grandmamma had ordered a special dinner of my favourite dishes
and I was allowed to sit up for it. She said to me, "You will remember
this dinner for the rest of your life as it is 4 s's, soup, salmon, sausages
and sparrow grass (asparagus)." On the other hand, I also remember
that when we were on holiday, a young couple in the hotel proudly
bringing their new born baby to her to be admired. She looked it
firmly in the eyes and said "You know I don't like little babies"
whereupon the poor little creature set up a great howl, and was
hastily carried away.

I think we all enjoyed our visits to Grandmamma as she was
interested in everything we did. She was only interested in the
present, and not at all interested or sentimental about the past; nor
were we really so we knew very little about her past, though we
loved reading "Pleasures of a Chaperon".

In the mornings she would go to picture sales at Christies, Sotheby's
etc., and buy paintings. She was always a law unto herself and would
decide who the paintings were by regardless of the information in
the catalogue. I remember telling her one day that the Italians had
come into the war as our enemies, and she said "They can't have, dear.
I just bought a Guardi this morning." Her "Fantin la Tour" was an
early English 19th-century flower painting, but she had no respect
for the masters and had no scruples in altering the paintings if she
thought anything was "out of drawing". The pride of her collection
of paintings was her "Sir Peter Lely" painting of a lady on which she
had painted a completely new eye on top of the varnish which made
it look rather odd, I thought.

She was very healthy and I can't remember her ever spending a
day in bed. I think she ignored her body if it got in the way of anything she wanted to do, but as she grew older, although her mind was

as alert as ever, she became less active and said to me once in her
99th year! "I have a word of advice to you. Never grow to be 98.
It's deadly dull." She was quite prepared for her death as, ever since
I can remember, there was a notice stuck over her vast mahogany-
encased bath. The paper was cockled with steam and all the ink
had run but it was still legible. It said: "If I should die in my bath,
turn on both taps until the bath is filled, my body will then float to
the surface and can be easily lifted out."

Grandmamma disliked antiques after having been brought up at
Rothamsted surrounded by them. She liked everything to be bright
and cheerful. When she moved to 6 Seamore Place she got on a ladder
and painted the plaster festoons of fruit round the ceiling in bright
colours. The staircase walls were decorated with canvas panels of
draped nymphs almost life size. I think one was riding a bull, but
she had some assistance with that one from the Italian footman at
No. 6. Her four poster bed was North African and came from an
Ouled Naile dwelling in Tangier. The carved pillars were painted
in bright colours with pieces of looking glass glued to them. She
had to buy it unseen as it was not respectable to enter the dwelling,
but a description of the bed was shouted down to her out of the
window as she stood in the street below. She bought it on the spot
and had it shipped to London. She also had four enormous caryatids
made of solid lead transported from Naples. She said the happiest time
of her life was when she finally married off her last daughter, Everilda,
in 1910 and had no more responsibilities. She then set off round the
world with a camera.

Soon after the bombing started in the Second World War, Grandmamma was left alone in the vast mansion in Park Lane with a
rather tipsy Irish cook, Mrs. Rook, who locked herself in the basement
every night. Grandmamma seemed quite unmoved, but attempts
were made by Everilda and Diane to get her to go to a nice "home"
in the country but she was quite adamant. I think the expression
she used was "over my dead body". Eventually she reluctantly con-
sented to go and stay with Sylvia in Wiltshire but she was soon
back again as she complained that the country was "deadly dull".
Everilda and Diane then found her a very pleasant retired SRN called
Miss Saunders with a yapping Pekingese. Miss Saunders became
devoted to Grandmamma. Grandmamma listened to the wireless and
read the papers and when a bomb was dropped in the vicinity Miss
Saunders had to wheel her off in a wheel chair to view the damage.
I think she preferred Miss Saunders to the members of her family
as Diane used to go regularly to have tea with her, to give Miss
Saunders time off, but Grandmamma wrote to her one day saying
'Dear Diane. Who is this grey-haired woman who insists on coming

to tea and interfering with me? I wish you would tell her to go away.' The letter was signed as usual 'Yrs aff : C.C.'

Grandmamma was made to sleep in the anti-room on the ground floor in a small iron bedstead from one of the maids' bedrooms, whilst Miss Saunders retired to the basement with Mrs. Rook who she became very friendly with; (a most ill assorted pair I would have thought).

The last time I saw Grandmamma, she was then in her 101st year. She was sitting bolt upright in the iron bedstead looking very frail with her lace cap on her head and her eyes tightly closed. I was greeted by a burst of yapping from Miss Saunders' pekingese. Grand-mamma opened one eye and said "The dog is more pleased to see you than I am," and those were the last words I heard her say.

I believe she was drinking a cup of tea one day when the cup dropped from her hand and she died.

THE PEOPLE IN THE BOOK

Skye was the issue of two families long established among the English country gentry. She married into another. The Lawes based their descent from Jacques Wittewronghele, born in the city of Ghent in 1531, who became the first squire of Rothamsted. Sir John Lawes's wife, Caroline, the mother of Skye, was a Fountaine of Narford Hall, the seat of one of the oldest families in Norfolk. The lineage of Walter Creyke, Skye's husband, is recorded from the beginning of the fifteenth century. All of them were people who moved in high society.

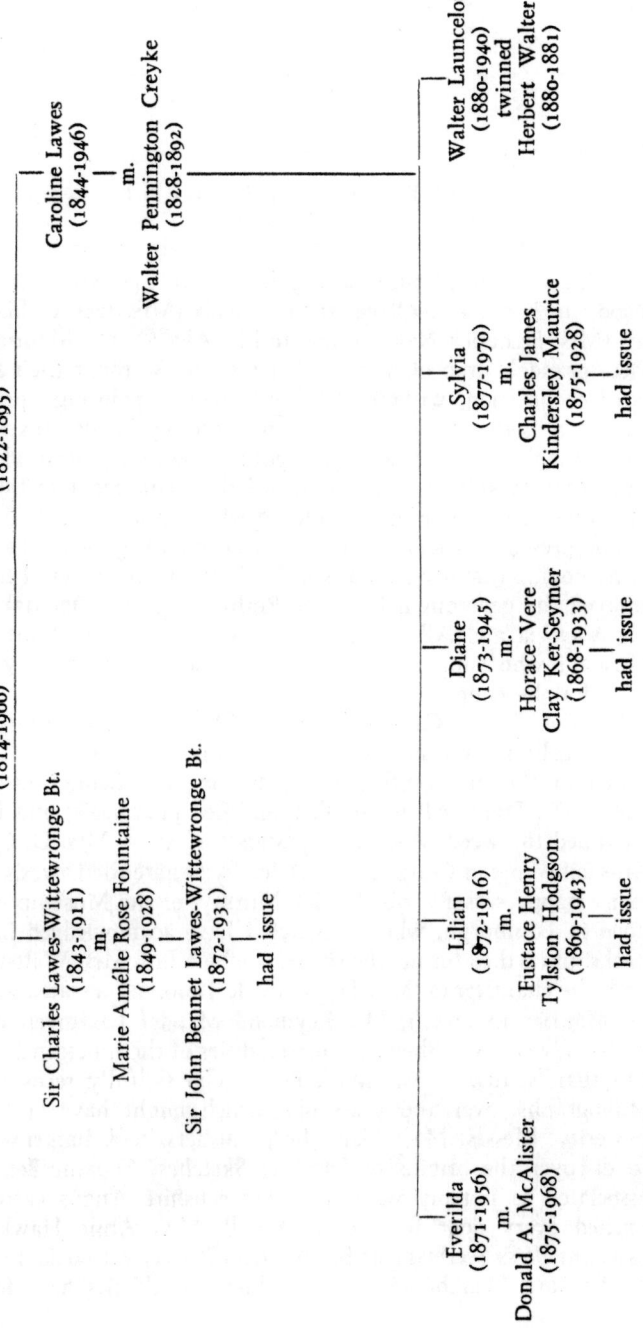

Sir John Bennet Lawes Bt.   m.   Caroline Fountaine
(1814-1900)   (1822-1895)

Caroline Lawes
(1844-1946)
m.
Walter Pennington Creyke
(1828-1892)

Walter Launcelot
(1880-1940)
twinned
Herbert Walter
(1880-1881)

Sir Charles Lawes-Wittewronge Bt.
(1843-1911)
m.
Marie Amélie Rose Fountaine
(1849-1928)

Sir John Bennet Lawes-Wittewronge Bt.
(1872-1931)

had issue

Sylvia
(1877-1970)
m.
Charles James
Kindersley Maurice
(1875-1928)

had issue

Diane
(1873-1945)
m.
Horace Vere
Clay Ker-Seymer
(1868-1933)

had issue

Lilian
(1872-1916)
m.
Eustace Henry
Tylston Hodgson
(1869-1943)

had issue

Everilda
(1871-1956)
m.
Donald A. McAlister
(1875-1968)

ACKNOWLEDGEMENTS

I am indebted, to an unusual degree, to Jean Ina (Mrs. Gerald East-wood); to Barbara Ker-Seymer; to Griselda (Mrs. Jack Blakiston); to Iris (Mrs. Frederick Newton) and to Mr. Alec Creyke Maurice, all of them grandchildren of Mrs. Walter Creyke. Without their sophisticated cooperation, without the family papers, paintings, prints and photographs that they have freely put into my hands, this record of a remarkable Victorian woman might have been lost to social history. I can only trust that I have returned the compliment to the family by telling Skye's great-grandchildren who she was.

The present baronet, Sir John Lawes, kindly gave me permission to photograph family portraits in his house in Guernsey. I have also enjoyed the generous help of the Rothamsted Experimental Station, the Victoria and Albert Museum, and the trustees of the London Museum who supplied me with the balloon map of May Fair in 1850 for the endpapers.

Lt. Col. R. T. Campbell-Preston, M.C., of Ardchattan Priory, courteously allowed me to look over his house in Argyll which was leased in the nineteenth century to Sir John Bennet Lawes. My friend Mr. Frank Allen, the distinguished pharmacist and botanist, identified the weed which now pesters the estate. Mrs. D. C. Leggat entertained me in Craig House, Dalmally, where the Lawes's spent so many happy seasons. Mr. Patrick Murray, of the Museum of Child-hood in Edinburgh, whose research I have acknowledged in former books, unearthed for me the cartoons which link Mrs. Walter Creyke with the character of 'Mrs. Ponsonby de Tomkyns', created by George du Maurier in *Punch*. Mr. Raymond Mander has given me most useful advice about theatrical personalities of the nineteenth century. My thanks, too, to Mr. Mark Bond, who skilfully recovered sepia photographs, over 100 years old, which might have been lost to posterity. Messrs. Macmillan, the publishers, took immense trouble to discover the origins of *Sporting Sketches*. Captain Ben Coutts, associated so notably with the Aberdeenshire Angus cattle breed, opened every door for me in Argyll. Miss Anne Hawkins, the assistant Press Secretary at Buckingham Palace, got books for me out of the Lord Chamberlain's office which I could not have found for myself. Lady Browning (Daphne du Maurier) has given me advice which has avoided at least one mistake.

From the Mansell Collection, I owe the woodcut of Park Lane in 1895 showing the Creyke's mansion. My thanks to the bursar of Rugby College, who put me right about one of Dr. Arnold's last students. My thanks, too, to readers of *Horse and Hound* who told me so exactly where Walter and Skye hunted. And, of course, to Portia Holland, this being the fourth book that she has typed, and retyped, for me.

Finally, and most of all, my love to Diane; otherwise Skye, Ina, Caroline. I trust that her ghost will feel that I have been fair to her memory.

SELECTED BIBLIOGRAPHY

Black's Guide to Scotland (1861)
Old Court Customs by Hon. Mrs. Armytage (1883)
Sporting Sketches by 'Diane Chasseresse' (1890)
Our Fathers by Alan Bott (1931)
Rothamsted by Sir E. John Russell (1942)
The Manor of Rothamsted by D. H. Boalch (1953)
Hatred, Ridicule or Contempt by Joseph Dean (1953)
Madame Sarah by Cornelia Otis Skinner (1967)
William Holman Hunt, my Grandfather, his wives and loves by
    Diana Holman Hunt (1969)
George du Maurier by Leonee Ormond (1969)
Victorian Heyday by J. B. Priestley (1972)
Memoirs of the Lawes-Wittewronges (Privately Printed)
Everilda (Privately Printed)
Rothamsted Experimental Station, by Edwin Grey (Privately Printed)

INDEX

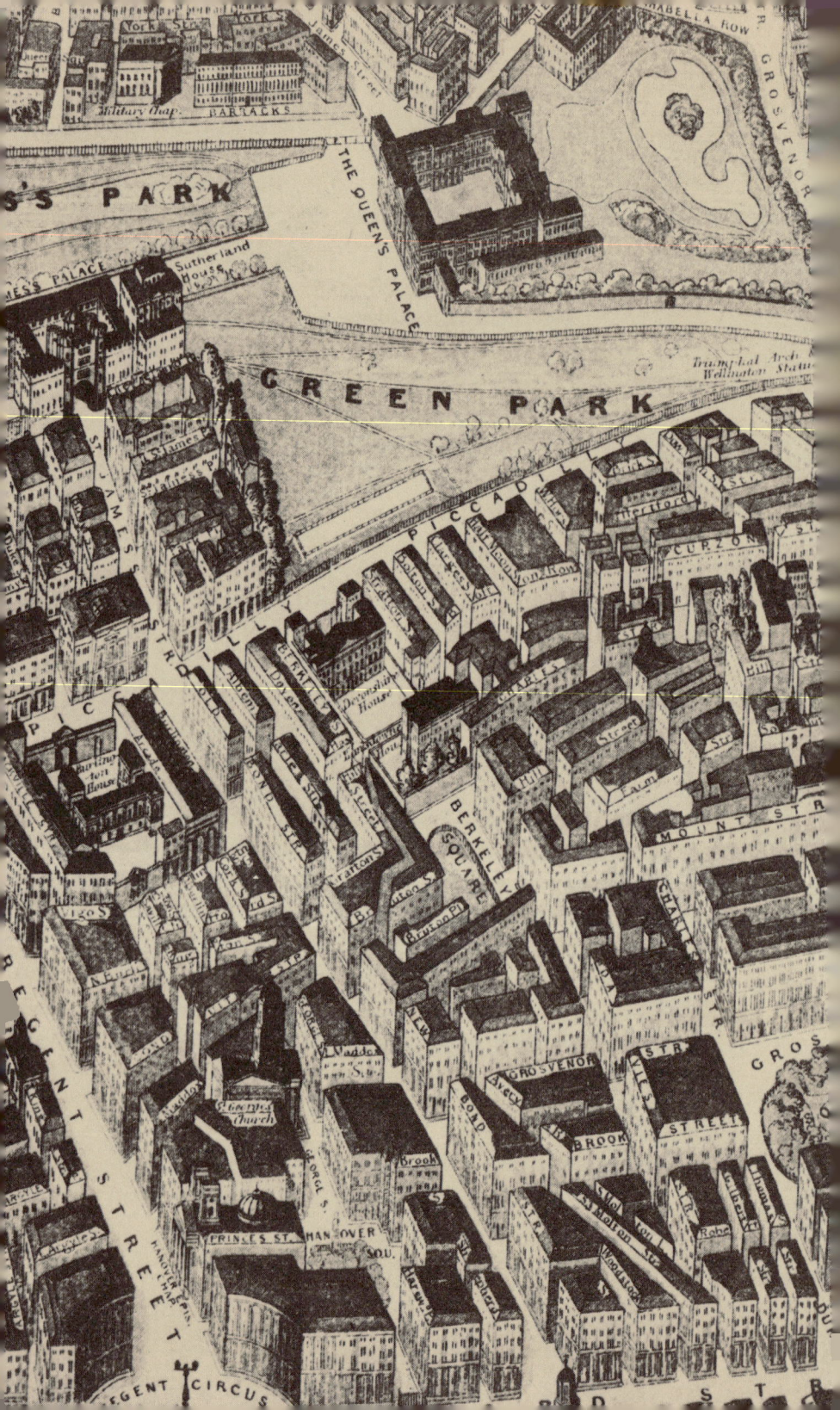